Understanding Japanese Society

With Japan now often leading the way in the establishment of the new global order comes an ever more crucial need to understand a society that is fascinating, but often confusing to the outsider. The third edition of this classic text brings the understanding of Japan into a global context and questions the stereotyped impression of the Japanese often held by those in the rest of the world.

Investigating Japanese society through the perspective of a local resident from childhood into adult life, Hendry brings her book fully up to date by covering all aspects of life in the early twenty-first century. She presents the effects on Japanese people of religious fanaticism, disaffection with politicians, the Kobe earthquake and the so-called 'lost-years' of economic recession, while simultaneously admiring the newly vitalised civil society which has emerged. By identifying a new acceptance of internal diversity, alongside a playful fascination with foreign fare, *Understanding Japanese Society* presents a more complex and positive view of Japan to counterbalance the oft-reported picture of economic doom and seriousness.

This book is an invaluable tool to students wishing to gain a comprehensive understanding of all aspects of Japanese society and culture. It will also enlighten those travellers and business people interested in learning more about the diverse lifestyles of the Japanese people.

Joy Hendry is Professor of Social Anthropology and Director of the Europe Japan Research Centre at Oxford Brookes University.

The Nissan Institute/RoutledgeCurzon Japanese Studies Series

Editorial Board

J.A.A. Stockwin, Nissan Professor of Modern Japanese Studies, University of
  Oxford and Director, Nissan Institute of Japanese Studies
Teigo Yoshida, formerly Professor of the University of Tokyo
Frank Langdon, Professor, Institute of International Relations, University of British
  Columbia
Alan Rix, Executive Dean, Faculty of Arts, The University of Queensland
Junji Banno, formerly Professor of the University of Tokyo, now Professor, Chiba
  University
Leonard Schoppa, Associate Professor, Department of Government and Foreign
  Affairs, and Director of the East Asia Center, University of Virginia

Industrial Harmony in Modern Japan
The intervention of a tradition
W. Dean Kinzley

Japanese Science Fiction
A view of a changing society
Robert Matthew

The Japanese Numbers Game
The use and understanding of numbers in modern Japan
Thomas Crump

Ideology and Practice in Modern Japan
Edited by Roger Goodman and Kirsten Refsing

Technology and Industrial Development in Pre-war Japan
Mitsubishi Nagasaki Shipyard, 1884–1934
Yukiko Fukasaku

Japan's Early Parliaments, 1890–1905
Structure, issues and trends
Andrew Fraser, R.H.P. Mason and Philip Mitchell

Japan's Foreign Aid Challenge
Policy reform and aid leadership
Alan Rix

Emperor Hirohito and Shōwa Japan
A political biography
Stephen S. Large

Japan
Beyond the end of history
David Williams

Ceremony and Ritual in Japan
Religious practices in an industrialized society
Edited by Jan van Bremen and D.P. Martinez

The Fantastic in Modern Japanese Literature
The subversion of modernity
Susan J. Napier

Militarization and Demilitarization in Contemporary Japan
Glenn D. Hook

Growing a Japanese Science City
Communication in scientific research
James W. Dearing

Architecture and Authority in Japan
William H. Coaldrake

Women's *Gidayū* and the Japanese Theatre Tradition
A. Kimi Coaldrake

Democracy in Post-war Japan
Maruyama Masao and the search for autonomy
Rikki Kersten

Treacherous Women of Imperial Japan
Patriarchal fictions, patricidal fantasies
Hélène Bowen Raddeker

Japanese–German Business Relations
Competition and rivalry in the inter-war period
Akira Kudō

Japan, Race and Equality
The Racial Equality Proposal of 1919
Naoko Shimazu

Japan, Internationalism and the UN
Ronald Dore

Life in a Japanese Women's College
Learning to be ladylike
Brian J. McVeigh

On the Margins of Japanese Society
Volunteers and the welfare of the urban underclass
Carolyn S. Stevens

Understanding Japanese Society

Third edition

Joy Hendry

RoutledgeCurzon
Taylor & Francis Group
LONDON AND NEW YORK

First published 1987
by Croom Helm

Reprinted by Routledge 1989, 1991, 1992
11 New Fetter Lane, London EC4P 4EE

Second edition 1995
Reprinted 1996, 1997, 1998, 2000, 2002 (twice), 2003

Third edition 2003, reprinted 2004, 2005
by RoutledgeCurzon
12 Park Square, Milton park, Abingdon, Oxon, OX14 4RN

Simultaneously published in the USA and Canada
by RoutledgeCurzon
270 Madison Ave, New York, NY 10001

RoutledgeCurzon is an imprint of the Taylor & Francis Group

Typeset in Baskerville by RefineCatch Limited, Bungay, Suffolk
Printed and bound in Great Britain by
TJ International, Padstow, Cornwall

British Library Cataloguing in Publication Data
A catalogue record for this book is available from the British Library

Library of Congress Cataloging in Publication Data
Hendry, Joy.
  Understanding Japanese society / Joy Hendry. – 3rd ed.
    p. cm. – (Nissan Institute/RoutledgeCurzon Japanese studies
series)
Includes bibliographical references and index.
  1. Japan – Social conditions.   I. Title. II. Series: Nissan
Institute/Routledge Japanese studies series
    HN723.5 .H46 2003
    306'.0952 – dc21
                                        2002153220

ISBN 0–415–26382–4 (hbk)
ISBN 0–415–26383–2 (pbk)

Contents

Figures

x   *Figures*

Series editor's preface

World news at the beginning of 2003 is dominated by the prospect of an American-led invasion of Iraq. North Korea is also targeted as the only non-Islamic member of President Bush's 'Axis of Evil'. In some ways North Korea – and policy towards it – represents an even greater potential danger to international order than does the situation over Iraq. Even though the North Korean economy is decrepit and broken down, its military could inflict massive destruction on Seoul, home to more than a quarter of the South Korean population and to 37,000 US troops. Japan is also within range of Pyongyang's rockets. The North Korean Government is practised in the art of countering threats with extreme behaviour. Even though this may be a 'hedgehog' reaction, its willingness to break international agreements over nuclear matters prompts grave concern. The South Korean Government sensibly pursues policies of engagement with the North, aiming to tempt North Korea out of its isolation and intransigence, and into the modern world. Despite mixed messages, there are some signs that the regime in the North would like to modernise, and that its nuclear bluster is aimed at winning external guarantees of security and of regime survival.

For Japan, the Korean situation represents a crucial test of foreign policy. The one-day visit to Pyongyang on 17th September 2002 by the Japanese Prime Minister, Mr Koizumi, had mixed results. Japan and North Korea signed an important joint statement, but further progress was frustrated by the issue of Japanese citizens spirited away to North Korea several years before. Later North Korean admissions about their nuclear development in breach of international agreements made further Japanese initiatives even more difficult.

A challenge to Japan of a different kind is provided by two related developments. One is the rapid economic growth of the People's Republic of China (or at least its coastal regions), and the success of Chinese exports to Japan. The other is the continued failure of economic policy to solve the problems of Japanese deflation and bank indebtedness. The Japanese economy is stalled while the Chinese economy is moving dynamically. Japan is still a huge economic power with a far higher standard of living than China, but her economy is stagnant.

Japan is thus faced with the combined effects of a worrying situation in Korea, an economically resurgent China and chronic failure of its economic policies. To this may be added another ingredient, namely generational change, since younger Japanese are paradoxically becoming both more nationalistic and more internationalist. They are less inhibited about championing symbols of nationhood and thinking of Japan as a major power, but also happy to interact more freely and naturally than their elders with people from other parts of the world, both at home and abroad. To adapt a phrase of Ronald Dore, the Japanese are still Japanese, but their Japaneseness is steadily evolving.

The Nissan/RoutledgeCurzon Japanese Studies Series goes back to 1986 and is approaching its sixtieth volume. It seeks to foster an informed and balanced, but not uncritical, understanding of Japan. One aim of the series is to show the depth and variety of Japanese institutions, practices and ideas. Another is, by using comparisons, to see what lessons, positive or negative, can be drawn for other countries. The tendency in commentary to resort to out-dated, ill-informed or sensational stereotypes still remains, and needs to be combated.

Professor Joy Hendry's many publications on Japanese society are well known. The present volume was first published in 1987, and this is the third revised edition of a book that has been widely popular. Her purpose is to orient the reader to the characteristics of Japanese society by reference to a number of common features. Among these are the salience of face-to-face relationships, the existence of a shared value system, the principle of reciprocity, attachment to the warmth of human feelings, adherence to norms of hierarchy, emphasis on cooperation, especially within coherent groups, playing down of individualism and the striving for equality. She well recognises that all of these play a role in most other societies, but she argues that it is the particular mix of them that characterises the society of Japan.

She devotes chapters to various aspects of Japan, comprising history, family, upbringing, community, education, hierarchy, religion, ritual, work, leisure, politics and law. Rather than attempting exhaustive treatment of them, she seeks to show how all these spheres of activity reflect – and in some cases deviate from – the dominant patterns of Japanese social life. In the modern world, of course, no society remains static or unaffected by a myriad of changing influences, local, national and international. Notions of individual autonomy are, for instance, becoming more prominent. It is the dynamic and creative nature of social life in Japan that constitutes so much of its fascination, and to this dynamism Joy Hendry is a gifted and sensitive guide. She also provides comprehensive and up to date advice about published research on the various aspects of her subject.

J. A. A. Stockwin

Preface to the third edition

The third edition of *Understanding Japanese Society* goes to press during a period of considerable concern within that country: concern about the recession and the state of the banking system, concern about a continuing fall in the birth rate, and concern about an apparent frivolity amongst the newest generation of young 'adults'. There is much to discuss, and much to worry about, but I suggest that there are also several things to celebrate, and it will be from this more positive stand that I would like to approach the topic.

In the 30-odd years since I first stepped off the Brazil-*maru* onto the shores of Yokohama, Japan has changed, and it has changed much in the eight years since I wrote the second edition of this book, but there are also lines of continuity. In this third edition of my attempt to make vital aspects of Japanese society clear to a newcomer to that country, I will try to give a flavour of both: the new, bright, brash Japan and the older, quieter, more subtle areas that lie alongside it. The first is plain for all to see, and it is often reported in the world's media, but the second needs a little ferreting out, a search nevertheless well worth taking on, and I hope this book will provide the reader with a useful and trusty companion for that task.

The first cause for celebration as Japan entered the twenty-first century is a more positive attitude than recently towards diversity among the people who live there. So many tired texts have repeated a largely mythological (though politically inspired) idea of homogeneity amongst Japanese people. This notion was never actually a fact, but represented a position largely adopted relative to the melting pot that is America, which for a while during living memory has been the main source of comparison, from both inside and out. Now books are instead emphasising the diversity that is to be found in Japan: the excitement of cultural and historical regional variation, a slightly nervous regard for increasing numbers of immigrants – some with Japanese origins – and the way that the formerly marginalised Ainu and Okinawan people are at last being given a proper voice.

A second, related cause for celebration is derived from an opposing spread of Japanese people in other parts of the world – making a living, making art and making a contribution towards alleviating world poverty and other problems arising in the global village to which Japan now belongs. Back in Japan, people know much more about Europe, the Middle East and other Asian countries than they did ten years ago, and they use that knowledge when choosing food to eat, a place to visit or when booking long-distance travel. In Japan, too, foreign visitors are more abundant and better accepted outside big cities than they were then, and the friends they make (which was never a problem) are more likely to know something about where they come from.

The Crown Princess gave birth recently, after eight years of childless marriage. In a country where the Imperial Line claims over two thousand years of continuity this was a cause for considerable celebration – except that the baby was a girl. In the second edition of this book I looked to the recently married Princess Masako, a potentially brilliant diplomat who gave up her career to become the wife of the Crown Prince, to pave a new way for women in Japan. Now perhaps she has a chance through her daughter to do just that. She has some models from more than one reigning Empress in ancient Japan, but the present Constitution allows only a male heir, so the first task is clear.

In fact there have been several changes at an official level for women in twenty-first-century Japan, and this situation would seem to be an example of a silver lining to one of the clouds of concern, namely the recent drastic drop in the birth rate. To encourage women back into giving birth, and men too to take time off and help rear their small children, new policies have been passed and support facilities have multiplied. This book addresses the effects of these new policies, but it finds even highly educated mothers preferring to remain in their communities rather than commute to work, and they are also contributing to a new wave of volunteering that has taken off in the past few years.

Volunteer work provides occupations for some of the increasing numbers of retired people at the other end of the worrying population pattern, too, and it contributes to a related new emphasis on the development of an active and responsible 'civil society' in Japan. Advocates of this movement see it as a way for Japan to take a maturer role of global citizenship and a general move towards achieving world peace and well-being for people throughout the world. Volunteering and the ideas of civil society were not unknown before in Japan, but reactions to the dreadful loss of the Kobe earthquake triggered a new impetus, and some dubbed 1995 as a 'first year of the volunteer'. Japan has also signed up for a greater commitment to United Nations Security and the Universal Declaration on Human Rights in the past few years.

The economic recession that has plagued Japan for the past decade has of course also brought about changes to employment practices, and indeed to employment possibilities, and these will be considered in some detail in this new edition. There is something of a silver lining here too, in my opinion, for new ideas have a better chance of being adopted in formerly conservative firms, and have contributed towards the creation of a more flexible political system. Some of the so-called frivolous young people are also making a virtue out of change by choosing short-term temporary employment while they consider paths for lives that they hope will be less stressful than those they saw their parents suffer. Many place a priority on the fun they can have, rather than the long hours of work and commuting that characterised the secure life of the previous generation, and for this they are criticised – of course. It will be interesting to see how they fare in the long run.

A superabundance of new material has appeared on Japanese society in the past few years and several authors have devoted themselves to that element of fun. Leisure, play and consumption are terms that abound in the titles of new volumes, but there is also serious work that has addressed darker topics of child abuse, school refusal and the shocking sarin gas attack in the Tokyo underground in 1995. The bankruptcy of a big chain store provided an illuminating theme for one important anthropological study, and others have examined the lives of workers in small firms and those seeking labouring positions for only a day at a time. Numerous authors have addressed the new emphasis on regional diversity and the immigrant communities that have burgeoned recently, and others have focused on changing attitudes to gender and sexuality, and to the imaging and practice of homosexuality in Japan.

So much anthropology of Japan has appeared in the past few years that it has been difficult to represent fairly all the material, or to do justice to those works I have cited. I hope that the snippets I have managed to include will whet your appetites and point the way to follow up your own interests more deeply. Another new source of material since the second edition is of course the Internet, and there are innumerable useful websites issued from Japan, particularly for statistics and up-to-date news stories, though the role of anthropological work for background, context and a deeper understanding remains unchallenged.

Acknowledgements for the third edition

I have received support from an enormous number of people while putting together this updated version of *Understanding Japanese Society*, and it is impossible to mention them all by name, though I am no less grateful for that. The Japan Foundation Endowment Committee funded an invaluable trip to Japan to visit all the sites of my previous research to get a feeling for change that has taken place since my last visits and sojourns in those places. I am therefore also indebted again to many of the same people who have helped me over the years, and I thank them once again for their patience with my questions and their willingness to chat. I would like to express special gratitude to those who gave me practical help and hospitality. These include Laura and Giichi Inoue and their friends in Okinawa, particularly the Kubas and Michiko Ikehara; Yukifumi Makita and her friends, the Sugiyamas, in Ishigaki-jima, for introducing me to a 'freeter' life; the whole Kumagae family in Yame, who welcomed me into their midst as always despite being in the throws of a family reunion; the Kawaguchis in Kurotsuchi, Kazuko Onishi in Tsu, where I made a reluctant brief foray into academic life but also discovered real evidence of a long-awaited return to the country; Yoko Hirose in the heart of fashionable Tokyo; Tom Gill in Yokohama, who entertained me along with students currently doing fieldwork; and Ushio Takahashi and the staff of Shirayuri Kindergarten in Tateyama. Jane Wilkinson introduced me to many of her good friends and contacts in the Ainu community in Hokkaido, where I was also reacquainted with Masahiro Nomoto, who gave me much useful information as well as hospitality in Shiraoi.

Many friends, students and colleagues, as well as six anonymous readers, have made suggestions and comments, initiated ideas, and directed me to readings I might not otherwise have found, and I list them with trepidation in case I have missed anyone, but I am grateful to you all. They are Catherine Atherton, Brian Bocking, Naomi Brown, Rupert Cox, whom I must also thank for arranging several wonderful side-trips in Japan, Matt Field, Tim

Fitzgerald, Hiroko Ford, Daniel Gallimore, Roger Goodman, who also read and commented on a whole draft of the text, Peter Grimshaw, Ruth Martin, Lola Martinez, Louella Matsunaga, Ayami Nakatani, Ian Neary, who also kindly commented on the last two chapters, Ian Reader, James Roberson, Glenda Roberts, Ayumi Sasagawa, Phil Sawkins, Mitch Sedgwick, who also gave a critical eye to Chapter 9, Katsunobu Shimizu, Kimie Shin, Carolyn Stevens, Noriya Sumihara, Nobue Suzuki, Ayumi Takenaka, James Valentine and Bruce White. Thanks also to Yoko Ono-Revidon and Simon Wright for suggesting some of the films at the end of the chapters. All errors of fact and judgement of course remain my own.

Introduction

There is plenty of access to information about Japan these days. It features abundantly in radio and television programmes, in newspaper articles and in splendid and spectacular films. Then there are exhibitions of Japanese art, live concerts, theatre, shows and demonstrations. There are also large numbers of Japanese people in most of the major cities of the world and they are usually happy to talk about and 'explain' their country. The image we receive is still one of industry and efficiency, even if the startling post-war economic success has now received a battering. We hear of the astounding, if sometimes shocking, achievements of the education system, but we can also see photographs of Japanese young people dressed up and even painted in bright and cheerful ways. For many foreigners, however, the Japanese people remain difficult to understand. How can this be?

One of the problems is that we generally apply our own standards of judgement when we look at other countries. It is, of course, difficult to do anything else. The press is trained to report on matters that are of interest to its consumers, and foreign correspondents are often summoned home when their reporting becomes too 'native', wherever they come from. They need to be tuned in to the perceived needs of their audience. Japanese people, themselves, are extremely adept at presenting themselves and their country in the way they think appropriate to a local audience, and they may also be keen to present a good image of their country even if they have private doubts. Many Japanese people abroad actually spend considerable time comparing themselves with other people and they formulate ways to present aspects of their own society which can be easily assimilated even if they are somewhat stereotyped.

Academics spend years studying Japan. They learn the language, they visit the country, they read Japanese books and they become experts in an area of Japanese life which happens to appeal to them. They write accurate and informative books about their particular specialities, and these books are usually good sources for further study, but they are often written for other Japanese specialists or for specialists in their own particular field. The field of social anthropology is one such field, and one of its main aims is to understand people on their own terms. Anthropologists try to see the world as the people themselves see it and then to translate this understanding back into language which their own colleagues can follow. It is only a small step further to write their findings in language that the lay reader or a new student can understand. This book aims to take that step and to introduce the non-specialist to the anthropology of Japan.

Japanese society is here presented, therefore, according to a social anthropological approach. The subject of anthropology has in some areas become tainted with a negative image of colonial arrogance, but Japan is a good case to dispel that idea. The aim is simply to introduce the world as it is classified and ordered by Japanese people. The reader is asked to suspend his or her own judgements and assumptions about how people should or should not order their lives, and try to imagine how a Japanese person might see things differently. There is, of course, great variety in Japanese society, as there is in any society, but just as Japanese people learn Japanese as their first language, they also learn to classify the world in a Japanese way, and they learn to perceive things from a Japanese point of view. An attempt is made here to present the world as it might be seen by someone growing up and living in Japan, covering as much as possible of its rich diversity.

The chapters move from a discussion of small social units, such as the family, school and neighbourhood, experienced by any member of Japanese society in everyday and ceremonial life, to larger institutions like companies, parliament and courts, which impinge in different ways on people's lives, depending on their position in society. Considerable attention is given throughout to the symbolic aspects of Japanese behaviour, the non-verbal ways in which members of Japanese culture communicate with each other, and particularly to the ritual behaviour in which they participate. Some principles will recur from one chapter to another, and the conclusion tries to bring together features common to all the different arenas discussed.

Women have not been given a special, separate chapter as the approach aims to include men, women and children at all stages in proportion to their participation in whatever the area of society being discussed. It is possible that the author's bias may lean slightly towards giving women priority over men, particularly in the ordering of the chapters, but this has the advantage of coinciding to some extent with the order of experience of most Japanese growing up and acquiring their cultural heritage. The bias is not, I think, strong enough to warrant the inclusion of a special compensatory chapter on the subject of 'Japanese men', though I will make reference here and there to the work of other authors on both men's and women's separate lives and views of the world.

The sources for this book are as far as possible anthropological studies, including those of the author. They are usually based on fieldwork, often carried out for long periods in the same place with a circumscribed group of people, so that various aspects of Japanese life have been experienced at an intimate 'grass-roots' level. Some of the studies have even been conducted in a single home, some have focused on one village or urban neighbourhood, and others have investigated a single school, factory, nightclub or wedding parlour. Other studies take a theme as a focus and examine its manifestation in different parts of Japan. The detailed content of each of the chapters of this book has been designed to draw on the rich fund of work available, for an understanding of these microcosmic views of Japanese society is ultimately the best means to understanding the macrocosmic view which will emerge gradually towards the end of the book.

In the few areas that have been little investigated by anthropologists but which nevertheless add an important dimension to an understanding of contemporary Japanese society, an attempt has been made to fill in the gaps using other sources available. Nothing has been barred, and I hope that the reader will benefit from this broad approach. In fact, the book was originally based on a series of lectures which were designed for the modular course at Oxford Polytechnic, now Oxford Brookes University. This course enables students to combine two major fields and a number of minor ones in the pursuit of their degrees, so it is particularly appropriate if they can relate the anthropological approach to the other disciplines in which they happen to be interested.

Further reading, novels and some often quite classic films are recommended at the ends of chapters with the aim of helping readers to pursue their own individual interests. The book, as a whole, is intended to open a door, to provide details about life in Japan which all Japanese know because they were brought up there. It explains the kinds of things that Japanese people probably wouldn't bother to tell you because they may not have noticed that everyone doesn't think like that. Or if they have, they just assume only Japanese people would understand these things anyway. As will be discussed in Chapter 1, Japanese people (like many others) tend to think of themselves as rather special and unique. Once the reader is armed with background information like this, it should be possible to achieve a deeper understanding of specialist books in other areas.

The intended audience is fairly broad. There were no prerequisites for the course at the Polytechnic for which the lectures were designed. Many of the students had some background in anthropology, others had taken a module or two about Japan, but there were also students who knew nothing of either area. In the same way, the book makes no assumptions about the readers' knowledge. It could be of value to anyone interested in Japan. It could form a useful companion to someone planning to visit, someone posted by his or her company, someone hoping to set up a subsidiary there. It will not provide details about how to do business in Japan, but it will give potential businessmen and women an insight into the way their Japanese counterparts may be thinking about an issue.

This book will also help someone studying the Japanese language to put the fruits of their learning into a social context. It will provide answers to questions which may arise about why things are said in the way they are, why some things don't appear to have an equivalent in Japanese and why there are several different ways of saying apparently simple words like 'come', 'go' and 'eat'. It will also help to explain Japanese words which seem to have no clear translation into English and in some cases, the understanding of such words will open a revealing window onto categories of thought fundamental to native speakers who use the language in their everyday lives. Not many Japanese words have been supplied in the chapters that follow. This is no language textbook, but without an understanding of the words that have been included, no one could claim a good working knowledge of the Japanese language.

1 Sources of Japanese identity

Historical and mythological foundations of Japan

INTRODUCTION

Japan is the nation of origin of some of the most exciting and successful individuals in the contemporary world. In the fields of art and architecture, film, fashion and music, even international politics and diplomacy, Japanese achievements take the world by storm and Japanese names abound. At the same time, stereotypes persist that Japan is a nation of well-organised groups, that Japanese people learn only by copying others, that they work too hard, play little and travel around the world on safely contained package tours. How can a people apparently so boring and conformist demonstrate such an extraordinary degree of innovation and creativity? Who are these people and what exactly do they share?

The string of islands that comprises the nation of Japan is situated at some distance from the Asian mainland and this geographical feature provides a natural boundary for marking off the Japanese people. Archaeological findings continually push back dates for the first evidence of human life on these islands, and early Chinese history reports the existence of a separate people over the sea. There have been many waves of influence into Japan from the outside, however, and the contemporary population shows considerable genetic diversity. Japan has recently played host to several immigrant groups, too, and regional and ethnic minorities form a small but important part of the population. Skill in adopting foreign ideas is one of the best known features of Japan. Using them to innovate within an existing framework is a less well-known but equally characteristic one, as we shall see.

Nevertheless, like other peoples, Japan seeks from time to time to consolidate its own special identity and to present that identity to others with whom it deals. This opening chapter will examine some of the sources and manifestations of that search. It will summarise some of the geographical and archaeological features that define the nation, historical events that have influenced it and the mythological stories that have been drawn upon to imbue the people with a symbolic unity. Such a summary will necessarily be cursory, but it will offer sources of national and personal identity, as well as providing a useful background for the book's main focus on modern Japanese society. It should also provide a frame of reference for understanding some of the chapters that follow. To pursue further some of the issues raised, readers may find useful two collections of articles, edited by Denoon *et al.* (1996) and Vlastos (1998), and an anthropological study of the way postage stamps were used in the formation of identity (Frewer 2002).

GEOGRAPHICAL IDENTITY AND THE EARLY INHABITANTS

There are four main islands that make up Japan, and some 3,900 smaller ones, stretching from the Soya strait separating the Kurile Islands claimed by both Russia and Japan in the north, almost to Taiwan in the south. From tip to tip, the length of the Japanese archipelago is just under 1,900 miles, and at its nearest point to the Asian mainland it is 120 miles from South Korea. There has been some fluctuation in the position of Japan's boundaries, and the peoples of Okinawa and Hokkaido can claim a rather different history, but the central islands have enjoyed a degree of isolation that made possible a long continuity of geographical identity. Since there has been written history, they suffered no real occupation by outsiders until after the Second World War, and the extraordinary weather conditions that deterred two Mongol invasions in the thirteenth century encouraged the inhabitants to see themselves as being blessed with divine protection.

This is an area of considerable geological disturbance, however, and it is likely that the earliest human beings settled or developed here long before the islands became separated at their extremities from the Asian mainland between 10,000 and 20,000 years ago. Early hunters and gatherers left various stone tools to mark their existence, and the oldest of these have been dated back some 500,000 years. They may or may not have survived to develop into the people known as Jomon, named after their attractive ropemarked pottery and dated from around 13,000 years ago to the third century BC, but this early ceramic period has provided a source of artistic origin for Japanese culture. Although there have been various theories about their fate, including the suggestion that they fled north and became the people now known as the Ainu, they certainly provide a source of identity for contemporary Japan. Kobayashi and Kaner (2003) is a good source for this period.

In fact there are different types and stages of stone tools, each of which may represent distinctive, unrelated groups and the ceramic remains, too, show considerable variety. There are also several ethnological theories about the origins of the Japanese people, who seem to combine characteristics of the ruling Tungus people of the north and the Austronesian people of the south. These theories have been proposed as a result of studies of similarities in language and social organisation, as well as by the examination of archaeological artefacts. It is more than likely that the islands of Japan have received many diverse influences since their first settlement, but a sense of continuity is encouraged, at least at a popular level, and archaeological findings are often reported prominently in the news media.

An interesting article by Clare Fawcett (1996) examines the way archaeological sites are used to foster a sense of identity in Japan, in particular the representation in several places of the next important period, known as the Yayoi. It was during this time, from about the third century BC, that metal tools and rice cultivation were introduced by an influx of people from the mainland, and during the next six hundred years or so elements are said to have developed of what is now regarded as true 'Japanese tradition'. Remains of Yayoi communities may be visited, and objects found there inspected, but houses, rice fields and grain stores have also been reconstructed to demonstrate the archaeologists' version of life at the time (see Figure 1.1). Children may dress in Yayoi costume, try their hand at

Figure 1.1 Reconstruction of a Yayoi period house, displayed at the Toro archaeological site in Shizuoka.

Yayoi tools and listen to lectures about their ancestral forbears. A detail that interested Fawcett (1996:70–1) was the emphasis on the cleanliness of the Yayoi people.

This Yayoi period is cited as the source of considerable cooperative activity in Japan, associated with the rice cultivation that was introduced at this time, and the selective access to bronze and iron metal objects is said to have encouraged social divisions and a system of social stratification. Objects were also assigned a religious significance, and the present style of the Ise shrine (see Figure 1.2), which contains some of the most sacred buildings, dates back to this period, as do the mirrors that adorn the innermost sanctum of most Shintō places of worship. The notorious samurai sword no doubt developed from the splendid spears that were

Figure 1.2   Some buildings of the Ise shrine, showing the roof structure characteristic of the Yayoi period. (Photograph courtesy of Bill Coaldrake.)

introduced, and one example of the cultural forging that is favoured in depicting Japanese identity is the idea that the fine decorative work often found along the blades combines a Jomon love of nature with Yayoi craftsmanship.

MYTHOLOGICAL ORIGINS OF JAPAN

The symbolic importance of these objects is made clearer when one turns to the mythological foundations of Japanese identity, recorded in eighth-century chronicles and taught as history in Japanese schools until the Second World War. According to these tales, the islands of Japan were created by a god and goddess named Izanagi and Izanami, who leaned down from the floating bridge of heaven and stirred the ocean with a jewelled spear. The first island was formed from drops of brine that fell from the spear as it was lifted out. The heavenly couple descended to this island, where they gave birth to what is referred to as an Eight Island Country. The sun goddess, Amaterasu, the ultimate ancestress of the imperial line and tutelary deity of the Ise shrine, was then created out of a bronze mirror held in Izanagi's left hand.

During some considerable turmoil that ensued in the heavens, caused particularly by Susano-o, her younger brother, Amaterasu is said at one point to have hidden herself in a cave, thus plunging heaven and earth into darkness. In their efforts to lure her out, the other deities used a bronze mirror again, and another goddess performed a comical dance with the aid of a spear, so that the ensuing laughter aroused Amaterasu's curiosity and she peeped out. Captivated by her own image in the mirror, she was lured out long enough for the cave to be closed behind her and the world was granted sunlight again. Amongst the paraphernalia used by the gods in this story to entice Amaterasu out of her cave were also some curved jewels, or beads, and, sometime later, when Amaterasu's grandson was sent down to earth to become the first Emperor, she presented him with three gifts, to this day regarded as the Japanese Imperial Regalia, namely a bronze mirror, a sword and a curved jewel.

According to the mythological accounts, the grandchild of Amaterasu and his companions spent six years of battle and adventure moving from the southern island of Kyushu, where many outsiders also first landed, through the Inland Sea, to the Yamato Plain in the central part of the main island of Japan. Here, the tale runs, he established a palace on the first day of spring in 660 BC and became the first Emperor Jimmu. The eighth-century account lists a continuous line of imperial rule from that time, although some of the rulers are said to have lived for well over one hundred years, and the records are now seen as written support for a later established supremacy.

This formation of an imperial line, said to be unbroken to the present day, provides another important source of Japanese identity. The Imperial Palace in Tokyo occupies a piece of land said at the height of Japan's economic success to have had a real estate value approximately equivalent to that of the whole of California. In southern Japan, at Takachiho on the Island of Kyushu, a cave may be visited where Amaterasu is supposed to have emerged, and versions of the dances may be seen at any number of Shintō ceremonies to this day (Averbuch 1995). When the Emperor Shōwa died in 1989, his funeral was the occasion for the greatest known gathering of heads of state. This emperor, known abroad as Hirohito, was personally charged to denounce his divinity at the end of the Second World War, and his funeral could be regarded as a special case, but the wedding of his grandson in 1993 also attracted extraordinary media interest at home and abroad. Stefánsson (1998) has a good description of this 'fairytale' wedding.

The long search of the Crown Prince for a wife had been a subject of such speculation that the media had been asked to curb their interest, and a similar situation arose when the marriage failed immediately to produce an heir. When the Crown Princess at last gave birth to a daughter on 1 December 2001 the discussion turned instead to the issue of whether continuity could pass through the female line. It was reported that the present rule of male inheritance had been introduced relatively recently, and Japan has precedent for female dominance in the historical record as well as the mythological one. Surveys seem to suggest that a majority of people in Japan would accept a change in the ruling to allow an Empress to inherit the position.

CHINESE HISTORICAL ACCOUNTS OF THE ANCIENT PERIOD

The earliest historical accounts of the Japanese people are to be found in ancient Chinese chronicles (Tsunoda and Goodrich 1951). In the second and third centuries AD these tell of a country of 100 kingdoms, some 30 of which had sent emissaries to China on business of one sort or another. They speak of an earlier male ruler, but after much warring amongst these kingdoms, the Chinese report that a kingdom named Yamatai gained supremacy in the third century under the rule of a queen named Himiko. She is reported to have lived hidden in the depths of a great, guarded castle, where she spent her time in communication with the gods, allocating the everyday affairs of state to her younger brother.

As it happens, the location of Yamatai, according to Chinese directions, falls in the middle of the Pacific Ocean, and there are at least two possible adjustments to their calculations that would be plausible. One would put this kingdom in the southern part of Japan, where there is later evidence of this type of sister–brother rule, and some recent archaeological findings in Yoshinogari in northern Kyushu were briefly identified with the site of Himiko's castle. The other, in the Yamato Plain, closer to the eventual documentation of the existence of a supreme imperial line, seems to remain the preferred one for the time being, however.

Here, impressive remains in the shape of large tomb mounds date back to this period and provide visible evidence of the existence of powerful leaders. The earliest burial mounds were built into natural hills, but these gradually became larger and more elaborate, taking a characteristic keyhole shape, now often observed most effectively from the air. Some thousands of these tombs have been discovered all over the west of Japan, and that discovered in 1989 in Kyushu seems to go back as far as 100 BC, but the largest was built in the fifth century AD in the Yamato area, now Osaka prefecture. Said to be the tomb of the Emperor Nintoku, this site occupies an area of eighty acres. It is 574 metres long, 300 metres wide and surrounded by three moats.

There is some argument amongst scholars about exactly when the Yamato rulers gained supremacy over the regional leaders and how far it extended. However, the archaeological remains and early written accounts provide us with an interesting record of this people, whose larger identity was becoming established. The buried riches of the rulers include ornaments and decorative objects, similar to ones found in mainland Asia, and there is also much in the way of military paraphernalia. Many of the tombs were originally decorated with terracotta figures known as *haniwa*, which represented houses, people, animals and objects of local everyday life, and the Chinese reports provide details of the customs and social organisation of the people themselves.

Society was already clearly stratified, with a ruling class that could call on the services of a large and cooperative working class. The latter was organised into hereditary occupationally specialised groups, known as *be*, which provided goods and services for the ruling families, or *uji*, each of which had control over a particular territory. It was for the leaders of these *uji* that the tombs were built, and their contents reveal that as time passed, the aristocratic lifestyle became increasingly sophisticated. As for the subordinate *be*, however, apart from the craftsmen, most of the population was probably involved in the subsistence activities of farming – in particular rice cultivation – and fishing.

The internal organisation of the *uji* was based on related family lines, with a main line, whose head was the leader or chief, and branch lines that were subordinate to the main one. The whole group observed rituals to remember the ancestors who had preceded them. The imperial line that established itself at Yamato was one of these *uji*, which claimed descent from the sun goddess, Amaterasu, and held as symbols of their authority the 'three sacred treasures' of mirror, sword and jewel. It maintained supremacy by using principles between the different *uji* similar to those that were used within them. These thus came to be ranked hierarchically according to the closeness of their relationship to the imperial line.

These principles of social and political organisation have provided Japan not only with a symbolic centrality and focus of identity, but also with a blueprint for social order that has been drawn on through the centuries. Its modern manifestations will be discussed in detail in subsequent chapters. The imperial line did not forever retain *de facto* political power, as will be seen, but it has continued to enjoy special status, and together with the religious foundation on which it was initially based, it has served again and again as a source of Japanese identity, not least in the ultra-nationalistic period preceding the Second World War.

JAPANESE HISTORY RECORDED:
THE ARISTOCRATIC AGE

In the seventh century, there was a great influx of cultural influence from China that brought far-reaching changes to Japan, and undoubtedly helped to consolidate the hierarchical system which had been established. Along with written script, which made possible the codification of the imperial supremacy, came the political doctrines and practices of Confucianism, the art and theory of Buddhism and the whole range of technology, arts and philosophy of a highly civilised people. The ruling families of Japan used the new, advanced culture to divide themselves further from the ordinary people, and they gradually became an aristocratic elite that lived an increasingly rich and sophisticated lifestyle.

The head of the chief Yamato family became an absolute ruler in the Chinese imperial style, and everyday affairs were now administered by a bureaucratic system, imported almost intact from China. Local offices were established in all the regions, and magnificent capital cities were built, again on a Chinese model. The first of these was at the site of the present city of Nara, but less than a hundred years later a new capital was founded at Heiankyo, now Kyoto. The names of these two capitals are used to refer to the historical periods of this aristocratic age. In 702, a set of laws, known as the Taihō Code, was instituted and promulgated, and a further Yōrō Code followed sixteen years later. For the first time, the entire country was brought under a single system of criminal and civil law (*ritsuryō*). The previous *be* were abolished, and farmers became free tenants of the state, each entitled to a standardised parcel of land for their own use.

During the five hundred years which followed the great incursion of Chinese influence in the seventh century a splendid court life developed in Japan. Arts and etiquette flourished, and the literature of the period remains as testimony of the achievements of the age. Two major historical/mythological chronicles, the *Kojiki* and the *Nihongi*, provide a wealth of information, as well as the written charter for the supremacy of the imperial line. There are also fine collections of early poetry, such as the Man'yōshū and the Kokinshū, and the famous writings of court ladies, the 'Tale of Genji' and 'Pillowbook of Sei Shōnagon', date back to the latter part of this period. Art and architecture also found an outlet in the Buddhist temples, which were built throughout the country, although the religious ideas remained for some time the preserve of the ruling elite.

It was during the later part of this aristocratic age that the imperial family gradually lost its political power to a family by the name of Fujiwara, who maintained a 200-year hegemony by means of skilfully arranged marital alliances. A matrilocal residence system was customary at the time, which ensured that if each emperor could be married into a Fujiwara family, the infant princes would also be brought up in a Fujiwara household, a system that aided alliances in the next generation. Political power fell more and more into the hands of the Fujiwara regents and chancellors, who succeeded one another almost as regularly as the emperors did, and for generations the emperors were little more than legitimising symbols of the authority of the ruling elite. At the temple of Chūsonji, in northern Japan, treasures of the Fujiwara family have been carefully preserved.

In the country at large, the bureaucratic system also began to lose its effectiveness, and the second half of this period witnessed a move away from Chinese models. Government again became the preserve of a few influential families. These shared the powers and duties of central government and consolidated their economic base by gradually establishing control over areas of cultivable land. The direct relationship between cultivators and the state was replaced by local bonds of dependence between farmers' families and those of their local superiors, who increasingly took responsibility for protection and law enforcement in their own provinces. The locus of power moved gradually away from the court nobles and into the hands of military leaders.

FEUDALISM AND *BUSHIDŌ*

In stark contrast to the artistic occupations of court life, these provincial rulers were concerned with the acquisition of military skills, and they developed a code of ethics that has become another major source of Japanese pride and identity. The samurai warriors, as they became, valued deprivation and rigorous discipline in the interest of building an impenetrable inner strength of spirit. They trained themselves to conquer fear and be ready to die at a moment's notice. Relations between them were based on hierarchical principles similar to those described above for the *uji* and loyalty to the ultimate leader was a paramount virtue. The principles of *bushidō* (or the way of the samurai warrior) were not specifically articulated until much later, but the military leaders who developed this set of values gradually came also to wield the greater political power throughout Japan.

Towards the end of the twelfth century, a period of civil strife culminated in the establishment of a powerful military headquarters in Kamakura by the ambitious leader of the Minamoto family, named Yoritomo. His supremacy was recognised, albeit somewhat reluctantly, by the emperor of the time, who eventually gave him the title of *shōgun*, commander of the entire military forces. From that time onwards, the powers of the court gradually diminished, and were only occasionally to regain any strength. In the fourteenth century, for example, an imperial uprising succeeded only in transferring effective power to another family, the Ashikagas. In fact, until 1868, the locus of power was to remain more or less effectively in the hands of a succession of shogunates.

The system that developed during this period has been described as feudal, because it was seen (loosely) to resemble the European feudal system as opposed to the bureaucratic arrangements that had been introduced from China in the seventh century. The country became divided into fairly autonomous provinces under the leadership of local lords. These commanded the allegiance of bodies of hierarchically organised supporters to whom, in turn, they granted rights to parcels of land. The farmers who worked the land were obliged to provide their superiors with rice and other foodstuffs, and in exchange they were supposed to receive protection. In practice farmers often suffered incidentally in battles waged between lords for supremacy over a particular area.

The lives of the warring samurai are relived regularly in film and television dramas in Japan, and these are known collectively as 'historical theatre'. Theme park versions of this period of history have also been created in various parts of the country, where visitors can examine the construction techniques of the castles that were built and buy reproductions of the weaponry used. Thanks to the extraordinary technological wizardry employed, they can also even experience the noise and mayhem of standing on a shuddering battlefield. A park near Nagoya called *Sengoku Jidai Mura* is one particularly fine example. Hearn (2002) is an exciting English-language novel set in the period.

THE TOKUGAWA (OR EDO) PERIOD

During the sixteenth century, the first explorers and missionaries arrived in Japan from Europe. They coincided with a period of some considerable strife between lords of different regions of Japan, as has been graphically, if not strictly accurately, described in James Clavell's novel *Shōgun*. The chief influences were Portuguese and Dutch at this time, but the success of particularly Jesuit missionaries, who were led by St Francis Xavier, was eventually counterproductive. Towards the end of the century, as the country was again brought under unified central control, Christianity was seen as a threat to the new social order that was being created, and the expulsion of the missionaries was ordered. This was only part of an eventual expulsion of all foreigners except the Dutch, who were allowed to occupy one island off the coast of Kyushu, and provided a continuing trickle of knowledge from Europe. Japanese were also banned from travelling abroad, and the country entered a two-and-a-half-century period of self-imposed isolation.

The new unity was in effect established by Toyotomi Hideyoshi, although the subsequent period is named after his eventual successor, Tokugawa Ieyasu, who consolidated Toyotomi's achievements and whose house remained in power throughout the isolation period. Between them they created and stabilised strict divisions between the various classes of people, and reinstated a degree of bureaucracy in the administration of the provinces. The samurai became a ruling military class, who lived in the castle towns, and they alone were allowed to carry swords. The rest of the population was divided into farmers (at the top), artisans (second) and (ironically at the bottom) merchants. The last two also lived in the towns. Priests did not fit clearly into the scheme, although their rank was fairly high, and there were also itinerant entertainers and others who remained outside the system at a lower level. Also separated were people outcaste because of defiling occupations, who were literally described as 'non-human'.

At the peripheries of this tight system, the Ainu in the north and the Okinawans in the south were actually encouraged in their quite considerable cultural differences (Morris-Suzuki 1996). This was a system of Chinese origin of expressing an identity for Japan in a world gradually growing in their comprehension, where colourful neighbouring (inferior) peoples were expected to pay tribute to the central power. The Shimazu clan in the southern Satsuma domain had invaded the Ryukyu Islands (later known as Okinawa) that had their own king, and a system of tribute they installed was reinforced by the shogunate. In the north, the Matsumae clan imposed unequal trade relations on some prominent Ainu, a practice interpreted centrally in the same way to reinforce the boundaries of this new unified identity of Japan.

The capital was established at the city of Edo (now Tokyo), and a system was set up to maintain the subjugation and support of the local *daimyō* (lords). Each had to spend part of the year in the capital city, leaving his immediate family there when he returned to his local province. Gardens built during this period to remind the families of their own regions may be visited in present-day Tokyo, and a huge and interactive Edo Museum depicts the life of the time. Each class had strict rules by which to live, and all activities, from cultivation to trade, were registered and controlled. Every family was by law to be registered with a local Buddhist temple, to help eliminate lingering Christianity, and these temples also kept a record of deaths as they occurred. It was during this period that the samurai ethic became a conscious 'way' of life, and, despite the lack of contact with China, Confucianism was again drawn upon to support the carefully regulated, hierarchical system that they guarded.

This period was for two centuries stable and relatively peaceful. In the middle of the nineteenth century, however, when Western ships began to press for access to Japanese ports, the strict social order had already begun to break down. The shogunate and various *daimyō* alike were suffering financial problems, merchants were becoming wealthy and people at other levels were expressing dissatisfaction. For some years there was a struggle between the Tokugawa supporters, who sought to revamp the shogunate, and new emerging leaders whose aim was to bring the emperor back into a more powerful position. The latter were eventually successful and the 'Restoration' of the 15-year-old Emperor Meiji in 1868 was the single event that led most effectively to the establishment of a central government and the introduction of Japan to the era now known as 'modern'. Shiba's (1998) book, *The Last Shogun*, depicts rather well the complicated power play of this period.

FROM THE MEIJI PERIOD (1868–1912) TO THE SECOND WORLD WAR

During the next fifty years, Japan was again exposed to considerable outside influence. The new leaders travelled to various European countries to seek models for their innovations, and trade relations were established, or re-established, with willing countries all over the world. This was a period of considerable cultural display in the Expositions and World Fairs that were held at intervals in all major cities of the world, and Japan sought to establish a role alongside the major powers of the time. Extraordinary art and architecture caused flurries of interest wherever the fairs were held, and the first period of *Japonisme* took Europe and then America by storm.

Within Japan, a comprehensive railway network was constructed, a post-office system was established and schools were opened gradually throughout the country. Western technology was introduced, and factories and industrial plants began to form the basis of new urban developments. Western material culture also spread quickly, as buildings, vehicles, clothes and even food were imported to suit the changing tastes of the modern population. The old class divisions were officially abolished, and all became equal in the eyes of the law. Attempts were made at either end of the country to turn the various Ainu and Okinawans into regular Japanese citizens, but now, according to ideas imported from Europe, they were to be 'civilised' into new ways of life. For the Ainu, this meant abandoning their hunting and gathering means of livelihood, and the Okinawans eventually lost their communal system of land ownership (Morris-Suzuki 1996:86–7).

There was considerable discussion and disagreement about the system of government that should be adopted, particularly about the extent to which there should be popular participation, and various European ideas were tried out on an experimental basis. The first political parties were formed in the 1870s by those who wanted to introduce a national assembly, but for some time the Meiji oligarchs resisted, and power remained entirely in their hands. They were also supported by a conscript army that was introduced in 1873. Work began on the drafting of a Constitution in 1882, however, and the posts of prime and cabinet ministers were created in 1885. Eventually, in 1889, a Constitution was promulgated which made provision for a bicameral parliament, with an elected House of Representatives and an aristocratic House of Peers, and a new legal system, based on French and German models, which was acceptable to the outside world.

By this time there was something of a reaction to all the European influence, and Japan entered a period of consolidation. Various institutions had been established which corresponded to the models on which they were based, but just as in the period following the great Chinese influence in the seventh century, Japan set about placing them on a firm local footing. This nationalistic period, which effectively continued until 1945, witnessed some swaying in the balance of power between the oligarchs, the military and the new political parties, but popular participation had only rather sporadic success, and the country was led into a series of wars. Carol Gluck's (1985) book entitled *Japan's Modern Myths* is an excellent study of the creation of identity and ideology in the late Meiji period.

The two successful forays into China and Russia around the turn of the century may be interpreted as further efforts of Japan to gain an equal footing with other great powers. The arts and architecture that impressed the wider world had nevertheless failed to remove Japan from a position of 'quaint Orientals' in the ranking, to our lasting shame, of anthropological studies of the time (see Hendry 2000: chapter 2 for further detail). These sought as much as anything to justify European incursions into great areas of the globe, and Japan's expansion at that time clearly used the British Empire as a model. Initial success in China, Russia and Korea undoubtedly helped to inspire the extraordinary self-confidence that was eventually to lead to Japan's own first experience of foreign occupation.

The build-up of extreme nationalism, which preceded Japan's attack on Pearl Harbor in 1941, drew on all the resources for national identity that Japan had at her disposal. The Shintō mythological foundations of the nation in the sixth century BC were taught as history in schools during this period, and the people were encouraged to think of themselves as ultimately related through their ancestors to the imperial family. Samurai values of inner strength and self-denial were held up as personal qualities to emulate in the pursuit of the Confucian principles of loyalty and filial piety. The Shintō notions which made service to the state an extreme form of filial piety to one's ultimate ancestral line, embodied in the Shōwa Emperor, apparently resolved an oft-discussed conflict between the demands of family, on the one hand, and military leaders, on the other.

DEFEAT AND SUCCESS

Japan's defeat in the Second World War has become a landmark in world history, not least because it coincided with the first and so far only use of atomic bombs in warfare. The Allied, though predominantly American, Occupation which followed led to another influx of foreign influence into Japan, this time largely from the United States. The defeated people sought again to learn from their evident superiors, and surprised their victors by apparently cooperating with their programmes of demilitarisation and democratisation. Japan's army and navy were first disbanded, and only much later allowed to reform as 'self-defence forces'. The legacy of this period may be found in strong peacekeeping and anti-nuclear movements that have persisted in the new post-war Japan.

Many other changes were introduced into Japan during the Occupation. A new Constitution was drawn up, which brought the principles of democracy firmly into the legal system, at least in theory. The education system was revised, particularly with the aim of eliminating propaganda and the harmful nationalistic elements, and the state branch of Shintō was abolished. There was a radical land reform programme, which removed land from absentee landlords and allowed farmers who were actually working it to buy it at very low prices. Incipient organisations, such as labour unions, which had been suppressed, were allowed to develop. Women were given a vote, and the minimum age for male suffrage was lowered from 25 to 20. A period of intense economic hardship followed, as the return of soldiers and overseas administrators combined with a post-war 'baby-boom' to put tremendous pressure on the country's depleted resources. Gradually, however, the Japanese people drew on their cultural strength again. Dower (2000) is a very readable source about this period.

The tremendous economic success that Japan has achieved since that time is another important element of world history and a source of pride for Japanese people. Elements of the explanation for this phenomenon will emerge gradually during the chapters of this book, for it is necessary to understand the social forces that underlie economic behaviour to make full sense of it. With that success came again the self-confidence to consolidate imported values with underlying Japanese ones that seem to persist just below the surface and a flourishing of extraordinary Japanese invention and innovation swept the wider world. This coincided with another period of reaction to outside influence, partly demonstrated in a search for identity and cultural heritage that became almost a popular obsession.

Hundreds of publications appeared, written by a variety of academics, journalists and amateur intellectuals, each of whom proposed theories to explain the special qualities of Japan in contrast with the rest of the world, which they tended to lump together. Many of these books reached the bestseller list, some have been translated into English, and numerous television programmes have featured interviews and information about the major contributors. Anthropologists have analysed this whole phenomenon as an example of 'cultural nationalism' (Yoshino 1992). Harumi Befu (2001) saw it as a means of filling a 'symbolic vacuum' left when more usual national symbols such as the flag and national anthem became tainted by association with doubts about Japan's role in the Second World War.

During Japan's role as co-host of the World Cup in 2002, however, such symbols were used freely and positively. The flags of the participating nations became amusing and apparently innocuous parts of body decoration, and Japanese fans were not averse to sporting those of another people once Japan had been eliminated. It seems then that the search for identity itself may have taken on a new role.

IDENTITY IN GLOBALISED JAPAN

It is not unusual for people to emphasise their uniqueness. Indeed, this is one of the ways in which groups of one sort or another define themselves as distinct from others surrounding them. In the more distant past it was with China and Korea that Japan sought distinctions. During the years when Japan became so successfully and so rapidly a major player in the industrialised world much contact was with partners of quite a different historical background, and it was significantly with the West that many of the self-defining comparisons were made. As we all enter the twenty-first century, and other Asian countries make notable contributions to the 'globalised' world order, Japan would seem to have achieved a more mature and balanced position in that world.

Some Japanese have gained this maturity by travelling abroad, and the growth of Japanese enterprise, entertainment and religion in other parts of the world was quite phenomenal in the closing decades of the twentieth century. Two important anthropological collections about aspects of 'global Japan' are those edited by Eades, Gill and Befu (2000), and Befu and Guichard-Anguis (2001), and reference will later be made to chapters within them. With the strong yen, foreign tourism was also rife, but other Japanese have learned of the world and their own past without ever leaving Japanese shores. My own recent research identified considerable sophistication in an abundance of cultural theme parks that displayed detailed depictions of numerous foreign countries, and even a miniature round-up of the development of world architecture (Hendry 2000, see Figure 1.3).

Buildings in Japan are influenced by many foreign styles, and an abundance of imported music, food and cinema provides direct experience of the tastes of the wider world. Some other anthropological studies are worth a mention at this point. The first, by the American anthropologist Gordon Mathews, who lives in Hong Kong with his Japanese wife, proposes a sort of dual identity for members of the new globalised world. His book *Global Culture/Individual Identity* (2000) discusses the way that so much cultural information is available these days that people may almost select an identity from a global cultural supermarket through their choice of home, work, food, music, reading and religious affiliation. Their upbringing, which they cannot change, is the other basic part of their identity, and his study of Japanese artists and musicians examines the extent to which these identify themselves with their Japanese 'roots' or the culture of their chosen musical forms. He finds that their views are quite varied, and some of the reasons for this variety will again emerge in the subsequent chapters of this book, but an important factor he mentions is that of generation.

Although young people have a tendency to distinguish themselves from

Figure 1.3 This miniature Leaning Tower of Pisa is just one of the numerous reproductions of architectural wonder visitors may inspect at Tobu World
Square in central Japan.

their parents in any society, the growth and change in Japan's place in the
global community within living memory has been so extraordinary that it
seems legitimate to seek genuine differences between generations in contemporary Japan. Two of my own students are writing up work on this
subject. One – Bruce White – finds varying sources of identity precisely in
relation to different levels of social and cultural contact. The youngest of his
rural informants make distinctions about the wider world based on experience beyond the imagination of their parents and grandparents while they
themselves probably have only a vague idea of the mythological stories
which their grandparents were taught as history. Their attitudes are quite
different as well, and this was one of the findings of my other student,
Ayumi Sasagawa (2002), whose focus is on highly educated women who do
not return to work after creating families. Some of the content of these
attitudes will also emerge in later chapters. Both have a paper in Mathews
and White (2003).

Other anthropological studies have identified some interesting discrepancies in the way that Japan is, and the way that it represents itself, both
inside and outside Japan. One book – by Emiko Ohnuki-Tierney (1993) –
examines the way rice is picked as one of the most important symbols of

Japanese identity, despite clear evidence that consumption of this basic food has diminished to quite small quantities. Japan's attachment to local varieties of rice has also caused entirely uneconomic behaviour in this economically highly developed nation, she argues, explaining its importance in ritual, in aesthetics and in defining basic principles of social organisation. A volume edited by Pamela Asquith and Arne Kalland (1997) entitled *Japanese Images of Nature* offers many examples of the way 'natural' features of Japan are sought as symbols of identity. This oft-cited 'love of nature' in Japan is contrasted with hideous cases of environmental degradation at home and abroad.

Finally, an excellent study by Rupert Cox (2002) on the way that Zen arts are used to represent Japan to the outside world, shows how the tea ceremony and the martial arts create an image of that country at odds with the way they are practised at home. We will return to this subject in Chapter 10, but Cox's research highlights the use of Japanese arts as an expression of identity, recently presented to the world at large as benign and aesthetically pleasing to offset prior negative impressions of excessive belligerence and economic might. Japan's early entry into the turn-of-the-century world recession is often presented in a negative way, but a kind of compensatory export of Japanese arts and accomplishments to the theatres and galleries of the world offers a most congenial contribution to the shelves of that global cultural supermarket.

REFERENCES AND FURTHER READING

Aikens, C. Melvin and Takayasu Higuchi, *Prehistory of Japan* (Academic Press, New York, 1982)

Asquith, Pamela and Arne Kalland, *Japanese Images of Nature: Cultural Perspectives* (Curzon, Richmond, Surrey and Hawaii University Press, Honolulu, 1997)

Aston, W.G. (trans.), *Nihongi: Chronicles of Japan from the Earliest Times to AD 697* (Allen & Unwin, London, 1956)

Averbuch, Irit, *The Gods Come Dancing: A Study of the Japanese Ritual Dance of Yamabushi Kagura* (Cornell University Press, Ithaca, 1995)

Barnes, Gina L., *China, Korea and Japan: The Rise of Civilisation in East Asia* (Thames & Hudson, London, 1993)

Befu, Harumi, *Hegemony of Homogeneity* (Trans-Pacific Press, Melbourne, 2001)

Befu, Harumi and Sylvie Guichard-Anguis, *Globalizing Japan: Ethnography of the Japanese Presence in Asia, Europe and America* (Routledge, London, 2001)

Bowring, R. and P. Kornicki (eds), *The Cambridge Encyclopaedia of Japan* (Cambridge University Press, Cambridge, 1993)

Coaldrake, William H., *Architecture and Authority in Japan* (Routledge, London, 1995)

Colcutt, Martin, Marius Jansen and Isao Kamakura, *Cultural Atlas of Japan* (Andromeda, Oxford, 1988)

Cox, Rupert, *The Zen Arts: An Anthropological Study of the Culture of Aesthetic Form in Japan* (RoutledgeCurzon, London, 2002)

——(ed.), *Japan and the Culture of Copying* (RoutledgeCurzon, London, 2003)

Denoon, Donald, Mark Hudson, Gavin McCormack and Tessa Morris-Suzuki (eds), *Multicultural Japan: Paleolithic to Postmodern* (Cambridge University Press, Cambridge, 1996)

Dower, John, *Embracing Defeat* (Penguin Books, London, 2000)

Eades, J.S., Tom Gill and Harumi Befu, *Globalization and Social Change in Contemporary Japan* (Trans-Pacific Press, Melbourne, 2000)

Fawcett, Clare, 'Archaeology and Japanese Identity', in Denoon *et al.* (eds), *Multicultural Japan: Paleolithic to Postmodern* (Cambridge University Press, Cambridge, 1996), pp. 60–77

Frewer, Douglas, 'Japanese Postage Stamps as Social Agents: Some Anthropological Perspectives', *Japan Forum*, 14, 1 (2002).

Gluck, Carol, *Japan's Modern Myths: Ideology in the Late Meiji Period* (Princeton University Press, Princeton, 1985)

Goodman, Roger, Ceri Peach, Ayumi Takenaka and Paul White (eds), *Global Japan: The Experience of Japan's New Immigrant and Overseas Communities* (RoutledgeCurzon, London, 2003)

Hall, John Witney and Richard K. Beardsley, *Twelve Doors to Japan* (McGraw-Hill, New York, 1965)

Hendry, Joy, *The Orient Strikes Back: A Global View of Cultural Display* (Berg, Oxford and New York, 2000)

Hunter, Janet, *The Emergence of Modern Japan* (Longmans, London, 1989)

Kawada Minoru (trans. by Toshiko Kishida-Ellis), *The Origin of Ethnography in Japan: Yanagita Kunio and his Times* (Kegan Paul International, London and New York, 1993)

Kobayashi, Tatsuo and Simon Kaner, *Jomonesque Japan* (Oxbow Books, Oxford, 2003)

Mason, Penelope, *History of Japanese Art* (Abrams, New York, 1993)

Mathews, Gordon, *Global Culture/Individual Identity: Searching for Home in the Cultural Supermarket* (Routledge, London, 2000)

Mathews, Gordon and Bruce White (eds), *Japan's Changing Generations: Are Japan's Young People Creating a New Society?* (RoutledgeCurzon, London, 2003)

Morris, Ivan Ira, *The World of the Shining Prince: Court Life in Ancient Japan* (Oxford University Press, Oxford, 1964)

Morris-Suzuki, Tessa, 'A Descent into the Past: The Frontier in the Construction of Japanese Identity', in Denoon *et al.* (eds), *Multicultural Japan: Paleolithic to Postmodern* (Cambridge University Press, Cambridge, 1996), pp. 81–94

Ohnuki-Tierney, Emiko, *Rice as Self: Japanese Identities through Time* (Princeton University Press, Princeton, 1993)

Sansom, Sir George, *A History of Japan* (3 vols, Dawson, Folkestone, 1958)

Sasagawa, Ayumi, 'Life Choices: University Educated Mothers in a Japanese Suburb', Ph.D. thesis, Oxford Brookes University, 2002

Stefánsson, Halldór, 'Media Stories of Bliss and Mixed Blessings', in D.P. Martinez (ed.), *The Worlds of Japanese Popular Culture: Gender, Shifting Boundaries and Global Cultures* (Cambridge University Press, Cambridge, 1998)

Storry Richard, *A History of Modern Japan* (Penguin Books, Harmondsworth, 1984)
Tsunoda, Ryusaku (trans.) and L.C. Goodrich (ed.), *Japan in the Chinese Dynastic Histories* (Perkins Asiatic Monographs, no. 2, South Pasadena, 1951)
Vlastos, Stephen, *Mirror of Modernity: Invented Traditions of Modern Japan* (University of California Press, Berkeley, Los Angeles and London, 1998)
Yoshino Kōsaku, *Cultural Nationalism in Contemporary Japan* (Routledge, London, 1992)

RELATED NOVELS

Clavell, James, *Shōgun* (Dell Publishing Co., New York, 1976)
—— *Gaijin* (Hodder & Stoughton, London, 1993)
Endō, Shūsaku, *The Samurai* (Penguin Books, Harmondsworth, 1986)
Hearn, Liam, *Across the Nightingale Floor: Tales of the Otori* (Riverhead Books, Penguin Putnam, New York, 2002)
Shiba, Ryotaro, translated by Juliet Winters Carpenter, *The Last Shogun: The Life of Tokugawa Yoshinobu* (Kodansha International, New York, Tokyo and London, 1998)

FILMS

Birth of Japan (*Nippon Tanjō*) (1959 Hiroshi Inagaki)
Deep Desire of Gods (*Kamigami no Fukaki Yokubō*) (1968 Shōhei Imamura)
The 47 Loyal Samurai (*Genroku Chūshingura*) (1941–2 Kenji Mizoguchi)
The Passage to Japan (*Fukuzawa Yukichi*) (1991 Shinichiro Sawai)

2 The house and family system

INTRODUCTION

In Japan, as elsewhere, life begins in a family and it is here that children build up a picture of the world. Family members are usually the first people they learn to classify, and the way in which these close relations are defined varies greatly from one society to another. The perception of relatives is also influenced by residential arrangements, and Japan has as many possibilities as any other modern society, but it is important not to draw conclusions based only on apparent similarities in lifestyle. Anthropologists have found that understanding the principles defining relatives, sometimes even quite different from the biological ones implied in English usage, is vital to understanding systems of classification used in the wider society. Kin relations are also inextricably associated with other types of relations, so that economic activities, political relations and religious practices may also only properly be understood when considered in the context of the kinship system.

The importance of kin relations in Japan should already be clear from the previous chapter, and though there has in practice been considerable regional and occupational diversity, the family has historically been the focus of considerable ideology. In the Meiji period, when Japanese intellectuals were reassessing the whole structure of Japanese life in preparation for the establishment of a new Civil Code, something they described as the 'family system' was a bone of much contention. Some saw a traditional model as essential for the maintenance of orderly social life, others saw it as a major hindrance to the progress they sought in their modern, internationalised world. The Civil Code of 1898 ended up as a compromise, but the debate continued at an intellectual level.

This Japanese 'family system' was based on a model approximated by samurai families in the nineteenth century, which was an essentially indigenous Japanese system, supported by an overlay of Confucian ideology. By 1890, there was already a growing feeling in conservative quarters that Western influence was getting out of hand, and an imperial rescript on education issued at that time made explicit the expected values of the system. It was to be learned by heart and recited daily by all schoolchildren. Educationalists of the time tended to be traditionalists, and as enrolment in schools was up to 98 per cent by 1909, the dissemination of these ideas was extremely efficient. There were of course variations in the practice of this 'family system', but its principles became common cultural property, and the model of family relations was used explicitly in many other areas of life.

The same 'family system' was blamed for all sorts of evils during the Allied Occupation, and it was virtually demolished legally in the 1947 Constitution. Modern Japanese life has in many areas become rather incompatible with the system in its traditional form, and Japanese social scientists used to predict its total demise. However, that old family system contains deeply held values and anthropologist Takami Kuwayama (2001:24) has argued that the ideas and attitudes derived from the system are far from extinct, even in the urban sprawl. An understanding of the traditional system will pave the way for appreciating its modern manifestations, and will also lay a foundation for later chapters where its value as a model will become evident. The system will therefore be described here in some detail before we turn to look at the variety of living arrangements found in contemporary Japan.

THE *IE*

The basis of 'the family system' is a unit that does not happily translate as 'family' at all. Indeed, the whole notion of a 'family system' was a concept created in the face of outside influence to explain Japanese behaviour in a comparative context. At any one time, the Japanese household may look rather similar to a domestic unit in any number of other societies, but at an ideological level, this unit is better described using the indigenous term *ie*. 'Family' in one of the senses used by European aristocracy, of a continuing 'line' requiring a definite heir in each generation, would be close in sense, but the word 'family' has several other shades of meaning. 'House' is a better translation, because *ie* may also signify a building, and the English term does again have a connotation of continuity, as in the expression, 'House of Windsor'.

Continuity is an essential feature of the *ie*. The individual members of a particular house, who need not always be resident, occupy the roles of the living members of that particular *ie*. The total membership includes all those who went before: the ancestors, now forgotten as individuals, the recently dead who are remembered; and the descendants as yet unborn.

It is the duty of the living members at any one time to remember their predecessors, and to ensure that the house will continue after they die (see Figure 2.1).

It was the *ie* as a unit that was regarded as owning any property which accrued to it in the traditional system, but in the Meiji Civil Code this property had to be registered in the name of a particular individual. There was usually an occupation associated with the *ie*, and members were expected to contribute to it as they were able, sharing its benefits without individual remuneration. Members were also expected to maintain the status of their particular *ie* within the wider community, and an individual who threatened to bring shame on the house could be cut off from membership. The continuing entity was more important than any individual member, and individual members were expected to find their *raison d'être* in the maintenance and continuity of the *ie*.

The affairs of the *ie* were ultimately managed by the head, although certain tasks and responsibilities could be delegated to other members. The head was legally responsible for all the members, who were subordinate to him, but again, if any particular head became despotic or detrimental in some other way to the house as a whole, he could be removed according to the decision of a wider family council. Within the house, the head was supposed to be given privileges, like being served first at meals and being allowed to take the first bath. Relations between members were

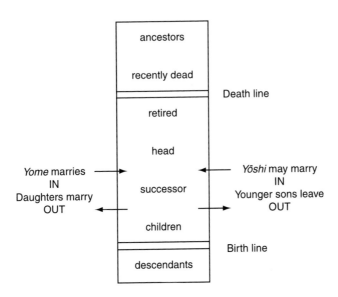

Figure 2.1 Elements of the *ie*.

hierarchically organised along lines of distinction based on age, sex and expectation of permanency in the house.

In general, the younger members of the house were seen as indebted to the older members for their upbringing, and in return they were expected to take care of the older members when they could no longer manage for themselves. The relations between generations were characterised by Confucian principles of loyalty and benevolence, so that sons and daughters would personalise their duty to the house as loyalty to their parents for benevolence received. Women were supposed to obey men, and a new bride her mother-in-law as well. Relations within the house were characterised less by love and affection than by duty and filial piety, and too close a relationship between a husband and wife, for example, could even be seen as detrimental to the house as a whole.

In each generation, one permanent heir would be chosen, and a spouse would be brought in to share the role of continuing the family line. Other members of that generation could stay in the *ie*, or return to it, but if they married they were expected to move out. The system that became codified was that of primogeniture, or inheritance by the eldest son, but there had been a number of regional variations, including first-child inheritance – male or a female – in some northern districts, and last-son inheritance in parts of Kyushu.

Again, the insurance of continuity was more important than the particular means, and all sorts of arrangements could be made to accomplish this aim. If there were no sons, for example, a son-in-law could be married in to take the role of successor, and this position of *yōshi* was a common one for non-inheriting sons from other houses. If there were no children at all, a new spouse could be sought, or a relative's child could be adopted, or the head could take a concubine to produce an heir, who would then be brought up by his wife. It was also permissible, if necessary, to adopt a totally unrelated child, so that the blood connection, while desirable, was not indispensable to the continuity of the *ie*.

The spouse brought in to marry the heir of a particular house was in a somewhat precarious position for a while. Any *ie* was regarded as having its own customs or 'ways', and although marriages were made preferably with houses of a similar standing, an outsider needed to demonstrate fitness to adapt to these ways. An unsuitable wife (*yome*) or *yōshi* could be returned to their house of origin for lack of general fitness, as well as possible barrenness. Such a resort could even be taken if an outsider fell ill in middle life, and became unable to carry on with his or her expected duties. Again, the *ie* is seen to take precedence over its individual members.

RELATIONS BETWEEN *IE*

A preferable possibility for a non-inheriting son was to set up his own house and start a new *ie*. This would be regarded as a branch of the main house, and in some areas there developed a strong wider group of houses which had all at some stage branched off from an original main one. These groups tended to maintain a stronger hierarchy in the north of Japan, based on when they were formed, but in the south such relations could be forgotten within a few generations. Groups of related houses, known as *dōzoku*, often cooperated in economic activities, too, and in the north of Japan the local political community was organised along these lines as well (see Figure 2.2).

In the early period of industrialisation many of Japan's big companies were formed in a similar way. The principle that branch houses owed

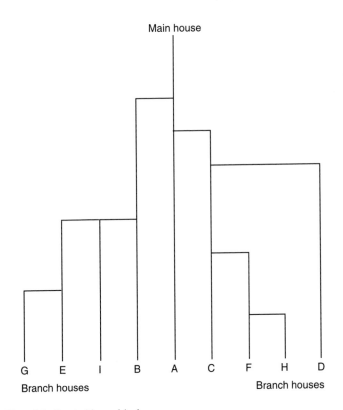

Figure 2.2 Dōzoku hierarchical group.

allegiance to the main ones was also exploited in the pre-war image that depicted every house in the nation as ultimately being a branch of the imperial family line. Thus one's allegiance to the *ie* could be translated into a wider allegiance to the Emperor, as head of the original main house, and the nation he represented could be pictured as one great family group. Similar principles operated in the great and small families of earlier periods, too.

THE *IE*'S LEGAL DEMISE

There have always been regional and occupational variations, particularly in marriage arrangements, and individual families developed their own idiosyncrasies within particular areas. Nevertheless, for centuries, the laws of the time generally supported a similar system, and the Meiji Civil Code simply introduced centralisation with modifications to the previous regionally varying codes. From 1881 families were to be registered with the authorities and they were registered as continuing units. Records reveal that families sometimes officially recorded arrangements in line with the new Civil Code, but in practice continued with something they found preferable. For example, first-son inheritance did not suit some families, yet they would register their eldest son as if he were the successor.

In the Civil Code drawn up during the Allied Occupation, the *ie* was abolished as a legal unit, and now a nuclear family has to be registered on its creation at marriage. All children are supposed to have equal rights to inheritance and they share responsibility for the care of their parents. The laws are drawn up according to the Constitution of 1947 which states: 'With regard to choice of spouse, property rights, inheritance, choice of domicile, divorce and other matters pertaining to marriage and the family, laws shall be enacted from the standpoint of individual dignity and the essential equality of the sexes' (Article 24).

It is clear that these values are imported directly from the West, and are at variance with the system described above. It was decided that the 'family system' was incompatible with the democratic state that Japan was to become, and it was discarded in legal form, along with other so-called relics of feudalism. These new values were taught in schools, and they have often been held up as ideals to be emulated. In many ways the family has altered in post-war Japan, but just as people found ways to cope with discrepancies between their own ideas and the law in the matter of the inheritance of the eldest son, so they are not necessarily too concerned with the legal code in other matters. In fact the notion of the *ie* continues to be held quite happily in many parts of Japan, and elsewhere its underlying principles pervade the nuclear families which appear on the surface to be quite independent. One clause in the new Civil Code actually makes provision for a certain amount of continuity, in that one member of a family needs to be chosen to take care of the genealogical records and 'utensils of religious rites' (Article 897). A closer examination of these religious rites will further elucidate the depth of these persistent ideas.

THE RELIGIOUS CHARTER

Within a house, the charter for the continuity of the *ie* takes the form of a Buddhist altar, or *butsudan*, where the memory of the ancestors is preserved (see Figure 2.3). When a member of the house dies, a tablet is made bearing the posthumous name given to him or her by the Buddhist priest who performs the funeral, and this is kept in the altar. These altars are found in most houses which have been allocated the responsibility for the care of departed forbears and thus the family grave, a duty codified since the Meiji Civil Code, and even included also in the new post-war code. Offerings are made regularly, and special memorial services are performed for the care of the soul at certain fixed times after death for a period of up to fifty or sixty years, depending on the region.

Once these memorials are complete, the 'recently dead' member of the family joins the general category of ancestor (*senzo*), and is then remembered in company with the other predecessors of the house. Some say that the *senzo* become Shintō deities once the Buddhist memorial rites are complete and the last memorial should therefore be a celebration, rather than an occasion of mourning. In any case, there is an idea that ancestors eventually merge into a kind of single spiritual entity, from which souls emerge for babies who are born, and this notion is distinct from Buddhist ideas found elsewhere.

In practice, the Buddhist altar symbolises the continuity and existence of the *ie*, and visiting members of the house will sometimes walk right past their living relatives to greet ancestors before they acknowledge the human beings present. Gifts received by the house are often presented to the ancestors before they are opened, or placed inside the altar after the wrapping has been removed. Members of the family may consult the ancestors about important decisions, and the doors of the *butsudan* are opened on special occasions so that the ancestors may participate.

Once a year there is a festival called *Bon* to remember the souls of departed ancestors, and people still make long trips all over Japan to visit the homes of their birth and original ancestors. Wives will also often leave

Figure 2.3 Families remember their departed members at the Buddhist altar in the home.

their marital homes at this time to visit their natal *ie*, and city families travel out to the country to visit the family *butsudan* and renew ties with the relatives of their youth. At New Year, too, similar visits are made, and both occasions are regarded as appropriate times for members of branch houses to pay their respects to their ultimate ancestors in the main house.

In many Japanese houses, there is also a Shintō 'god-shelf', which is associated with the imperial ancestress Amaterasu Omikami. Offerings are made here too, and amulets and talismans purchased during visits to Shintō shrines will be kept on this shelf. The Shintō shelf is cheaper, usually less conspicuous than the *butsudan* and the offerings are less abundant, but it is hard not to draw a parallel between these two places of reverence. Although no one emphasises these links much today, it seems likely that this 'god-shelf' still serves a symbolic purpose in identifying members of every household with the ultimate ancestors they share as members of the Japanese nation.

DOMESTIC ARRANGEMENTS

In some parts of Japan to this day, members of a family living under one roof will conceptualise their unit as a continuing *ie*. This is particularly the case if the house has been passed down through several generations, and even if all the generations are not present a scattered family may see themselves as only temporarily separated. In other cases, couples of two generations may live in close proximity, an arrangement not dissimilar from an older one found in certain regions of Japan where an *inkyō-ya*, or retirement house, was built close to the main family home. It is said that one needs to be near enough to be able to carry hot soup from one house to the other without having to heat it up again.

'Continuing houses' tend to flourish where there is an *ie* occupation, or the house owns its own land. Some family businesses share a site with the family home, and two or more generations may share the burden of the work. Where considerable investment has been made into the property or business, it is economically sensible for parents to encourage their children to carry on the line. Doctors, for example, must invest a hefty sum if they want to build their own hospitals and clinics, and the benefits are really only reaped in the next generation if their children become doctors, or at least hospital managers. The entrance requirements for medical school are so stringent that medical families sometimes send their pre-kindergarten children to classes to try and give them a head start over their peers.

In rural areas, too, the continuing *ie* is still common, though the success with which continuity is maintained depends very much on local circumstances. Farmers, for instance, need a lucrative cash crop, or some additional source of income, if they are to thrive. In Kyushu, where I carried out research myself, the cultivation of tea and chrysanthemums – aided by electric light – has been enough of an incentive to keep a son in many houses, though it seems to be becoming increasingly difficult to find wives to share that kind of work. In other parts of rural Japan, farmers have brought wives from Korea and the Philippines to maintain the family prosperity. An anthropological study carried out in the location of a ski resort, however, demonstrated that an injection of new economic prosperity can work wonders for the success of the continuing family (Moon 1998).

Today the majority of Japanese families live in urban areas, and for most there is no longer a physical *ie* which has been passed down through the generations. Typically a married couple will set up home in a rented apartment, perhaps with the long-term goal of eventually buying their own freestanding house. Statistics about living arrangements in Japan show a decreasing proportion of three generation families, but the proportion of couples with children is also decreasing, and in 2000 stood at just under one-third. Little can be discerned from these figures about how many units are entirely independent and how many still have obligations to each other. It is not unusual for an elderly parent to move in with a son or daughter in later life, for example, or perhaps to come and live near enough to share hot soup. Other young people living with their children have only sporadic relations with the previous generation.

In the late 1980s, a new version of intergenerational living became popular in the 'three-storey two-family' house, much advertised in urban areas. These houses may make use of land owned by an older generation but developed into a new house with the salary of their son or daughter and their family. Typically the house is built with a ground floor for the older couple, who will have their own entrance and an independent kitchen and bathroom. The first floor then houses the main living rooms of the younger family and perhaps the parental sleeping area while the third floor provides study-bedrooms for the children. According to the research of anthropologist Naomi Brown (2002), who worked in a company marketing this form of accommodation, the apartments of families related through a daughter are more likely to include an inner staircase, but they may well still be registered for statistical purposes as two separate units.

In fact, according to the housing statistics, there has been a steady increase in the proportion of couples residing without children, and single-person households have increased dramatically. Between 1970 and 1990 the latter increased by 50 per cent and the proportion of houses solely occupied by couples increased by more than 60 per cent. By 2000 they were approximately one-quarter and one-fifth of all households respectively (*FFJ* 2002:18). Many of these are couples, or widows and widowers, whose children have left home, but it is impossible to tell whether or not they are near enough to help out. Other single-person households are young people before marriage, and the age of marriage is steadily rising. Some are those whose marriages have broken up, and there is also an increase in the divorce rate and the proportion of single-parent families. Finally, there is apparently an increase both in the number of people who choose not to marry at all and those who decide, though married, not to have children. Jolivet (1997) has some interesting personal accounts.

There are of course various reasons for changes such as these. An excellent book by Wim Lunsing (2001), entitled *Beyond Common Sense*, takes as its subject the people who have rejected the 'common sense' of marriage and 'normal' family life. He argues that it became much more acceptable to live alone in the last couple of decades of the twentieth century. Thus single women who would previously have bemoaned such a state now point to its advantages, especially if they espouse feminist principles. It has also become much more acceptable to be openly homosexual in Japan and an increasing number of gay men live alone rather than creating a marriage of convenience as had been more common in the past. Lesbians are more likely to create a home together, he found, and he cites such a situation as one of the most common forms of alternative lifestyle beyond single-person households.

Sexuality is not the only factor influencing change, however, and the post-bubble recession has been blamed for a tendency for young people, married or otherwise, to postpone settling into the constraints of family life. Difficulties in finding long-term employment is almost certainly a contributory factor, but the youngsters known as 'freeters' have probably been given that name partly because they value the freedom it gives them to try out various ways of life. A couple I met in the warm southern regions of the Okinawan islands had moved there from large cities to enjoy swimming and diving for a few years, and they did menial jobs to pay their way. Some young people with quite well paying jobs have been dubbed 'parasite singles' because they continue to rely on parental support, perhaps even living in the family home, instead of setting themselves up and having children of their own.

Some of the negative spin placed on situations such as these stems from publicity about a demographic problem that has been brewing for decades in Japan. The first part relates to life expectancy, which is the longest in the world, and should therefore be a cause for celebration. However, coupled with this is a decline in the birth rate that is also amongst the most severe, and forecasts predict that by 2040 one third of the population will be over 65 while only 11 per cent will be under 14 (*FF J* 2002:10). Although the decline in family support would appear to have been less sharp and severe than earlier predicted, this 'greying of society' is often cited as a cause for serious concern. One aspect of the problem relates to the growing numbers of old people in Japan who, for whatever reason, are unable or unwilling to rely on relatives to see them through their final years.

Several innovative ventures have been seeking to create a new image, summed up somewhat sarcastically as the 'silver business', or the 'silver boom' – 'silver' being the designated positive version of 'grey'. Glenda

Roberts (1996) found an example of this kind of support for healthy retirees in Silver Talent Centers, local government-sponsored work programmes meant to help older people re-connect with their communities, earn pocket money and stay healthy by remaining active and involved. While such goals were fulfilled for many participants, class differences tended to keep white-collar retirees away from the largely manual jobs, such as parks mainten-ance, home help, crafts and light manufacturing. For these, another area of burgeoning activity has been as a volunteer in community projects and taking part in creating the new 'civil society', a subject we will hear more about in later chapters.

Roberts also noted a gender imbalance in membership of the Silver Talent Centers, with men forming two-thirds, stemming from a family reluctance to allow grandmothers to go out to work as it is considered unseemly. This may be related to the nature of gender roles in the house-hold as the household activities that older women maintain are central to their identities, whereas men who were salaried lose their identities upon retirement and cast about trying to fit in somewhere. Although previously the elderly could stop worrying about supporting the household, Roberts found that many of these seniors were using their earnings as gifts to daugh-ters-in-law or grandchildren, in anticipation of a time when they would need to be cared for and could no longer reciprocate.

A study by Kinoshita and Kiefer (1993) makes a clear and readable summary of the contemporary situation for those who choose not to depend on their children. Entitled *Refuge of the Honored*, the book eventually focuses on one of the earliest 'retirement homes' to be created, and charts its progress through a period of nine formative years. Kinoshita lived in the community, with his family, participated in all its activities and became a well-known figure to the management and local residents alike. They shared with him as they experienced them the trials and tribulations of creating community life from scratch, and he followed up particular issues over a continuing period to see how they would develop. The results are laid out in comparison with experiences reported elsewhere, and they are placed in the context of the overall Japanese facilities available for this section of society, as well as of studies carried out in other parts of the world.

Refuge of the Honored documents the retirement lives of relatively affluent members of Japanese society, however, and two papers published by anthropologist Diana Bethel (both 1992) report on the state of affairs in an old people's home run by the social welfare system. She makes clear that institutionalisation represents a failure to achieve the Confucian ideal of filial piety for ageing parents to live with their children, and that in their darker moments the residents are only too aware of this, but she also describes the way they come to terms with their situation. Some are even pleasantly surprised by the camaraderie that they experience. They try to establish familiar patterns of social life, and engage in traditional practices such as gift-giving amongst themselves.

It is not only old people who fall through the family net, of course, and anthropologists have also taken an interest in people of other ages who find themselves to some extent thrown upon the wider society for their care. An interesting book by Roger Goodman (2000) provides a wealth of information about Japanese children's homes and other aspects of the social welfare system (see also Chapter 9). The material is set in an international context, but Goodman finds that principles of the continuing *ie* are helping to maintain a very Japanese style of facility, typically run as a kind of family business. Tom Gill (2001) spent considerable time examining the lives of men who largely live on the streets of Tokyo, and one chapter of his book describes movingly the makeshift homes they create for themselves free of former family ties. Another useful book by Carolyn Stevens (1997) documents the various forms of welfare that are meted out to these same groups.

INTERPERSONAL RELATIONS BETWEEN THE GENERATIONS

Even within a continuing house, there is sometimes conflict about the expectations. The older generations would like the *ie* to continue, partly for the sake of the ancestors, perhaps also for the sake of the household occupation and for the practical needs that they may have in their old age. Yet they know that the current emphasis on individual rights demands that they should allow their children to choose their own lives. In the past people gave service to the house by taking care of senior and junior generations, knowing that they owed their livelihood to the former, and in the confidence that the latter would reciprocate in later years. It thus comes particularly hard on the generations who have given service to find that modern ideology no longer supports their case. It is thought to be a poor way to end one's life in an old people's home, and the elderly are inclined to pray for a quick death.

In practice, many old people do still spend their later years close to their families, whether it be in the family home, or moving to, or near to the home of one of their children. Very often there will be a successor who regards their care as his duty. There is still a strong sense of obligation to the older generation in Japan, whether co-residence is practised or not, and the three-storey houses with separate entrances would seem to offer a good compromise. Increasingly, however, parents opt to stay with their daughters' families, as was mentioned for the two-generation city houses discussed above. In other cases siblings will share the responsibility by visiting their parents while they can manage by themselves in the family home, and later move them into the largest of their houses, or to facilities nearby.

Despite the law that inheritance should be divided equally between all children, family land or property often cannot stand division, and non-inheriting children will sometimes sign away their rights for the sake of the *ie*, especially if one of their number agrees to take responsibility for the family home. The non-inheriting sons may then receive a contribution towards house purchase or education, and daughters customarily receive a trousseau on marriage. These forms of aid are given in lieu of inheritance, and to some extent represent a relinquishment of the joint responsibility for the older generation, although if something should prevent the successor carrying out his duties, other children may step in to help out. Such arrangements do not always work out smoothly, of course, and there are cases where the construction by one sibling of a three-storey/two-generation house on the family's expensive land in Tokyo has resulted in lawsuits from the other siblings.

Another change is that while it used to be the case that a junior wife would give up outside work to take care of her elderly parents or parents-in-law when they could no longer cope alone during the day, there is more outside support these days. If the younger members of a house are out at work all day, they may take the elderly to a day-care centre, just as they will take their young children. Such institutions are mushrooming throughout Japan, partly as a response to the falling birth rate, and sometimes facilities for both dependent groups are sited close to one another on the principle that it is good for young and old to have contact. An interesting anthropological study by Leng Leng Thang (1999, 2001) found that the results of such a policy are not always as successful as the original planners had hoped, though it seems clear that at an ideological level they appear to compensate for a decline in multigenerational living.

All these modifications to the relations between generations have in turn modified interpersonal relations within the house. The strictly hierarchical system has inevitably broken down at the ideological level. In practice it was often not quite as strict as it was portrayed, but there is little doubt that the senior generations had more power and authority in the past than they do now, and the younger ones were certainly more burdened with specific duties. Nevertheless, the reciprocal concern between generations seems to be alive and well in many families, whatever their living arrangements, and the principles of benevolence for loyalty between parent and child have yet to be eradicated at their original level.

Two anthropological studies document the strong ties of obligation and ideological continuity persisting at the highest level in Japanese families regardless of living arrangements. One of these recounts the way that women agree to and cope with strategic marriages within the long-standing business families that stand at the pinnacle of enormous Japanese corporations (Hamabata 1990). The other is about families of the former nobility, officially dissolved in 1947, but still acting out their lives as representatives of an important social elite in Japanese society, notably because of the depth of their family line (Lebra 1993). For different reasons, each of these groups invests considerable effort into perpetuating the family system and both books offer an intimate and highly informative view of the areas of Japanese society they have chosen to highlight.

MALE–FEMALE RELATIONS

According to the Confucian principles which were brought to apply to the indigenous family system men were superior to women, who were expected to attend to their every need. Marriages were arranged by relatives according to the appropriateness of background and social status, and love between husbands and wives was thought to be inconsistent with the filial piety which demanded that attention be paid to the needs of elders and children before those of a spouse. For men, affairs outside the home were not only accepted, but also even expected, whereas until 1908 a woman could be killed with impunity by a husband who discovered her in an adulterous act. A woman was taught that her chief duty in life was obedience, first to her father, then to her husband and his parents, and finally, when widowed, to her son.

Married women were usually also outsiders in the house, and for some time after their marriage they also came under the subjection of their mothers-in-law. In fact the word commonly used for a young wife (*yome*) has the literal meaning of woman of the *ie*, and in the early years of marriage a young wife would be at everyone's beck and call. Women were responsible for cooking, cleaning and washing, but they also took an active part in the household occupation, and small children could well be left to the care of a less able-bodied member of the family, such as a grandmother or grandfather, during much of the day. Child care was not exclusively a woman's role, and young wives in the village where I worked complained that they missed much of the fun of rearing their children since they were stronger than their fathers-in-law for the productive work.

Indeed, in many parts of the country women played a much stronger role than these Confucian ideals would suggest, and in indigenous ideology women have held important ritual roles as well, such as those described in the previous chapter for the Empress Himiko. These are still well documented in Okinawa and an anthropological study by Arne Røkkum (1998) entitled *Goddesses, Priestesses and Sisters* analyses some of these female roles. Within the continuing houses in Kyushu where I worked family decisions were often made in council and the influence of the women could be considerable, although this obviously varied from house to house. Men were expected to represent their houses, and they would be seated in top positions at official gatherings, but the locus of power was never as simple as these formal arrangements would suggest. Indeed, apron-clad women were often called from the kitchen to clear up important public matters.

Marriages in the country were based on mutual attraction in pre-Meiji times, and young people were given freedom to establish their own relationships and even monitor those of others in the community. The distant unions developed by the samurai class were often arranged to cement strategic alliances, just as Hamabata describes for the former *zaibatsu*, and although such arrangements spread for a while throughout all social classes, love marriages have now become acceptable again. Arranged meetings known as *miai* have been used to good effect throughout Japan to introduce young people to others from a background thought appropriate by elder relatives, and many couples have benefited from such a system (Chapter 8 has more detail). In continuing houses, it is helpful if an incomer can get along with the other members of the house as well as their spouse, although accommodation for the newly weds is sometimes quite private these days.

In nuclear families, especially those of men who work for big companies, it has become common for a woman to stay at home, keep house and attend to the small children, and she is usually entrusted with the family finances as well. Some women take this role so seriously that they are called 'professional housewives', a role very often involving considerable input to the children's education as well as research into household products, the nutritional value of food for the family, and so on. In many parts of Japan housewives have set up cooperatives for buying food directly from producers, partly to cut out the expensive middlemen and partly to have some control over the production process. One of these groups in 1989 was awarded an international prize for creating an alternative economy based on 'cooperation, human contact and ecological sustainability' (Hendry 1993).

However, more than 50 per cent of married women do actually go out to work, and many others help in a family business, or take piecework into the home. The role of the grandparents is still strong with regard to child care, and women who do go out to work are often able to draw on this resource, at least for part-time aid. It may be seen as a reciprocal benefit for the shared or close living quarters, although many young mothers in cities too report that they would prefer to stay at home with their children.

Sasagawa's (2002, referred to in Chapter 1) work with highly educated mothers who do not return to work after giving birth would seem to suggest that if the resources are there it has even become an option of preference. Other women take a period off while their children are very small, and then accept a part-time job so that they can return home in time to collect their children from their day nurseries, or be there when they come in from school.

There are, of course, women who want to pursue a serious career, or simply to work the same long hours that men do, and these may decide not to have children at all. As we saw above, the numbers of houses occupied by single people or couples is fast increasing and many of these involve childless women. Women in nuclear families are also seeking more cooperation from their husbands in the running of the home and some men genuinely seem to be making an effort to comply (see Ishii-Kuntz 2002, for example). Academic families of my own experience include several where men and women have worked out a sharing of the roles of child care so that they can both continue their careers, and in one case, the father seemed a lot more concerned about his son than the mother did. Somehow even the most helpful of husbands still seems to take precedence as if by right in a clash of interests, however.

As for other domestic tasks, a visit I made to Matsushita's Museum of Technological Developments in Osaka in the year 2000 suggested that it will only be a few years before almost anything can be done by remote control. Access to light switches, doors, shutters, bath heaters and rice cookers may all be made from a mobile telephone so that a call home can answer the door bell, attend to security, organise a comfortable environment and cook supper. The development of such technology may help working wives to manage their homes from a distance, but it can also make it easier for people to live quite well on their own so it may not solve the problems associated with the drop in the birth rate. On the other hand a disembodied greeting as one returns home may not be quite the same thing as a bit of human contact.

THE FAMILY AS A MODEL

If much of the 'family system' has been modified within the domestic realm, discourse about the *ie* and its underlying principles are still used as forms of ideology in other areas of society. Kuwayama's (2001) comprehensive survey of work on the subject demonstrates the way that the principles of the *ie* are used as a source of Japanese cultural identity, contrasted with a perceived Western emphasis on individualism and individual rights. An ongoing debate that illustrates this contrast is concerned with the issue of dual surnames within one family. Raised in the context of the post-war Constitution that advocates the 'essential equality of the sexes', the issue was advocated largely on behalf of women who want to be allowed to keep (and officially to register) their own names on marriage. Arguments against draw heavily on the value of the *ie*, Kuwayama argues, and the issue remains unresolved. Ironically, perhaps, an *ie* can choose the surname of either partner as it had sometimes to accommodate an incoming male to continue the line, but this does not satisfy the protagonists of change.

The situation illustrates one of the basic ideas taken from the ideology of the family system in Japan, namely that of putting the house before the individual needs of its members, and this principle is referred to in many other areas of Japanese life. The subject will recur in later chapters, but the all-embracing nature of the large Japanese company has been cited as a good example, and it has been argued that for company employees the company itself has taken over the traditional role of the *ie*. In the way that parents expected loyalty from their children, a company superior expects total loyalty from his subordinates, and the individual's real family should come second. In exchange, the superior will take care of the individual and his family, if necessary, even to the extent of arranging a marriage for him. In practice, there has been change here, too, and an increasing number of employees will at least sometimes offer family reasons for leaving their offices early.

An ethnographic study carried out with employees of the National Railways in Japan, before they were privatised into regional sections, illustrates very clearly the way the family model was used and manipulated within a particular work context. Paul Noguchi (1990) describes the way that the image of the family was constantly invoked by the authorities in the slogan 'One Railroad Family', but he also noted that the ideology was open to different interpretations at different levels among the employees and at different times in their careers. His analysis of the system is based on two longish periods of participant observation, and his work reveals some of the immense complexity found in working relations based on these principles of family cooperation. Dorinne Kondo's (1990) work in a confectionery factory (see Chapter 3) also illustrates the use of this model.

The idea of giving loyalty in exchange for benevolence may be referred to as appropriate for pairs of relationships in various walks of life, and the expression *oyabun/kobun*, or parent-part/child-part, is sometimes used to describe such relations. It has been used for bonds between teacher and pupil, master or mistress and apprentice, landlord and tenant, and, in particular, criminal and accomplice. Like the bond between parent and child, it implies that these relationships are expected to last, and the beneficiary expected to consult and visit the benefactor even unto death if need be. Evidently the family and the ideology associated with it has much in the way of preparation for the world outside. More specific aspects of this preparation will be presented in the chapter that follows.

REFERENCES AND FURTHER READING

Bernstein, Gail Lee, *Haruko's World: A Japanese Farm Woman and Her Community* (Stanford University Press, Stanford, 1996)

Bethel, Diana, 'Alienation and Reconnection in a Home for the Elderly', in Joseph Tobin, (ed.), *Re-made in Japan* (Yale University Press, New Haven and London, 1992)

—— 'Life in *Obasuteyama*, or, Inside a Japanese Institution for the Elderly', in T.S. Lebra, *Japanese Social Organisation* (University of Hawaii Press, Honolulu, 1992), pp. 109–34

Brown, Naomi, 'Under One Roof: The Evolving Story of Three Generation Housing in Japan', in John Traphagan and John Knight (eds), *Demographic Change and the Family in Japan's Aging Society* (State University of New York Press, New York, 2002)

Dore, R.P., *City Life in Japan* (University of California Press, Berkeley, 1971), section III

FFJ – Facts and Figures of Japan (Foreign Press Centre, Japan, 2002)

Gill, Tom, *Men of Uncertainty: The Social Organization of Day Laborers in Contemporary Japan* (State University of New York Press, New York, 2001)

Goodman, Roger, *Children of the Japanese State: The Changing Role of Child Protection Institutions in Contemporary Japan* (Clarendon Press, Oxford, 2000)

Hamabata, Matthews Masayuki, *Crested Kimono: Power and Love in the Japanese Business Family* (Cornell University Press, Ithaca, 1990)

Hendry, Joy, 'The Role of the Professional Housewife', in Janet Hunter (ed.), *Japanese Women Working* (Routledge, London, 1993)

Imamura, Anne E., *Urban Japanese Housewives* (Hawaii University Press, Honolulu, 1987)

Ishii-Kuntz, Masako, 'Balancing Fatherhood and Work: Emergence of Diverse Masculinities in Contemporary Japan', in James E. Roberson and Nobue Suzuki, *Men and Masculinities in Contemporary Japan: Dislocating the Salaryman Doxa* (Routledge, London, 2002)

Jeremy, M. and M.E. Robinson, *Ceremony and Symbolism in the Japanese Home* (Manchester University Press, Manchester, 1989)

Jolivet, Muriel, *Japan: The Childless Society* (Routledge, London and New York, 1997)

Kinoshita, Yasuhito and Christie W. Kiefer, *Refuge of the Honored: Social Organization in a Japanese Retirement Community* (University of California Press, Berkeley, 1993)

Kuwayama, Takami, 'The Discourse of *Ie* (Family) in Japan's Cultural Identity and Nationalism: A Critique', *Japanese Review of Cultural Anthropology*, 2 (2001)

Lebra, T.S., *Above the Clouds: Status Culture of the Modern Japanese Nobility* (University of California Press, Berkeley, 1993)

Lunsing, Wim, *Beyond Common Sense: Sexuality and Gender in Contemporary Japan* (Kegan Paul, London, New York and Bahrain, 2001)

Moon, Okpyo, 'Is the *Ie* Disappearing in Rural Japan? The Impact of Tourism on a Traditional Japanese Village', in Joy Hendry (ed.), *Interpreting Japanese Society* (Routledge, London, 1998)

Noguchi, Paul H., *Delayed Departures, Overdue Arrivals: Industrial Familialism and the Japanese National Railways* (University of Hawaii Press, Honolulu, 1990)

Ochiai Emiko, *The Japanese Family System in Transition: A Sociological Analysis of Family Change in Postwar Japan* (LTCB International Library Foundation, Tokyo, 1997)

Plath, David, 'My-car-isma: Motorizing the Showa Self', *Daedalus*, 119, 3 (1990)

Roberts, Glenda, 'Between Policy and Practice: Silver Human Resource Centers as Viewed from the Inside', *Journal of Aging and Social Policy*, 8, 2/3 (1996), pp. 115–32

Røkkum, Arne, *Goddesses, Priestesses and Sisters: Mind, Gender and Power in the Monarchic Tradition of the Ryukyus* (Scandinavian University Press, Oslo, 1998)

Stevens, Carolyn, *On the Margins of Japanese Society: Volunteers and the Welfare of the Urban Underclass* (Routledge, London, 1997)

Thang, Leng Leng, 'The Dancing Granny: Linking the Generations in a Japanese Age-integrated Welfare Centre', *Japanese Studies*, 19, 2 (1999), pp. 151–62

—— *Generations in Touch: Linking the Old and Young in a Tokyo Neighbourhood* (Cornell University Press, Ithaca, 2001)

—— 'Touching of the Hearts: An Overview of Programs to Promote Interaction between the Generations in Japan', in Roger Goodman (ed.), *Family and Social Policy in Japan: Anthropological Approaches* (Cambridge University Press, Cambridge, 2002)

Traphagan, John and John Knight (eds), *Demographic Change and the Family in Japan's Aging Society* (State University of New York Press, New York, 2002)

RELATED NOVELS

Ariyoshi, Sawako, *The Twilight Years* (Peter Owen, London, 1972)

—— *The River Ki* (Kodansha International, Tokyo, 1981)

Enchi, Fumiko, *The Waiting Years* (Kodansha International, Tokyo, 1986)

Futabatei, Shimei, *An Adopted Husband* (Greenwood Press, New York, 1969)

Tanizaki, Junichiro, *The Makioka Sisters* (Picador, London, 1979)

FILMS

The Ballad of Narayama (1983 Shōhei Imamura)

The Family Game (*Kazoku Geemu*) (1983 Yoshimitsu Morita)

The Makioka Sisters (*Sasame Yuki*) (1983 Kon Ichikawa)

Muddy River (Doro no Kawa) (1981/2 Kōhei Oguri)
My Stiff-Necked Daddy and Me (1983 Shun Nakahara)
Tokyo Story (Tokyo Monogatari) (1953 Yasujirō Ozu)
Torasan series (Yōji Yamada)

3 Socialisation and classification

INTRODUCTION

Having looked at the ideological position of the family in Japanese society in general, we shall now focus on the very heart of the home to look at the world that is first presented to a Japanese child. Socialisation is the means by which an essentially biological being is converted into a social one, able to communicate with other members of the particular society to which it belongs. A child learns to perceive the world through language, spoken and unspoken, through ritual enacted and through the total symbolic system that structures and constrains that world. Through socialisation a child learns to classify the world in which it lives, and to impose a system of values upon it.

Much social learning of this sort happens so early that culturally relative categories are often thought to be 'natural' and 'normal' until a person moves out of his or her society of upbringing. Then there is a tendency to describe foreigners as 'strange', 'dirty' or even 'stupid', since their assumptions about the world are different. During the Second World War, for example, the Japanese were described as 'pathologically clean' by their enemies in the United States. It is thus interesting to look at the early training of children in a particular society to try and identify important categories being imparted to them. An understanding of these categories can pave the way for a deeper understanding of relations in later life, and headings found in this chapter cover aspects of Japanese interpersonal relations which are also described elsewhere for adult behaviour.

In Japan, the early period is particularly interesting because mothers and other caretakers of small children are quite assiduous in their efforts to train children in the way they regard as fit and proper to do things. 'The soul of the three year old lasts till a hundred', a saying runs, and it is up to the adults around to mould that soul. There is also some degree of consistency amongst the adults involved in many of their ideas about how children should be trained. There are, of course, regional variations and differences based on social status and occupation, but there are also certain features that seem to be common throughout Japan, no doubt aided by the almost universal influence of television, newspapers and magazines. In this chapter the most important of these common features have been picked out and their role in shaping the child for its membership in society will be discussed. The socialising role of the kindergarten will also be presented in some detail. Nearly all children are sent to a kindergarten or day nursery for a period of a year or more before they enter school, and this seems to be regarded as an important part of their early education, although it is not compulsory. It is particularly the introduction it provides to interaction with the peer group that is considered important, and thought best to take place before school entry. Various aspects of relations within this group are quite clearly defined and again appear under headings which could also apply to adult interaction. Teachers share many of the principles of the approach used in the family at this early stage, which provides some continuity in introducing the new experience of life in a large group.

UCHI AND *SOTO*

Some of the earliest acquired ideas which are most difficult to dislodge in any society are those associated with dirt and cleanliness. It is all very well to have an understanding at a theoretical level about different kinds of upbringing, but it is much harder to accept behaviour that one's own early training has presented as revolting or disgusting. It seems likely, therefore, that a system of classification associated with notions of dirt and cleanliness is held rather deeply, as Mary Douglas (1970) has pointed out. In Japanese society the distinction between *uchi* and *soto* is an example of such a deeply held part of the system of classification.

Uchi and *soto* translate roughly as 'inside' and 'outside' respectively, and they are probably first learnt by a child in association with the inside and outside of the house in which it lives. They, or parallel words, are also applied to members of one's house as opposed to members of the outside world, and to members of a person's wider groups, such as the community, school or place of work, as opposed to other people outside those groups. The importance of this distinction, and its association with dirt and cleanliness, is illustrated by looking at the ways it is used in training small children.

First of all, *uchi* and *soto* are associated with the clean inside of the house, and the dirty outside world, respectively. Japanese houses almost always have an entrance hall where shoes, polluted with this outside dirt, are removed, and it is one of the few inflexible rules enforced by Japanese adults that small children learn to change their shoes every time they go in and out of the house (see Figure 3.1). The anthropologist, Emiko Ohnuki-Tierney, has discussed this practice (1984: chapter 2) in terms of the notions of hygiene involved, and she explains that outside is regarded as dirty because that is where germs are thought to be located. This 'outside' is anywhere where there are other people, or other people have been, and the concept is succinctly expressed, she argues, in the term *hitogomi*, which sounds like 'people dirt', although the actual reading of the Chinese characters for the word simply means crowds.

Moreover, this distinction between the physical inside and outside of the house is reinforced by the use of ritualised phrases of greeting or parting which are uttered when one crosses the threshold, or by those remaining behind to greet or see off others who are coming or going. These phrases are pretty fixed and invariable, and adults take special care to pronounce them carefully with small children, who soon learn to copy them at the appropriate time. Further associations with the supposed pollution of the outside world are expressed in the way children are encouraged when they come in to wash, change and, in some houses, even to gargle, again to eliminate the germs they may have encountered while out.

In the country, children are sometimes held out over the verandah at the side of the house to urinate, and once over the threshold of the front door,

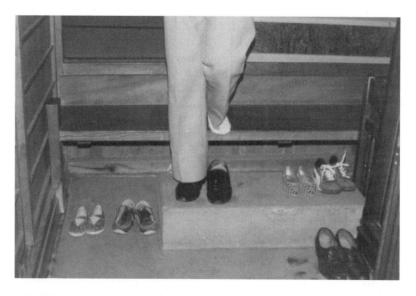

Figure 3.1 A porch for removing shoes is found at the entrance of every Japanese home. It marks clearly the distinction between *uchi* and *soto* worlds.

anywhere seems to be appropriate for the urine of a small child, even directly in front of the entrance. The toilets of a country house are often physically quite separate from the other rooms, and in most houses a special pair of toilet slippers is provided, which distinguishes this 'dirty' area from the main part of the house. The gaping hole of old-fashioned facilities was a real danger to children, as is the often steep drop found at the entrance of a house. Thus, an approach too close in either of these directions will elicit negative response from caretakers, and associate the outside with a danger of falling as well as with possible infection. A similar association will be made in a city house, but for practical reasons is more likely to be concerned with traffic and the anonymity of the city streets.

This association of the outside with danger and fear is actually encouraged in some families, especially by older people, perhaps partly because it seems to work as an effective means of keeping a child close at hand. It is opposed to another association that is consciously built up of security with the inside of the home. Parents take trouble to anticipate the needs of babies and small children, to give them in the early years the abundant attention which they see as necessary to create security and trust in a child, and also to elicit cooperation in following the directives of themselves and other adults. Punishments are avoided where possible, but if their use is necessary, they are often associated with the outside world, rather than with members of the inside of the home. Thus threats may be made about demons, policemen and passing strangers, and a severe punishment is to put a child out of the house altogether.

This is an example of the way in which these concepts, once internalised, may be strategically manipulated, an important aspect of Japanese social relations that will arise again and again. It has been analysed in detail in a collection of papers edited by Jane Bachnik and Charles Quinn (1994) which includes consideration of the concepts by Hamabata and Kondo, whose work on business families and companies was mentioned in Chapter 2.

TATEMAE **AND** *HONNE*

Another way in which the distinction between *uchi* and *soto* is made clear to a child is found in changes in the behaviour of adults depending on whether they are inside or outside the house. Put rather simply, this difference in behaviour corresponds to the difference between *tatemae* or public behaviour and *honne* or one's real feelings. In fact, this association is by no means clear cut, because members of the family will have close relationships outside the home, and will behave 'publicly' if outsiders are invited into the house.

However, the initial physical distinction is applied gradually to the circle of people with whom the child comes into contact, and it will learn to recognise the *uchi* and *soto* relations of its family, by participating in changes of behaviour in appropriate circumstances.

Such participation is gradually but firmly encouraged by adults, who will adjust their own levels of politeness according to the situation, and demonstrate to a child about how to adjust his or her level, too. Japanese language has quite clear speech levels, which are chosen according to the relationship between the people involved in a conversation, as well as the context in which they find themselves. The use of polite language also makes possible the maintenance of a certain distance between conversants, therefore protecting 'inner feelings' from the probings of an outsider. Other distinctions in Japanese which correspond to that between *tatemae* and *honne*, can be translated as 'front' and 'rear' (*omote* and *ura*), 'face' and 'heart' (*kao* and *kokoro*), 'mouth' and 'stomach' (*kuchi* and *hara*), and the ability to distinguish between them is regarded as a measure of maturity (Doi 1986).

It should be clear, however, that the distinctions are dichotomies only at an ideological level. In practice, there is a range of levels of politeness which varies depending on situations and a variety of relationships, and there are various degrees of closeness as well. A child probably first learns the distinction between the immediate family and the outside world, but will gradually come to recognise wider *uchi* groups, such as relatives, close neighbours, age-mates and so on, as his or her experience broadens. Even for each of these 'inside' groups, a slightly different type of behaviour will be appropriate.

The importance of these distinctions cannot be overemphasised in explaining features of Japanese society, as will be shown in later chapters, for it is in choosing the appropriate 'face' or 'wrapping' for a particular occasion that one is able successfully to fulfil one's social role in the world. The 'inner self' is recognised, and children are taught to understand their own selves so that they can project this understanding and devise behaviour which will consider the inner feelings of others. The conscious awareness of different sorts of *tatemae* behaviour is learnt only gradually, and it is associated with the emphasis placed on another important aspect of Japanese social relations, namely harmony.

HARMONY: RECIPROCITY AND HIERARCHY

The concern of adults to create a secure and attentive environment for a small child is part of this wider emphasis in Japanese society on harmony in social relations. It is, of course, an ideal that may or may not be achieved in practice, but much of an adult's training of children is based on the assumption that one should work towards this ideal. Thus, from the very beginning, one should try to maintain a congenial atmosphere with a small child, teaching it the proper way to behave for the sake of behaving properly, rather than for praise or to avoid punishment. An ideal child is a 'bright', cheerful child (*akarui, meirō*) and, once past the baby stage, a crying child is described as 'strange' or 'peculiar' (*okashii*).

This emphasis on harmony also applies to relations between the child and others with whom it may come into contact, and adults take pains to help children playing together to avoid situations of dispute. If a fight does break out, some time will be spent establishing what happened, and who should apologise, with full consultation of the children involved themselves. An apology must then be made clearly, and accepted by the injured party, so that play can resume happily. Two important principles are drawn upon in establishing guilt in such a case, and the same principles are used in pursuit of the aim of establishing and maintaining harmonious relations. They are the principles of hierarchy and reciprocity.

Reciprocity

Reciprocity is called upon constantly in the way adults teach children to think of others before they act. Essentially it is the principle of 'do as you would be done by' which is being invoked here. Thus a child is exhorted to think of how it would feel if another child were to do to it what it is doing to another child, how it would like it if another child refused to lend a toy when it wanted to borrow one, how it would feel if another child snatched its toy . . . and so on. A child must be trained out of its natural selfishness – the word used for selfish, *wagamama* is made up of *waga* (self) and *mama* (as it is) – rather implying an untrained state. This is part of a wider general encouragement of children to try and put themselves in the shoes of others before acting.

Hierarchy

It is of course asking a lot to expect very small children to project themselves in such a way and the other important principle, that of hierarchy, helps to resolve this problem. Children are made aware of their relative ages from a very early stage, and in case of dispute, an older child is encouraged to give in to a younger child 'who is not yet old enough to understand'. Such encouragement seems to emphasise the long-term advantages of being older, despite temporary deprival, and it seems to be rather a successful method of solving sibling rivalry, as well as quarrels within the neighbourhood. It has the incidental effect of emphasising the superior role, and the responsibility and benevolence associated with it, before the inferior role. This order of learning must be somewhat more palatable than the reverse.

In the family, older children are addressed by younger ones with a term meaning 'older sister' or 'older brother', sometimes as a suffix to their names, and adults make use of this form of address when eliciting 'good' behaviour, perhaps as a demonstration to a younger child. Similar distinctions are made in the wider circle of children in the neighbourhood, for example, and new children entering the group will always be asked their ages before play can proceed. When adults ask children to play with babies or their younger siblings, they may use a form of request which can be translated as 'do the favour of . . . ', projecting onto the older child a verb which is used for action from a superior to an inferior, and smaller children will learn to ask an older child to play using the converse of this form, used from an inferior to a superior.

These verbs and terms of address form part of the system of speech levels mentioned above, and it can be seen that the beginnings of such distinctions are being learned very young. The hierarchical distinctions within a house are sometimes thought appropriate ones to emphasise in teaching a child to use polite language, especially where there are three or more generations living together, but the distinction between *uchi* and *soto* may override these differences, so that children will be taught to address the grandparents outside the home more politely than those inside. Speech levels themselves vary greatly with social background, but the general principle of using hierarchy as a means of trying to achieve harmony is widespread.

KINDERGARTEN: EQUALITY

For a period varying between one and several years before children enter school they will attend a kindergarten or day nursery, which is said, among other things, to introduce them to 'group life' in preparation for school. The class will form a new 'inside' group for a child, a new *uchi*, to be opposed to the outside world, and various ritual procedures emphasise the nature of the group. Again children must remove their outside shoes when they come into the classroom, usually changing into special indoor shoes, and they may also have to change their clothes. As the day begins there will usually be some routine activity that the children learn and go through together involving elements such as songs, chants, movements in time to music and the reading of the register. There will be a similar routine at the end of the day as the group breaks up.

In contrast to the basically hierarchical relations found in the home and neighbourhood, when children enter kindergarten the emphasis within the class is on the essential equality of members of the group. The children may wear uniform, or at least smocks, aprons or badges to make them alike, and they have identical sets of equipment for their activities. The other children in the class are all referred to as 'friends'. These are not special buddies chosen by each child, but up to 39 other children with whom any one child is now to pass a substantial proportion of each day. Of course, any child will form special attachments, and children will also know their relative ages, strengths and so on, but members of the class are regarded as symbolically equal, and this equality is expressed in several ways.

Duties and privileges, for example, are shared out equally by means of a rota system. Thus children take it in turns to be on duty for break and lunch service, which probably involves handing out food and drinks, and also perhaps seeing that the other children are sitting properly before they give the signal to start eating. The children on duty may also be responsible for lining their classmates up for a trip to the hall, and they will probably also take any roles of privilege for the day, like presenting flowers to the altar in an institution with a religious foundation. In this way roles that could, if taken out of context, be interpreted as hierarchical, like service, authority and privilege, are equally distributed among all the members of the class. As will be seen elsewhere in Japanese society, apparent hierarchy is often contextual rather than based on any inherent differences in status.

Again, there is much emphasis on creating and maintaining a congenial environment for small children, and before a child even enters kindergarten much is made of the 'fun' it will have there. Ben-Ari's (1997) study of a Japanese day nursery includes a wonderful chapter that focuses on this aspect of life in a pre-school establishment which well complements a wider emphasis in studies of Japanese child care on training and 'control'. This is another part of the emphasis on harmony as an ideal in social relations, and quarrels that arise are investigated and apologies made. Children are expected to be happy, and anyone who is not, like the crying child, is classed as 'strange' or 'peculiar'. A child who shows reluctance to participate is encouraged to join in, but, if it refuses, it will simply be ignored, as the teacher goes about the business of making life 'fun' for all the other children.

This form of classification sets apart a child who appears to be unhappy, by moving it out of the main group and emphasising its difference from the other children. Taken together with the association already established of security with *uchi*, and fear with *soto*, and the emphasis on equality of members of the group, this form of ostracism is usually rather effective in encouraging participation. The threat of removal from the group is also used as an effective sanction when an individual child fails to comply with the teacher's directives. A small child at this stage is keen to be just like its mates, and teachers take advantage of and encourage this propensity, making it unattractive to be 'different', at least in a formal context. The well-known and classic autobiographical story of Totto-chan (Kuroyanagi 1982) is an exception that would seem to prove this rule. Now a popular TV personality in Japan, the author describes how she failed to fit into her class at school until she was eventually moved to another rather special school (see Chapter 5 for further detail about such schools).

PEER GROUP PRESSURE

Teachers also take advantage of the propensity of children to impose rules upon themselves (cf. Piaget 1932), allowing much of the discipline of the group to be generated by the pressure of the peer group. Thus, for example, at the beginning of the day, the routine in which the children participate is initiated by a tune on the piano or organ, played continuously by the teacher until all the children are sitting, or standing in their positions ready to begin. Those who are slow hold up the whole group, and they are urged by their classmates to hurry up. The same principle is put into practice before break and lunchtime, when the added incentive of hunger ensures rapid cooperation.

In a similar way quarrels are resolved by asking children who witness a dispute to pass judgement on the situation, and decide who was at fault and should therefore apologise. Teachers also appeal to the whole class when pointing out the recalcitrant behaviour of one of their number, asking whether such behaviour is acceptable, and if not, what kind of behaviour is. The personalised collective term *mina-san* is used to address and refer to the whole group and its needs, and an individual whose behaviour is to the detriment of *mina-san* is made to feel most uncomfortable. The children are also encouraged to take care of the kindergarten property in the name of its corporate owners, *mina-san*.

COOPERATION

In general, cooperation is also encouraged in a number of other positive ways. Classroom walls are invariably decorated with cooperative creations to which each child has contributed, like nets full of individually fashioned fishes, or woods full of trees. Marching in formation is another cooperative activity practised in some kindergartens, as are orchestras or choirs. The kindergarten where I worked in Chiba prefecture had an 80-piece orchestra, largely composed of 6-year-olds, who played tolerable renderings of popular Mozart and Vivaldi pieces. The annual sports day usually emphasises cooperation over individual competition, and children are encouraged to exert themselves for the sake of the class, or the area where they live, rather than for their own glory. Popular events include the tug-of-war and the three-, five- or seven-legged races, where cooperation is essential for success.

Stories and plays presented to or put on by the children also tend to emphasise the advantages of cooperation over individual endeavour. A Japanese version of the 'Three Little Pigs', for example, usually has the first two little pigs escape the attacks of the Big Bad Wolf so that they can join the third pig and cooperate in their efforts to entice him down the chimney into the cooking pot. The more usual version found in England, the home of the story, has the first two little pigs being eaten up for their lack of foresight, whereas the third pig uses his individual cunning and cleverness to defeat the wolf. Television programmes for children often reiterate this theme, as a single hero tries unsuccessfully to defeat the monster, or other alien force, until he gains the cooperation of other victims of the danger.

A much more detailed analysis of the activities of Japanese monsters and super-heroes forms the content of an interesting paper by anthropologist Tom Gill (1998). He argues that despite constant pressure for change in order to maintain audience ratings and market spin-off products, television programmes feature recurrent themes that can be traced back to ancient supernatural beliefs. Using a character called Ultraman as a case to consider in detail, he compares the way programmes surround Ultraman with brothers and other family relatives on whom he could rely in his quest to defeat monsters, with the American character Superman, who always acts on his own. Gill also looks at the way colours are used to code different characters and mark certain themes such as the numbers and hierarchical arrangements of members of gangs of heroes. He concludes that television dramas play an important classificatory role that children need (everywhere) as they build up a sense of security and confidence about the ordering of that world. Threats to the order increase the value associated with those who restore it.

SELF-DEVELOPMENT

It should be emphasised, however, that the development of the individual child is not neglected in all this collective activity. In the home, the child is, of course, given much individual attention, and one of the first things it is taught as a baby is to respond politely, with the term *hai*, to hearing its own name being called. Parents fill in detailed forms about their children's personal attributes, faults, friends, likes and dislikes, on entering them into kindergarten, and the teachers come to know their charges very well. They pick out individual children for praise or reprimand, and they seek ways of dealing with any individual problems they may have. They also maintain close communication with the parents of each child, and in public kindergartens they visit each child's home at least once a year.

Each child has its own property to take care of in the kindergarten or day nursery, albeit identical to the property of other children, but it must name and be responsible for its own personal set. It also has personal property at home, and early training includes the specific encouragement to attend to the maintenance and care of these items. Some of the aims of early training, shared by parents and teachers alike, are to develop personal qualities such as perseverance, concentration, effort, independence and self-reliance. Indeed, one of the aims stated by parents in sending their children to preschool educational establishments is to help them to develop these qualities.

Another often stated aim is that children should learn to think for themselves and understand themselves in order to understand others. By understanding their own needs they are thought to be able to understand the needs of others, and so to work out appropriate behaviour in any situation. They need, parents say, to understand the limits imposed on their self-interest by the needs of others and the collective needs of the wider group that they join in educational establishments. Thus, a child will gradually learn to exercise self-control in the interest of appropriate social relations.

Pre-school establishments are also places where children play within their own peer groups, and Ben-Ari's (1997) book, mentioned above, places a refreshing emphasis on the point of view of the children. He cites various hilarious examples of humour and mischief he observed in the day nursery where he worked, not least in the way the children played with the elements of his own name which in Japanese may be translated as 'excrement' and 'ant'. Their use of irony and word play is also set up in opposition to the organisational arrangements made by the teachers, although they rarely undermine them completely. Such critical creativity is often ignored in studies of establishments for children, but Ben-Ari's work demonstrates its importance in allowing individuals to position themselves personally within a social situation, to engage in power games with their peers and with the establishment, and to introduce the possibility of change through time.

This last factor is interesting, for it assigns to very young members of society the possibility of power to contribute to innovation in social life. The head of the kindergarten where I worked, originally in 1981 but with regular return visits through to 2002, noted change in the expectations of parents who were gradually placing more and more emphasis on 'free play'.

This meant that children were less and less well prepared for behaviour in the school classroom, she felt, and she noted recently that parents come to complain if they didn't like something, which they never did before. We will see in Chapter 5 how these changes may be filtering through into the educational system, but it is interesting to consider that changes in emphasis at home may also influence the way that kindergartens and day nurseries respond to their charges. On the other hand, contrary to popular perceptions in the world at large, the encouragement of innovation and creativity is not new in Japanese society, as we discussed in Chapter 1, and Ben-Ari's study may simply be identifying how early this starts.

SELF IN THE WORLD

An individual child still learns to enjoy the advantages of its new identity as a member of a collective group in pre-school establishments, and it sees that it is in fact in its own interest in certain circumstances to put self-interest second. This principle is important throughout school life, and indeed, for many Japanese, on into adult life in relations at work or in the local community. The success of a company, for example, is presented as dependent on the cooperation of its individual members, and the success of the members is then presented as directly dependent on the success of the company to which they belong. Individuals may therefore express satisfaction in being part of a greater entity such as this, but none of this means that they lose their own sense of personal identity within the social context, and they may continue to apply the ability they acquired at pre-school to be humorously critical.

Many writers have discussed the Japanese concept of self. There are so many American studies that those of us who are neither American nor Japanese can probably learn as much about America from these studies as we can about Japan! Indeed, some explicitly compare Japan and America. These studies are good in the sense that they debunk the stereotypical view of Japan as a group-oriented society often opposed to America where the individual is supposed to be paramount. In practice, as anthropologists are well aware, all societies have some behaviour which is practised in groups of one sort or another and they all certainly have 'individuals'. Japan has a superabundance of the latter, as anyone who has ever visited will know, but it is also very good at training children, and therefore adults, sometimes to put their own needs second to those of a wider group.

One of the barriers to understanding is related to the overlap in the English meaning of terms such as 'individualism' and 'individuality', for the Japanese words that translate these concepts have quite different connotations. The word for individualism (*kojinshugi*) is seen as little different from that for 'selfishness', or *wagamama*, which, as we saw above, implies an undesirable, untrained state (Hendry 1992). Although associated with 'democracy' and other apparently positively valued aspects of Westernisation, which were introduced after the Second World War, it has been accepted only slowly and reluctantly. The word for 'individuality' (*kosei*), on the other hand, soon became an ideal, and is sought in the pursuit of personal interests and achievements, perfectly acceptable as long as they don't interfere with one's obligations to others.

A collection entitled *Japanese Sense of Self*, edited by Nancy Rosenberger (1992), aims to use studies of Japanese lives to contribute to anthropological efforts to understand the issue of self 'outside of Western assumptions'. The editor explains that in this volume the self and the social are studied as interactive rather than as opposing processes, in other words they seek to ask: 'how do the self and the social constitute one another?' Notions like 'the multiplicity of self, or the multiple and changing positions that constitute self' are considered, and in one chapter Joseph Tobin focuses specifically on the learning process within a kindergarten context. He examines the way children learn to distinguish and move smoothly between the controlled behaviour expected in relatively formal *omote* or *tatemae* situations and the free and easy behaviour of the *ura* or *honne* ones. His research draws on the work of Doi Takeo (1986) in his book *Anatomy of Self* which examines in great detail the concepts of *omote* and *ura*, but Tobin emphasises that it is the *kejime* or distinction between the two which is important at the kindergarten stage.

Jane Bachnik's chapter in the same volume develops this notion of *kejime* and its importance for 'defining a shifting self in multiple organizational modes' in adult life. For those who wish to push further with this fascinating subject of self and society in Japan, Bachnik's work here and in her volume edited with Charles Quinn (1994) is of high quality and probably the most technically sophisticated approach available. Another important book is *Crafting Selves* by Dorinne Kondo (1990), an excellent account of life in a small family sweet-making factory in Tokyo, where the author spent a year working. She constructs a fascinating analysis of the sources and discourses of self and identity, including a fairly detailed analysis of her own self-identity as a Japanese American working as an anthropologist and therefore investigator in her country of origin.

Two further books seek to take their readers into the hearts and lives of 'real people' in their examination of self and society in Japan (and America). The first is a direct comparison between *What Makes Life Worth Living* in Japan and in the United States, and it introduces very specific cases of named individuals and their struggles to 'make sense of their worlds'.

Gordon Mathews (1996) writes well and the book is an absorbing and informative read. The second is a collection of papers again, entitled *Lives in Motion: Composing Circles of Self and Community in Japan* (Long 1999). It moves through various stages of the life course, with reference to home, work and play, and brings out too the importance of relations with the dead in Japanese society. The contributors include Japanese scholars as well as some important American anthropologists and the papers are intriguing and eloquent.

CONCLUSION

Looking at the lives of adults demonstrates the importance of the early learning we have considered in this chapter. Children understand that they can either cooperate with the activities of the kindergarten group or be left out, either be happy or laughed at as 'strange' and 'peculiar'. But this cooperative individual is not losing its *individuality* or individual identity by participating in collective activities. It is merely demonstrating one of the 'faces' it learns to have for different situations. This 'face' is part of the *tatemae* or 'public' behaviour appropriate in this particular context, and an individual will have several such 'faces' for different situations.

These different 'faces' are reflected in different speech forms used on different occasions, and none of them negates the existence of a complete self, using them all. Just as *tatemae* is distinguished from *honne*, one's real feelings or intention, behaviour in the group context may be distinguished from the individual who is acting out a role as member of the group. A child who falls down in front of his or her playmates will make every effort to avoid crying and being called 'strange', despite considerable pain. In another context – perhaps with a kind-hearted grandmother – the tears may be adjudged appropriate to gain sympathy and special treatment. A similar fall, when a child is entirely alone, may be more quickly overcome. These different 'faces' are recognisable in other societies, but they form an integral part of the system of classification in Japan.

By looking at the early training of a small child we have in fact only touched upon subjects which other studies have discussed in much greater detail as important 'keys' to understanding Japanese people and their ways of thinking. We have, however, isolated some very important indigenous concepts that will recur in the chapters that follow. Parents of small children receive a great deal of support and information about their role in Japan, and this is considered to be an important time to mould a child for future life. Research on the subject is disseminated through lectures, books and television programmes, and parents thus receive a kind of socialisation of reinforcement as they go about their task.

For ourselves, by seeing how these important concepts are first introduced in childhood, we can, I hope, get a feel for how they are acquired by a native speaker. Armed with this 'feel', we can proceed to venture out into the wider world outside the family.

REFERENCES AND FURTHER READING

Bachnik, Jane and Charles J. Quinn (eds), *Situated Meaning: Inside and Outside in Japanese Self, Society and Language* (Princeton University Press, Princeton, 1994)

Ben-Ari, Eyal, *Body Projects in Japanese Childcare: Culture, Organization and Emotions in a Preschool* (Curzon, Richmond, Surrey, 1997)

Doi, Takeo, trans. Mark Harbison, *The Anatomy of Self: The Individual Versus Society* (Kodansha International, Tokyo, 1986)

Douglas, Mary, *Purity and Danger* (Penguin Books, Harmondsworth, 1970)

Gill, Tom, 'Transformational Magic: Some Japanese Super-heroes and Monsters', in D.P. Martinez (ed.), *The Worlds of Japanese Popular Culture: Gender, Shifting Boundaries and Global Cultures* (Cambridge University Press, Cambridge, 1998)

Hendry, Joy, *Becoming Japanese: The World of the Pre-school Child* (Manchester University Press, Manchester, 1986)

—— 'Individualism and Individuality: Entry into a Social World', in R. Goodman and K. Refsing (eds), *Ideology and Practice in Modern Japan* (Routledge, London, 1992)

Kondo, Dorinne, *Crafting Selves: Power, Gender, and Discourses of Identity in a Japanese Workplace* (University of Chicago Press, Chicago and London, 1990)

Kuroyanagi, Tetsuko, trans. D. Britten, *Totto-chan: The Little Girl at the Window* (Kodansha, Tokyo, 1982)

Lebra, Takie Sugiyama, *Japanese Patterns of Behavior* (University of Hawaii Press, Honolulu, 1976), chapter 8

Long, Susan Orpett, *Lives in Motion: Composing Circles of Self and Community in Japan* (Cornell East Asia Series, Ithaca, New York, 1999)

Mathews, Gordon, *What Makes Life Worth Living? How Japanese and Americans Make Sense of their Worlds* (University of California Press, Berkeley, Los Angeles and London, 1996)

Ohnuki-Tierney, Emiko, *Illness and Culture in Contemporary Japan* (Cambridge University Press, Cambridge, 1984)

Peak, Lois, *Learning to Go to School in Japan: The Transition from Home to Preschool Life* (University of California Press, Berkeley and Los Angeles, 1991)

Piaget, J., *The Moral Judgement of the Child* (Routledge & Kegan Paul, London, 1932)

Rosenberger, Nancy (ed.), *Japanese Sense of Self* (Cambridge University Press, Cambridge, 1992)

Smith, Robert J., *Japanese Society: Tradition, Self and the Social Order* (Cambridge University Press, Cambridge, 1983)

Tobin, Joseph J., David Y.H. Wu and Dana H. Davidson, *Preschool in Three Cultures: Japan, China and the United States* (Yale University Press, New Haven, 1989)

RELATED NOVEL

Ishiguro, Kazuo, *Pale View of Hills* (Penguin, Harmondsworth, 1983)

4 Community and neighbourhood

INTRODUCTION

Outside the family, the next unit of social organisation that Japanese people experience, whatever their walk of life, is the neighbourhood. The nature of this unit will vary considerably according to its location, and within the same location according to gender, occupation and generation. There is also great regional variety in Japan that depends too on environmental circumstances. A visitor to a town or city hall will usually encounter a display of local crafts and products, as well as photographs of the choice scenic views in the area. However, there are again certain expectations for neighbourly behaviour which are perceived as characteristically Japanese. They are used as an ideological prototype for marketing and other purposes, as a practical model when setting up new communities and as a yardstick for disapproval when there is little consistency with actual behaviour.

One example of common neighbourly behaviour follows on well from the previous chapter, for it is generally in the neighbourhood that children make their first friends. Where physically possible, children are allowed out to play in the immediate vicinity of their house from the age of about 3. This early freedom is made possible by the cooperation of adults living in the area who keep an informal eye on clusters of tiny playmates who should happen to be roaming nearby. It is, of course, not possible for families who live on major roads to participate in such activities, but even in the largest cities there are plenty of residential areas with quiet unsurfaced roads, and apartment blocks may well open out into an enclosed play area for the use of residents.

When children begin to go to school, or even kindergarten, they will often line up together at a certain time each morning to walk together as a group. The older children are expected to take responsibility for the smaller ones as they make their way through the streets. In rural areas, too, children will cross the fields in crocodile formation, or, in more remote regions, they will take a bus together. Even within the school, children from each neighbourhood meet from time to time to discuss activities within their own community, and rules may be drawn up for the holidays based on the children's own ideas about how best they should behave. This group forms another experience of *uchi* affiliation.

Such neighbourly cooperation is not limited to children. Adults participate in neighbourly activities in a variety of ways, more or less compulsorily, depending on where they live and how long they or their forbears have been in the community. Until the modern period 90 per cent of the population of Japan lived in rural villages, and these paid taxes as a unit to their feudal lords. Villagers were not very free to move out of their own area, but there was considerable autonomy within the communities, and they developed effective ways of living together on a long-term basis. Towns, too, were composed of neighbourhoods which developed their own identities and they characterised each other through them. To this day, communities of all sizes draw on a fund of such historical traditions to support their current organisation, as we shall see.

A Japanese expression defines the immediate neighbours on whom one might need to depend in times of emergency literally as 'the three houses opposite and one on either side' (*mukōsangen ryōdonari*). It is generally thought to be important to maintain good relations with at least this minimal group, even those who have little to do with the wider community, and occupants of urban apartment complexes sometimes lament the breakdown of the system. Families moving into a new house or apartment will often take token gifts round to their close neighbours in order to establish relations with them, and housewives tend to maintain close links with at least some of their near neighbours. It is also in the interest of men and women who work in a neighbourhood – in shops and other services – to cooperate with one another, although out-of-town shopping malls are said to be putting paid to some of these long-term relations as well.

This chapter will present the principles, the variety and some of the consequences of this neighbourly interaction, which will again set the scene for further communication. A community is a good focus for anthropological study and a number of books and articles set in Japanese communities are listed at the end of the chapter. They will be referred to from time to time, but a reader who would like to get a real feel for the combination of security and constraint implied is encouraged to examine one or more cases in detail. Several older studies are also mentioned for those who might be interested in the amount of change that has taken place.

We will in fact see that community life has two apparently conflicting roles to play. On the one hand, it is the stage for a new kind of local society that is developing throughout Japan in a recent enthusiasm for 'civil society' and local volunteering activities. At the same time, it also provides a focus for something of a nostalgic ideal, both in urban areas that seem to have lost the community spirit and in rural areas that have been abandoned by their youth. Occasionally, former villages have actually been preserved for tourists to visit, and an interesting revival movement has brought some comfort to lonely city dwellers at the same time as revitalising areas of rural deprivation.

JAPAN'S ADMINISTRATIVE DIVISIONS

Japan is divided, for administrative purposes, into 47 prefectures, with prefectural offices, and municipal bodies encompassing 665 cities, 1,992 towns and 576 'villages', each with its own autonomous government and elected assembly (*Japan Statistical Yearbook* 2001). The English terms used here are somewhat misleading, however, as the towns and cities often include quite rural areas within their boundaries, and the 'villages' are usually collections of sparsely scattered small communities. Thus a small 'city' may well include within its boundaries a central area which resembles an English town, and a number of outlying settlements which would probably be classed in English as villages. To avoid confusion, then, the term 'village' will subsequently be used here for the type of settlement that the word would normally evoke in English.

These settlements usually form the smallest sub-divisions of the wider administrative zones in a rural area, and the corresponding unit of urban areas, which may have the same name in Japanese (*chōnai*), will here be called a neighbourhood. All these smaller units are used for the purposes of postal addresses, policing and school allocation, but also to maintain a register of every resident and his or her original home if that is different from the present one. Often these administrative units coincide with more natural divisions, but they are revised from time to time, and older allegiances tend to survive in certain situations.

A degree of local autonomy, even at neighbourhood level, makes it difficult to generalise for the whole of Japan, and local areas anyway like to emphasise their special features. The Ainu people in Hokkaido and the Okinawans in the southern islands can draw on a distinctive cultural heritage, as can communities of immigrants such as Koreans, Chinese and Japanese Brazilians, but regions can generally summon some local diversity. Communities based on specific occupations such as agriculture, fishing and mountain work also have for long had characteristic features, but they all share participation in the nation that is Japan and that brings several constraints. We will start here with one relatively stable rural unit to demonstrate some examples of considerable neighbourhood interaction, intersperse the description with examples of the variety found in other areas and then turn to look separately at urban life.

RURAL COMMUNITY LIFE

It is appropriate to start with a rural community, despite the lesser overall population, for the sites of production of Japan's long-held staple food are regarded as an important source of tradition. As we saw in Chapter 1, rice is still a source of identity despite declining consumption. Growing rice requires considerable cooperation, and the mechanisms developed for this purpose defined neighbourly relations in no small way. The crucial process of transplanting seedlings from boxes to fields requires artificial flooding, which must be coordinated between all the farmers who share the same water sources for their irrigation channels. The supply needs to be monitored carefully during the early period, and if one family took more than their share it could spell disaster for their neighbours. The old feudal practice of assessing a whole community for its quota of tax, to be paid in rice, meant that those who had more often had to subsidise those who had less, so it was in everybody's interest for each family to have a successful harvest.

In modern rural communities the economic base is usually very different. With the use of machines, chemical fertilizers and insecticides, even rice production has become less time-consuming, so that fewer people are required to provide the country's needs, which are anyway diminishing rapidly as rice consumption drops. There is also less need for cooperation to accomplish the basic tasks of production. Cash crops, such as tea, fruit, flowers and vegetables, have become more prevalent, and in many areas, populations have been greatly depleted by young people especially moving off to work in cities. Elsewhere, a substantial proportion of villagers commute to a nearby town to work, and in the northern snowy areas some spend the entire winter away seeking seasonal work in an urban area.

The community where I have done fieldwork over a quarter of a century has managed to adapt very well to changing circumstances, so it provides a good base line for comparison. It is largely agri/horticultural, with several families specialising in the production of tea and/or chrysanthemums. The plush glass greenhouses that surround the village attest to their success. Many families do have at least one member who goes out of the village to work, however, and several practise no farming at all. As elsewhere there has been a drop in the birth rate and an increasing number of single-person households. Nevertheless, all the houses participate in local festivals, and many of them are still continuing *ie* with ancestors who lived in the same village before the present occupants. Current residents have thus inherited much of their neighbourly interaction from their forbears, and though it has been modified, the village is a contemporary example of a relatively stable unit of the type which was common in pre-industrial Japan.

The basic unit of population in such a community is the *ie*, and questions about the size of the community are usually answered in numbers of houses, though even here reference is made to the falling birth rate and a consequent shortage of children. At village meetings, one member of each house is required to attend, and the same principle operates for all village obligations and communal activities. Much neighbourly interaction is also carried out between houses, rather than between individuals, and people tend to describe each other as 'the grandmother of House X', or 'the father of House Y', and so on.

Our village coincides with a local administrative unit of the 'city' to which it belongs. Much communication with the city hall is carried out through the head of the village, a person elected for a fixed term by an assembly of the *chōnaikai*, itself comprising heads of all the houses. He is responsible for the collection of dues for the maintenance of village build-ings and for lighting, for road and path repair, and where possible, for the settlement of disputes which arise amongst the villagers. In practice, the first of these tasks is carried out by the houses in strict rotation. Within three smaller neighbourhood groups, one house is responsible for the collection of dues each month and a member of the house goes round to all the others and collects up the money. This duty passes to another house at the end of every year. The repair of roads and paths is another task shared out equally among the houses. Most comply with the directive, but there is a standard fine charged if any should fail to do so. Streams and smaller paths are taken care of in a similar way by the houses that use them.

Similar practices are found in many urban areas as well, and the way the tasks circulate to everybody in turn is reminiscent of the way roles are shared out in the kindergarten. It probably has an equalising effect, too, despite other hierarchical differences. Since everyone has to collect dues, everybody pays up, and they even thank the collector for coming. Before the days of bank transfers, local taxes were paid in this way too, and if one house could not afford them for some reason, their neighbours would chip in to help out, a measure designed to avoid bringing shame on the whole community. Even now, the poorer residents of a neighbourhood may be allocated a lower sum to contribute to community funds, or even be excused payment altogether.

The order in which houses take on the responsibility for these collections is also the order followed by a 'circulating notice-board' which brings news

Figure 4.1 The circulating notice-board ensures that residents of a community are kept informed about events taking place there. It also keeps neighbours in touch.

from the city hall, from the head of the neighbourhood, or from someone else wishing officially to circulate all their neighbours about something. This board is brought to the door by the previous person on the route, and it must be stamped as seen, and carried round to its next destination. This regular circulation of news ensures that every house keeps in touch with at least two other houses, and it also allows the authorities to maintain contact efficiently and cheaply with every house in their administrative zone.

Security is another concern of the community as a whole, and young men of the village serve for a few years in a voluntary body which stands ready to help out in case of need. Usually their active role is in fire-fighting, and they meet once a month to check the village fire engine and practise the drill for using it. This is an important supplement to the professional fire service operated at city level, because members of the group are usually working in the neighbourhood and can be very quickly on the scene if they are required. The prevalence of wood and paper in Japanese houses means that swift action is essential in case of fire to prevent it spreading throughout a neighbourhood. These groups are found throughout Japan and are also ready to act in case of other disasters such as floods or earthquakes.

Another task of the whole community is the care of places of worship in the village. These include the shrine of the tutelary deity, who is thought to protect the residents of the community, and a couple of other sacred places, which are situated within the village boundaries. Groups of houses take responsibility in turn for each of these places, cleaning the buildings, maintaining the grounds and celebrating the periodic festivals associated with them. The largest festivals involve the whole community, but they are organised by the groups of houses to whose charge they fall in any particular year. This charge is passed on ceremonially after the major festival. Again, these are duties that surround community sacred places throughout the country.

That this is a neighbourly duty as much as a religious one is illustrated in the village where I worked by the way that even houses which have turned to a new religion are expected to take part. If they refuse, they are ostracised to some extent for their failure to cooperate. Formal ostracism is used occasionally in Japanese communities to express disapproval of 'some action regarded as antisocial'. This *mura hachibu*, or 'village eighth-part' was very effective in pre-modern closed communities, because neighbours would cut off all communication except that absolutely necessary for survival (the 'eighth-part'), and few families could survive such an ordeal without conforming. It can be seen that the tactics of the kindergarten have a tried and tested basis in traditional village life.

At a more microscopic level, strong links are developed between immediate neighbours within this wider community. These houses are usually close enough for frequent chance interaction, and they are also the ones to whom one turns in times of need. A death in one house will bring representatives round immediately from the closest neighbours to take over the practical arrangements for the funeral, and a birth will likewise elicit visits and practical help, if necessary. Similar participation is virtually automatic on the occasions of marriage, house-building, sickness or disaster such as fire. These closest neighbours may not be personal friends, but they are those on whom one can rely in an emergency, and even people who work outside the community offer their help freely because they know that they may need help in the future.

On an individual level, villagers may have further allegiances in the neighbourhood to their age-mates, those people with whom they have moved through school, and in the case of women who married into the community, those who arrived at around the same time. In the part of Kyushu where this village is located, these groups used to be very strong, starting during childhood, meeting regularly and adjusting to suit changing circumstances. They formed another support group in times of need or celebration, and they were often an individual's closest companions. Young people seem less interested in such activities now, though groups of older members of the community continue, and they are still found elsewhere. They save on a regular basis for outings – in the past the money was used to send the members at least once during their lifetimes to the shrine of the Imperial Ancestress at Ise.

Another series of associations based on age are for members of the community as they pass through particular stages in their lives. These are similar to age-grades found by anthropologists in other parts of the world. In this community there is a children's group, largely for members of primary school, the fire-fighters, a group of housewives and one for old people of retirement age. Elsewhere, there are youth groups, associations of young wives and one for men 'in the prime of life'. Such groups may have an important role to play in the organising and carrying out of festivals, and they may have sporting events arranged nationally and outings together as well. Old people's groups have been revived all over the country as part of the national concern with the welfare of the burgeoning numbers of retired people, who may also take responsibility for various tasks of benefit to the whole community. They have sporting and social events, and games such as 'gateball' (a version of the English game croquet) and 'grand golf' are popular.

Finally, at a more informal level, there are various places where neighbours meet regularly to exchange news and gossip about each other. Shops are one possibility, and in the community where I worked a retired shopkeeper still keeps open a public area where locals may pass the time of day, though she has minimal stock. Another might be a communal bath house, and though the village facility closed some years ago when everyone had constructed their own new bathrooms, a larger public *onsen* (hot spring resort) is a popular addition to the wider neighbourhood. *Onsen* are visited all over Japan, and public baths known as *sento* have a social function as well as a hygienic one in urban neighbourhoods (Clark 1994). A children's play area is another place for young caretakers especially to meet, and my village of research installed swings and slides in the shrine compound.

It can be seen then that community life involves companionship, but also a series of demands and obligations, and in fact there are others that have not been mentioned. Any one house is called upon regularly to send members to participate in tasks, activities and exchanges, and in many cases there is little choice but to join in. On the other hand, membership in such a community brings security in the face of danger, comfort in times of need and entertainment and social life to the very doorstep. Like the kindergarten child, villagers have little choice about participating, but they also realise the advantages of belonging to such a community. Some villagers who move away to a city for a period when they are young return later and settle down in the village, and as we shall see, some city dwellers are now seeking to make a new life in the country.

URBAN NEIGHBOURHOODS

An urban neighbourhood may draw on similar principles, but life is generally much less constrained in terms of participation, and in a study of *Contemporary Urban Japan* John Clammer (1997) argues that interaction for most people is more likely to be based on quite different networks. Hoards of people commute long distances to work, they relax in bars in the vicinity of train stations, and for shopping and dining they have a whole wonderland of possibilities. As for neighbourhoods, Clammer writes 'people who live in them work outside of them, most inhabitants originated elsewhere, friendship networks entirely transcend them and patterns of spatial movement for shopping and entertainment entirely ignore them'. What unifies most urban Japanese, according to Clammer, is 'a common culture of consumption', and he cites magazines and advertisements as shared sources of knowledge (1997:30).

This may be the case, and there have indeed been many recent studies that have chosen consumer behaviour as a topic for research. One interesting focus, for example, has been on department stores, which opened in Japan along Western lines over a century ago as places to learn about new products and their uses as well as to buy them (MacPherson 1998 has several articles). Public spaces such as roof gardens provided novel and interesting locations for people to meet and relax, restaurants and drinking establishments were opened, exhibitions installed and visits became social outings as much as shopping expeditions. Some of the companies that invested in department stores also funded private railway lines and situated the stations and stores side by side as mutually constitutive sources of custom. Other small businesses followed suit, and these areas became veritable communities of commuters – shopping, eating and drinking on their way between home and work.

Nevertheless, most of these city dwellers have homes too, and even if they are out much of the day, the neighbourhood has a role to play in their lives. An interesting anthropological study carried out in a recently developed housing complex in western Japan describes how neighbours organised themselves to secure acceptable services for their community, both from the developer and from local government (Ben-Ari 1991). They set up a citizens' action group called a *jichikai*, a word that emphasises their desire for a degree of self-governance. This study also illustrates the different attitudes to a community between outsiders moving in and those with houses going back through generations, for the new housing was amalgamated with an old village, and the degree to which neighbours felt obliged to participate in local activities was quite variable. In the country people may complain about the obligations they feel to participate in communal activities but, when asked, most of them join in. In newer communities people feel more at liberty to avoid participation. Evidently the ultimate sanction of *mura hachibu* would have considerably less force in an urban area, although informal ostracism may well continue.

The emphasis was a little different in another anthropological study entitled *Native and Newcomer*, carried out in a commuter 'bed-town' which had engulfed a number of older communities within the wider metropolitan area of Tokyo. Jennifer Robertson (1991), who had actually spent her childhood in this area, also found participation in local events and activities different for 'natives' and 'newcomers' but this time it seemed to involve a policy of deliberate exclusion from long-standing associations of all but families established for several generations. The community thus organised itself into tiers of relative natives, or relative newcomers, running parallel but different sets of organisations. Clearly participation is important to people even if it isn't compulsory. However, a picture emerges of deep and divisive rifts despite a community-building movement based on the harmony that was supposed to have existed amongst the pioneering occupants of the original seventeenth- and eighteenth-century communities.

A study carried out in a more established merchant neighbourhood in Tokyo also describes very forcibly how traditional features of neighbourhood organisation are invoked to justify modern social organisation, although there is ample evidence to show that this so-called tradition is not based on historical continuity (Bestor 1989). Bestor's study again illustrates a situation where there is conflict between the local government's ideas for and demands on the local people and their own activities organised through the effective *chōnaikai*. This demonstrates that the neighbourhood is not merely a small administrative unit of local government but retains a degree of autonomy, too. For example, when the official boundaries of the community were altered in a way that did not suit the residents, people just ignored them for all practical purposes except house-numbering. Cooperation at a local level has made it possible for the community to maintain its own cohesion here.

In fact in urban areas there are many organisations with the same names and apparent functions as those already described for a rural community whether people take advantage of them or not. Bestor's study lists a women's group, a senior citizen's group, a festival committee, a merchants' association, parent–teacher associations, school alumni clubs, politicians' support groups, a volunteer fire brigade and various groups based on hobbies. The *chōnaikai* organises traffic safety campaigns, drills in preparation for disasters such as earthquakes, maintains street lights in back alleys and sprays the whole area with pesticide in the hot summers. Other local groups

Figure 4.2 Local residents carry a portable shrine around the neighbourhood amidst much jollity during community festivals.

organise children's outings, trips for adults and a series of annual events including a New Year's party, a springtime cherry-blossom viewing party, a summer folk-dance festival and an autumn festival for the local Shintō deity.

Festivals bring members of a community out together to celebrate all over Japan, and since they often involve carrying or pulling a portable shrine around the whole neighbourhood, they serve to strengthen the residents' perceptions of their boundaries within a wider area. They also offer an opportunity to express divisions with that same community, and an excellent detailed analysis of an annual festival held in a pretty large town in the mountains of central Japan illustrates this tension perfectly. *The Rousing Drum* demonstrates the intricate relationship between the festival and local politics, its potential to incorporate and even legitimate change, and its importance in marking community identity (Schnell 1999). The prosperity and diversity of Japan's local festivals, urban and rural, provides ample evidence of both continuing participation in community life, harmonious or otherwise, and a concern to maintain distinctive local characteristics.

There is, however, much variation in levels of involvement in urban areas, and where residents are mostly commuters, local activities will be more important to housewives and children. Women have proved to be excellent organisers within the neighbourhood, and even in a suburb still under construction that I visited in Chiba City, effective groups were operating for housewives and children, and there was already a strong consumer protection league. Ayumi Sasagawa's (2002) study of highly educated housewives who give up good jobs to rear their children – mentioned in Chapter 1 – suggests that even quite young women gain considerable satisfaction through setting up facilities for themselves and their children within the local community. Many claim they would rather do this than commute to a distant office, and as they get older they may – if they can afford it – turn to voluntary work, an activity shared by the retired.

Lynne Nakano (2000) carried out a study of volunteering in Japan and she, too, found that particularly women made the choice to become involved because they prefer a local lifestyle that also allows satisfaction and status superior to the one they would achieve in a part-time job. Retired men who get involved in community volunteering activities point out that they may be passing up greater wealth, and even a superior standard of living, but they prefer a caring role to the emphasis on materialism and individual success that characterise the mainstream workplace. In fact the Japanese government has for long been encouraging private citizens to get involved in caring for the needy in their communities as a way of saving welfare expenses, but it has been largely a grass-roots movement that has burgeoned in the 1990s.

The recent emphasis on 'civil society' in Japan was fuelled by the failures of central government at the time of the Kobe earthquake in 1995, when small groups of volunteers totalling more than a million people stepped in to bring rescue and relief at a very local level. This year was also dubbed 'the first year of volunteerism in Japan', and the media apparently praised volunteers for 'reinventing traditional forms of village co-operation' (Nakano, p. 94). In fact, as the work carried out earlier than that by Carolyn Stevens (1997, referred to in Chapter 2) clearly shows, there were people ready and willing to volunteer help for the needy, but they themselves tended to be marginalised along with the people they cared for. A good summary of the history of volunteering and 'civil society' in Japan may be found in a chapter by Victoria Lyon Bestor (2002), which points out that

many of the contemporary groups have their roots in community organisations like those described above.

Finally, parks in towns and cities offer spaces to meet neighbours, as do
shrine compounds, and here the older people meet to play gateball and
grand golf, as they do in the country. After school, children turn out to enjoy
themselves and another facility found widely in Japanese communities are
the loud speakers that call them home at dusk. The ones close to an urban
area where I lived with my children for a while used to play the opening
bars of Beethoven's Fifth Symphony to annouce this informal curfew. The
same speakers are used to make announcements about emergencies, such as
approaching inclement weather, and during our stay we were reassured
about a volcanic eruption on a nearby island which had set our shutters
shuddering in a strange and, at first, inexplicable way. The public baths
are another popular meeting place in urban neighbourhoods, as already
mentioned, as are the ubiquitous 24-hour convenience stores.

DECLINE AND REGENERATION OF
COMMUNITY LIFE

In urban areas of Japan, however, these public spaces are just as likely to
be full of strangers as to offer opportunities to chat with neighbours, and
there is apparently much yearning for an old-fashioned idea of community. This longing is expressed in the idiom of lacking a *furusato* or
'hometown' to return to, and it is associated with a nostalgia for a disappearing past. Whether people feel like this or not, the advertisement culture that urbanites are said to share regularly fuels such a nostalgia,
invented or otherwise. A book by Marilyn Ivy (1995) that includes an
analysis of railway company campaigns to encourage internal Japanese
tourism has the intriguing title of *Discourses of the Vanishing*. Vanishing or
otherwise, city dwellers seem to travel about Japan seeking to enjoy the
benefits of the countryside, and the destinations they choose cash in on this
furusato discourse.

At the same time, many studies in rural areas tell tales of decline, and
they all bring news of change. In some cases this is positive, like the transformation provided by a ski resort in Moon's (1989) mountainous fieldwork
location, and the delights but also problems brought by tourists to a diving
community studied by D.P. Martinez (1990). Brian Moeran's first report of
a potting community was tellingly entitled *Lost Innocence* (1984, see also
1998), however, and an older book by Robert Smith (1978) about changes
over a twenty-year period was subtitled 'the price of progress'. Another
study even set out to describe the devastating effect of international

opposition to whaling for a Japanese community (Kalland and Moeran 1992). What then are the urban tourists visiting?

In the 1980s there was a nationwide movement to revitalise Japan's countryside and substantial government grants were made across the board to rural municipalities to give them an incentive. This provoked a great range of responses in different parts of the country, usually reflecting their own characteristic features, and one was to invest in the production and marketing of a single special product which might draw visitors to its source (Moon 2002). A related scheme was for members of declining rural communities to 'adopt' fictitious relatives, offering city folk who had no country ties a *furusato* so that they could re-establish the rural roots they felt they had lost. The idea was to give people the opportunity not only to visit the area and be taken care of in rural surroundings, but also to receive regular parcels of country produce when they returned to the city (Knight 1998). Post offices offered application forms for the programme.

Both of these schemes drew on and encouraged the wave of nostalgia for rural Japan that was washing over the country, and other areas went on to transform quite mundane daily traditions into tourist fare. In the central highlands of the largest main island of Japan, for example, an entire rural community has been preserved in an area formerly known as Hide, with occupants present only in door name plates and recorded stories. Visitors who pay a small entrance fee may watch the demonstration of local crafts, also available for purchase, and on snowy winter evenings there is a sound and light production that draws a bevy of amateur photographers to capture the charming rural scene. On Shikoku Island there is a similar village, reconstructed from old houses and work buildings brought from different parts of the island, and accessed by means of a narrow footbridge suspended across a gorge by an old method that uses thickly twisted vine twine.

An area of central Japan with unusually large family houses marked by their steep thatched roofs has even been designated a UNESCO World Heritage Site, though the residents are still in occupancy, and a recent study (Carle 2002) reports that they complain of living in a state of 'frozen preservation'. This is due to severe restrictions on changes they can make to the outside of their houses, though inside they can live pretty much as they like. Some of the locals offer accommodation to tourists, and when I was in the area, we ate supper cooked at an old-style hearth while a video was shown that depicts the lives of contemporary villagers in glorious Technicolor. I also visited a public toilet building, charmingly thatched in the style of the house roofs, but inside offering a heated seat, a veritable array of motorised washing and drying options and an automatic flush system (see Figure 4.3).

Some of the most attractive neighbourhoods in Japan these days are those that have been preserved, or often actually recreated to attract

Figure 4.3 The small building here emulates the local roofing style that has been granted World Heritage Status – inside is to be found an extremely high-tech public toilet.

tourists. The hiding of the electricity and telephone wires that mar much of urban Japan is one of the secrets, but the encouragement of tourist income based on an image of community charm is a good incentive to keep up overall appearances. In many areas districts of former samurai houses have been smartened up for visitors, though some of the dwellings may still be occupied. Okpyo Moon (1997) examined the case of the old feudal castle town of Aizu Wakamatsu, in the northern region of the main island, where an organisation described as the Aizu Retro Society has brought about a transformation of shops and businesses. Local traders dress in pre-modern costumes and chat to one another in a strong local dialect. The town thrives as a tourist attraction, but she reports that the activities have also provided for local people a new identity and a sense of pride in their neighbourhood.

At times, however, the arrival of tourism actually interferes with the genuine activities of local people. John Knight (2002), for example, reports a friction between the hunting and gathering practices of the mountain people where he worked, and city people who come hiking in the countryside. For the former, these may also be recreational pursuits, but hunting with guns brings danger to the tourists, who are in turn seen as plundering the herbs and mushrooms the local residents have for long enjoyed collecting. In Hokkaido, Ulrike Nennsteil (2002) reports another conflict between local fishermen and the tourists illegally filching the source of their livelihood. These studies raise an interesting modern conflict between the economic advantages of encouraging a nostalgic urban yearning for 'back to nature' activities associated with rural life, and the degradation of the environment it brings about in practice.

Some city dwellers have actually started moving out to rural locations, and John Knight (1997) reports a parallel set of longer term conflicts between organic farmers and those who have inherited their horticultural techniques from their forbears. In theory the relationship between the two groups could be one of assistance and tutelage, he suggests, but in practice the ideologically-minded organic farmers claim that the locals have become too industrialised and they must instead learn directly from the soil. Ultimately, however, newcomers such as these help to generate a real revival of rural life, and local councils can only encourage them in their quest to repopulate areas suffering from overall decline.

In 2002 I encountered another new rural group while visiting a friend in a city in Mie-prefecture. She had had built for herself a beautiful mountain retreat in an idyllic location on the edge of a valley, complete with open hearth and picture windows from which to admire the view (see Figure 4.4). At present this is her weekend home, but as she approaches retirement from a position as a professor of nursing, she is toying with the idea of adding a small health farm. Here she would offer a few select customers week-long courses of good food and fresh air designed to boost the immune system. Less than two hours' drive from the large cities of the Kansai region, this is becoming an increasingly popular area for second homes, but there is also a growing community of artists, potters and others who can work from home with the aid of a computer. The quality of life seemed good, and neighbourly relations friendly – and they thought it an improvement on the anonymity of the urban sprawl.

CONCLUSION

Whether the community is new or old, Japan has a rich fund of models for neighbourly interaction, and it is not difficult for the demands of local circumstances to be tackled by drawing on these models, whether at an ideological level or in practice. The principles of knowing and caring about one's neighbours have been strongly upheld in Japanese community life, and evidence seems to suggest that these are still held to be important. In new neighbourhoods, as in apartment complexes, women in particular have been reported to complain of loneliness and a lack of neighbourhood

Figure 4.4 A city woman enjoying her country retreat.

interaction. Elsewhere, it is no doubt women like these who are drawing on the traditions of neighbourhood interaction to solve their own problems of isolation.

Various aspects of the system of classification outlined in previous chapters have re-emerged here. For long-term communities, the *uchi/soto* distinction is clearly applied again at this level, as it is in most areas for housewives and children. The importance of reciprocity is made very clear, and the strict sharing of duties between houses reiterates the principles of equality and cooperation. There are of course hierarchical differences between houses based on economic resources, or older factors such as the *dōzoku* relations discussed in Chapter 2, but this chapter has concentrated attention on the neighbourhood as a conceptual unit, and at this level, at least, houses are for most purposes treated equally. In the next chapter we will encounter further expressions of equality, but also the first serious experience of the building of hierarchical difference for a child growing up in Japan.

REFERENCES AND FURTHER READING

Ben-Ari, Eyal, *Changing Japanese Suburbia: A Study of Two Present-Day Localities* (Kegan Paul International, Tokyo, 1991)

Bestor, Theodore C., *Neighborhood Tokyo* (Stanford University Press, Stanford, 1989)

Bestor, Victoria Lyon, 'Toward a Cultural Biography of Civil Society in Japan', in Roger Goodman (ed.), *Family and Social Policy in Japan: Anthropological Approaches* (Cambridge University Press, Cambridge, 2002)

Carle, Ronald D., 'The Way of the Roof: Heritage Preservation and Tourism Development in the Heart of Japan', Ph.D. thesis, University of Edinburgh, 2002, pp. 136–9

Clammer, John, *Contemporary Urban Japan: A Sociology of Consumption* (Blackwell, Oxford, 1997)

Clark, Scott, *Japan: A View from the Bath* (University of Hawaii Press, Honolulu, 1994)

Dore, R.P., *City of Life in Japan: A Study of a Tokyo Ward* (University of California Press, Berkeley, 1958)

Embree, John, *Suye Mura: A Japanese Village* (University of Chicago Press, Chicago, 1939)

Fukutake, Tadashi, *Japanese Rural Society* (Cornell University Press, Ithaca, 1972)

Ivy, Marilyn, *Discourses of the Vanishing: Modernity, Phantasm, Japan* (Chicago University Press, Chicago, 1995)

Japan Statistical Yearbook (Bureau of Statistics, Ministry of Public Management, Home Affairs and Post and Telecommunications, Japan, 2001)

Kalland, Arne, *Shingu, A Japanese Fishing Community* (Curzon Press, London and Malmo, 1980)

Kalland, Arne and B. Moeran, *Endangered Culture: Japanese Whaling in a Cultural Perspective* (Curzon Press, London and Malmo, 1992)

Knight, John, 'The Soil as Teacher: Natural Farming in a Mountain Village', in Pamela Asquith and Arne Kalland, *The Culture of Nature in Japan* (Curzon, Richmond, Surrey and Hawaii University Press, Honolulu, 1997), pp. 236–56

—— 'Selling Mother's Love: Mail Order Village Food in Japan', *Journal of Material Culture*, 3, 2 (1998), pp. 153–73

—— 'Hunters and Hikers: Rival Recreations in the Japanese Forest', in Joy Hendry and Massimo Raveri, *Japan at Play: The Ludic and the Logic of Power* (Routledge, London, 2002), pp. 268–84

MacPherson, Kerrie L. (ed.), *Asian Department Stores* (Curzon, Richmond, Surrey 1998)

Martinez, D.P., *Making and Becoming: Identity and Ritual in a Japanese Village* (Hawaii University Press, Honolulu, 2003)

—— 'Tourism and the *Ama*: the Search for a Real Japan', in Eyal Ben-Ari, Brian

Moeran and James Valentine (eds), *Unwrapping Japan* (Manchester University Press, Manchester, 1990), pp. 97–116

Moeran, Brian, *Lost Innocence* (University of California Press, Berkeley, 1984)

——*A Far Valley: Four Years in a Japanese Village* (Kodansha International, Tokyo, New York and London, 1998)

Moon, Okpyo, *From Paddy Field to Ski Slope* (Manchester University Press, Manchester, 1989)

——'Tourism and Cultural Development: Japanese and Korean Contexts', in Yamashita Shinji, Kadin H. Din and J.S. Eades (eds), *Tourism and Cultural Development in Asia and Oceania* (Penerbit Universiti Kebangsaan, Bangi, Malaysia, 1997), pp. 178–93

——'Countryside Reinvented for Urban Tourists: Rural Transformation in the Japanese *Muraokoshi* Movement', in Joy Hendry and Massimo Raveri, *Japan at Play: The Ludic and the Logic of Power* (Routledge, London, 2002), pp. 228–44

Moore, R.M., *Japanese Agriculture: Patterns of Rural Development* (Westview Press, Boulder, San Francisco and London, 1990)

Nagashima, Nobuhiro and Hiroyasu Tomoeda (eds), *Regional Differences in Japanese Rural Culture* (Senri Ethnological Studies no. 14, National Museum of Ethnology, Osaka, 1984)

Nakane, Chie, *Kinship and Economic Organisation in Rural Japan* (Athlone Press, London, 1967)

Nakano, Lynne Y., 'Volunteering as a Lifestyle Choice: Negotiating Self-Identities in Japan', *Ethnology*, 39, 2 (2000), pp. 93–107

Nennsteil, Ulrike, 'Illegal Fishing and Power Games', in Joy Hendry and Massimo Raveri, *Japan at Play: The Ludic and the Logic of Power* (Routledge, London, 2002), pp. 259–67

Norbeck, Edward, *Takashima: A Japanese Fishing Community* (University of Utah Press, Salt Lake City, 1954)

——*From Country to City: the Urbanisation of a Japanese Hamlet* (University of Utah Press, Salt Lake City, 1978)

Robertson, Jennifer, *Native and Newcomer: Making and Remaking a Japanese City* (University of California Press, Berkeley, Los Angeles and Oxford, 1991)

Schnell, Scott, *The Rousing Drum: Ritual Practice in a Japanese Community* (University of Hawaii Press, Honolulu, 1999)

Smith, Robert, *Kurusu: The Price of Progress in a Japanese Village 1951–1975* (Stanford University Press, Stanford, 1978)

Smith, Robert J. and Ella Lury Wiswell, *The Women of Suye Mura* (University of Chicago Press, Chicago, 1982)

Stevens, Carolyn, *On the Margins of Japanese Society: Volunteers and the Welfare of the Urban Underclass* (Routledge, London, 1997)

FILMS

As Iwate Goes: Is Culture Local? (Asian Educational Media Service, 1998 and 2001)

The Ballad of Narayama (1983 Shōhei Imamura)

Ella's Journal (documentary by Robert J. Smith and Ella Lury Wiswell about *Suye Mura* – Asian Educational Media Service, 1998)

My Neighbour Totoro (1988 Hayao Miyazaki)

Neighbourhood Tokyo (documentary by Ted Bestor about his community – Asian Educational Media Service, 1988)

Torasan series (Yōji Yamada)

5 The education system

INTRODUCTION

Having examined some of the enormous variety in the type of neighbourhood in which a child might find itself growing up, we shall turn now to a part of that process which is at least in theory much more predictable. Although children do find themselves learning about their regional location, and possibly too about the economic activities on which their families depend, the education system in Japan is carefully regulated by central government with the aim of providing an equal and comprehensive basis for learning. At the state schools attended by the vast majority of children, a standard form of Japanese language is expected, regardless of dialectical differences used at home, and the geography and history of Japan place local communities within a broad national context. Schools are thus an important source of shared knowledge and national identity, and throughout the compulsory period of education, quite a uniform understanding of the wider world.

It is through this education system too that many people seek their path in that world. In some of the 'continuing houses' described in Chapter 2 an eldest son may be assured of a future occupation as long as he is willing to follow in the footsteps of his forbears. If the business of the *ie* prospers, his younger brothers may even be provided for as well, and a daughter might find her house connections lead to a prosperous marriage. In the modern urban world, however, this customary practice is no longer possible for most families, and parents look instead to the education system to provide their children with the qualifications necessary for building a future. This is also a clear opportunity for children to work towards goals beyond the confines of their present situation, and for parents well established in careers which they cannot pass on, this is the only avenue for continuity.

Once children enter school, it becomes almost their whole life. Chapter 3 described how kindergarten or day nursery prepares a child for this new role as a member of a class and as a cooperating member of a peer group of equals. This peer group now takes its place at the bottom of a clearly defined hierarchy, and children will from the time they enter school identify themselves with their class. It is much more common in Japan for children to be asked which school year they are in, rather than how old they are, and an answer to the question places the child at a stage of development recognisable to anyone. Other children then identify them as seniors or juniors in the system, and appropriate behaviour ensues. For only a tiny minority of less than 1 per cent of children will parents choose a private school in the early stages, although this possibility increases as children get older.

School uniforms or badges are worn for many public occasions unconnected with school, and the wider world is thus able to classify its younger members according to the occupation proper to their age. Much of the responsibility for children passes to the hands of their teachers, and an accident or incident involving a child is likely to be reported to the school as well as to the child's parents. Unseemly behaviour, even if out of school hours, reflects badly on the school, and teachers may well want to be involved in any disciplinary action that arises. Even during the school holidays, children are expected to attend school at regular intervals, and activities are arranged to occupy the period when they are not there. Too much free time for children is thought to be dangerous and school trips are also a regular feature of a child's life.

It is evident, then, that school has an important shaping influence for a person growing up in Japan, and the system of classification imparted already by parents and kindergarten teachers provides a basis for this further development and elaboration. The emphasis on the importance of the right environment for a child's development continues, and one of the underlying assumptions of the system is that every child should have an equal chance to share the benefits of the system. The following sections will examine the official education system and its characteristics, supplementary institutions that are associated with it, some of the consequences of the system for children and their families, and recent moves for change in the light of criticism.

COMPREHENSIVE EDUCATION FOR ALL

For over a hundred years, Japan has had a school attendance record of above 98 per cent, and there is consequently a rate of literacy as high as any in the world. Since centralised universal education was introduced in the Meiji period, the possibilities for attendance have gradually increased, both at the earlier compulsory levels and for those who wish to pursue their studies further. The present system was crystallised after the Second World War. It aims to be egalitarian and co-educational for the period of compulsory schooling, which comprises six years of primary school and three years of middle school, and meritocratic for three further years of high school and the range of universities and colleges which follow.

For the first nine years most children attend their local public schools, and there are clearly defined catchment areas which should not be crossed. As was mentioned in the last chapter, primary school children from particular neighbourhoods gather at a fixed meeting point each day to walk to school together, and from time to time various activities within the school are organised along neighbourhood lines. All children enter school in the April after their sixth birthday, and they move up together each year, regardless of academic performance. Thus the *uchi* group, which probably formed rather casually in the neighbourhood and may well have been reinforced at kindergarten or day nursery, is quite likely to stay together until graduation from middle school. At middle school, cohorts from more than one primary school will come together, and the primary *uchi* group will by then be expanded to include other factors such as belonging to the same 'homeroom' or school club.

Throughout the nation, tuition at this compulsory level is provided for all, in subjects outlined by the Ministry of Education, without much streaming according to ability. Teachers have detailed plans to follow, so that children in the same grade may on any particular day be covering the same ground in Hokkaido as they are in Okinawa. The Ministry must approve the textbooks, and their writers are occasionally instructed to rewrite whole passages to reflect the image the Ministry deems appropriate. Courses in morals and social studies form part of the curriculum, and at the primary level children all over Japan are being socialised through this education in a rather uniform way. In secondary schools teachers have more autonomy in how they deal with the morals course, which is often the subject of political controversy.

The content of these courses is not unchanging, however, and the textbooks in use before the Second World War were banned by the Occupation Government because they helped to propagate the nationalistic fervour which led Japan into defeat – they taught Japanese mythology as history, as discussed in Chapter 1. The associated Shintō ideology was also banned from schools in the immediate post-war period. The values which were subsequently taught were for a while very Western, mostly American, with the lives of heroes such as Benjamin Franklin being held up as models for the children. Gradually courses have become more 'Japanese' in content, and suitable Japanese heroes have been brought in to localise the value system being advocated. However, the content of school textbooks remains a topic of considerable controversy, particularly in the way that it now depicts periods of war and imperial expansion. This has long been a bone of contention for countries such as Taiwan and Korea that were occupied by Japan, but general issues associated with the Second World War are also a source of conflict. Minority groups such as the Ainu are also seeking greater representation.

Order is maintained in elementary schools in much the same way as it is in kindergarten, with teachers allowing the force of peer pressure to play a strong contributory part. A 'homeroom' class is perceived as a group of equals throughout the system, with duties and privileges being shared out as fairly as possible. On the whole, discipline is reasonably good in the early stages, and children effectively keep themselves in order in the way outlined already in Chapter 3. Classes are divided up into small groups, which are responsible collectively for various tasks (see Figure 5.1). The behaviour of each member therefore contributes to the overall ability of the group, and the children learn to help one another. The principle of considering the needs of the collectivity as well as one's own personal desires thus continues to be emphasised in schools.

William Cummings's (1980) book *Education and Equality in Japan* provides considerable information about how the principles of equality are inculcated in Japanese schools. To give just a couple of examples, he cites the way the children themselves take it in turns to bring food over to the class-room and serve it out for lunch, and the way they are also responsible, with their teachers, for the cleaning of the premises. He regards such activities as part of the children's moral education, because they learn that 'no work, not even the dirty work of cleaning is too low for a student; that all should share equally in common tasks; the maintenance of the school is everyone's responsibility' (1980:117). He points out that Japanese teachers aim to 'develop "whole people", rather than some narrow aspect of individual potential' (1980:104), and much time is spent in non-academic activities such as music and sports.

Cummings is mostly concerned with education at primary level, and his major thesis, that Japan's schools have had a transforming egalitarian effect on society, would seem to reflect this emphasis. Children are aware of their seniors and juniors, according to school year, but since all move through the system together it is only a matter of time before any child reaches the top class. They are also aware of differences of ability, but these are played down, or channelled into group benefit, and competition between individual children is not encouraged at this stage, even during the school sports day. Amongst the children themselves, there are inevitable comparisons, however, and when they move through to middle school, in the April after their twelfth birthday, they become more important.

Figure 5.1 Classes of up to forty-five children are managed by dividing them into smaller groups, which work together and take collective responsibility for their activities.

A clear understanding of middle school education depends on an understanding of the differences in the high school system, which are discussed in the following section, and there we encounter the opposing hierarchical principle again. Middle schools prepare pupils for the more serious academic instruction they will receive when they go on to high school, but they also attend to the development of the child as a whole person, aware that the ages of 13–15 are a crucial period of change. A good overall study of this period in children's lives discusses in some detail the role middle schools have of 'guiding' their charges through puberty and it looks also at the way various children themselves steer a course between work and play (Fukuzawa and LeTendre 2001). The encouragement of extra-curricular school 'clubs' – common interest groups covering activities such as sports, music and other hobbies – allows time for the enjoyment of an activity of personal choice and also a degree of individual expression among all the communal activities. Their membership typically cuts across classes so that seniors help to train juniors in the pursuits involved and members of the same club may spend a lot of time together. Schoolmates in other classes are now referred to as 'seniors' or 'juniors', especially where club activities are concerned, and the consequent expectations and responsibilities are part of the education process.

SELECTION FOR HIGH SCHOOL AND BEYOND

Although some 96.9 per cent (in 2001) of middle school graduates move on into high schools, there is at this stage a considerable range of schools available (*FFJ* 2002:159). The students who are best qualified academically are able to continue into institutions that are ranked in any area for their success in placing graduating students in good universities. There are also a number of vocational high schools, which include training in commercial and technical skills, domestic science and fields of local importance such as agriculture or forestry. There is sometimes also a night high school, so that students can work during the day if necessary. In most areas there is also a variety of private high schools, which are sometimes of lower status than the public ones, but which provide an academic track for children who fail to gain access to the best public schools. Although it was not intended when the system was designed some of these private schools have become more prestigious than the local public schools.

In stark contrast to the previous emphasis on equality of education, entry into high school is based on merit, and is fiercely competitive. At this stage students are free to apply to any of the high schools within commuting distance of their homes, and acceptance is based on the results of an entrance exam set by the school, sometimes together with a report from their middle school. There used to be far more applications for the academic high schools than there were places, although the drop in the birth rate has affected schools in some areas. Nevertheless, the graduates of the best schools are likely to gain admission to correspondingly prestigious universities and, as we shall see in the next chapter, the quality of one's university is again reflected in the quality of employment which one can then go on to obtain.

A useful (if a little dated) anthropological analysis of the high school system and its social context is provided in Thomas Rohlen's (1983) book *Japan's High Schools*, which is based on research carried out in the city of Kobe. Rohlen spent six to eight weeks in each of five high schools, which range across the spectrum of possibilities. He found that many children, even in the specialist and night schools built to prepare less academic children for practical employment, were still hoping to gain entrance to university or, at least, to a two-year junior college. This is not the case everywhere, however. Indeed, in the rural area of Kyushu where I carried out my own fieldwork, the agricultural and commercial high schools were considered to be quite acceptable choices, although children who do well enough to enter an academic high school are not discouraged.

In many areas, local factors are quite influential, as a newer book by Okano and Tsuchiya (1999) is at pains to point out. Subtitled *Inequality and Diversity* this study of the Japanese education system focuses on the *process* of participation in the system the government provides and examines the difference in experience according to other social factors. In theory the system is a meritocracy, providing equal opportunities to all children who enter the school that should reflect only their ability and willingness to work hard. In practice, however, there are other factors involved and Okano and Tsuchiya consider the influence of gender, poverty and elitism through the presentation of detailed specific cases. They also discuss the situation for specific minority groups such as Koreans, formerly outcaste people and newcomers to Japan from other parts of the world.

Rohlen also found a striking correspondence between socio-economic circumstances and the high school a child ended up attending. He administered questionnaires to second-year pupils in each of the five schools studied, and found unmistakable correlations between the prestige of the school and the education of the parents, the facilities at home for study and the general stability of their families. One of the worst cases presented by Okano and Tsuchiya was related to unstable family life (1999:86–7) and Goodman (2000) has reported a dismal lack of educational success amongst the occupants of children's homes. It is evident that the emphasis on equality so thoroughly instilled in the early years is heavily tempered by the time a child enters high school. Indeed, Rohlen comments that he can think of no other inclusive social institution in Japan that comes closer to a simple class structure than the structure of urban high schools in cities like Kobe (1983:129).

INEQUALITY AND SUPPLEMENTARY PROVISION

This evidence of inequality in high school populations is related to the use made by families who can afford it of supplementary educational facilities, which abound in Japan. The most common form of supplement to the public system is found in classes held after school for tutoring in particular subjects. Some of these classes start before children even go to school. At this stage they follow quite a variety of pursuits, which may represent the development of individual interests, such as music, painting and martial arts like *kendo*, but a minority of children will already be studying academically orientated subjects such as English or maths. Primary school pupils may also go to classes to learn calligraphy or the piano, but by the middle school level, when pupils are preparing for high school entrance, the emphasis focuses on preparation for exams in the compulsory subjects.

From this stage onwards, until a university place has been secured, it has been reported that some children spend several evenings a week rehearsing the basics of maths and English until nine or ten at night, and then return home to study alone until the early morning. These classes (known as *juku*) are expensive, however, and some families are able to afford more and better ones than others can. Nor do most families have the space to allow each child his or her own workroom. Those who do have the resources may opt for a private middle school to help their children gain a place in one of the better high schools, but this represents only about 5 per cent of all children. Some public middle schools have a better reputation than others do, and since children are allocated to these on the basis of residence, some may even be lodged, in theory or in practice, with friends or relatives in the appropriate part of the city. Country families sometimes move mother and children to Tokyo solely for the sake of the children's education.

Although most children in Japan attend public primary schools, in areas where private middle schools have a particularly good reputation, competition for entry again encourages affluent parents to seek private primary schools to prepare their children for middle school entrance. These in turn come under pressure for entry, and there are even kindergartens that aim to prepare children to enter prestigious primary schools. In Tokyo some of the prestigious private universities have schools of all levels attached to them, and a child who gains entry at the bottom has a very good chance of moving smoothly through to the top – a system compared to an escalator. The problem then becomes one of gaining entry to the kindergarten and in Tokyo there are even tutorial institutions that accept children of 1, 2 and 3 years of age (Ohki 1986). Prices are very high, however, and there is no question here but that a wealthy elite is being separated off at a very early age.

In some kindergartens it is felt that the problems which can arise in trying to assess children of 3 years of age are too great, however, and they choose instead to test the mothers. This is not entirely inappropriate, for mothers in Japan often become very involved in the education of their children. The wives of company employees in particular seem to make a career of the supervision of their children's education. From an early stage, these mothers spend time studying manuals of advice on the best ways to bring up their children, and the most dedicated will continue to purchase publications supplementary to the school courses in order to keep one step ahead for as long as they are able. They will frequently discuss their child's progress with the homeroom teacher, and generally contribute to the school's welfare through the Parent–Teacher Associations.

Such mothers form something of an elite within the system at large, however, as many mothers go back to work once their children enter school. On the whole, a strong contributory factor would seem to be the occupation of the father. Good economic circumstances are clearly vital in that the 'education mama', as such mothers have become known, must be supported financially in order to be fully active in this respect, but it seems likely that more than this is involved. In my view it could well be related to the ability or otherwise of the family to pass on its lifestyle to its children. The offspring of employees of prestigious companies must do well in the exam system if they are to gain their own place in such a firm and follow in their fathers' footsteps. Their fathers can help economically, but their (maintained) wives take on the role of manipulating the system.

Another supplementary provision offers a kind of safety net for families whose children fail to gain a place in the university of their choice directly from high school. These are last-ditch private cram schools that provide intensive training for one or more years for second and subsequent sittings of the entrance exams. Rohlen's figures (1983:84) suggested that a quarter to a third of the applicants for higher education in any one year were from these 'cram schools', a proportion roughly equal to the number of students who failed to gain a place. Since that time, however, the combination of a drop in the birth rate and the ravages of economic recession have put some of these schools out of business altogether. Similarly, a friend who runs after school classes reported in 2002 that his numbers were down to one-third of their maximum attendance. Overall statistics also suggest that cram school numbers are dropping, but less drastically (http://jin.jcic.or.jp/stat/stats/16EDUA1.html).

Another aid to teachers helping parents and children to make decisions about which high school or university to choose when making applications is supplied by companies that offer tests on a commercial basis. Modelled on the school and university entrance tests, these tests classify the children who take them in comparison with their peers. A ranking for each examinee may then be compared with figures published by the same companies about the marks necessary for entry to particular universities or high schools. Some pupils will take these tests as regularly as twice a month as they work hard to improve their scores. The results have apparently become so influential that middle school teachers rely heavily on them in advising parents where to place their children's applications for high school entry.

All this emphasis on entrance examinations does not, of course, always affect the lives of children positively. The media, in Japan and abroad, tends to emphasise the strain of keeping up and the lack of time to play, and it was for a time reported that there was a high rate of suicide among school children in Japan. There has also been a good deal of fuss about violence in school and at home, particularly involving middle school pupils, and horrific cases resulting in the death of schoolchildren, at the hands of both a fellow pupil and a teacher, shocked the nation. Bullying was reported to be a major problem for a while, but special centres set up to provide phone-in help for victims have apparently had some success, for the figures are reported to have halved between 1995 and 2000 (*FFJ* 2002:161).

In the past few years, however, increasingly large numbers of children are refusing to go to school at all, and those who miss more than thirty days per year have doubled between 1991 and 2000 (http://jin/jcic.or.jp/stat/stats/16EDU91.html). An interesting article by the medical anthropologist Margaret Lock (1988) examined in some detail this phenomenon of 'school refusal', a subject that has been another focus of attention in the Japanese media. Lock cites cases which have been diagnosed as a specific 'syndrome' and she reports on the treatment administered, but her article also places Japanese attention to this phenomenon in the context of contemporary ideas about the breakdown of traditional social values. Blame is laid at the door of the 'fragile nuclear family' or the 'new middle class', including a 'selfish' mother and/or an absent father, although there is little hard evidence to demonstrate any such correlations. Indeed, discrete enquiries among the children of some of my friends in Tokyo suggest that going off to have fun is not an uncommon reason for being out of school.

At one level the press coverage accorded these unpleasant aspects of school life would seem to be directly related to the shock they deliver to the more usual expectations of the audiences concerned. The Western press finds Japanese schools unbearably uniform, and seizes on examples of rebellion as signs of pathology in a social system that seems to deny the very individuality that they regard as so important. In Japan these incidents are news because they undermine the order which has been such an all-pervading part of the education system. In other advanced industrialised nations violence and bullying in schools are often so commonplace that they cause little or no stir in the outside world. Truancy is also quite common. In Japan, these problems have put particular pressure on long-standing committees set up to discuss an overall reform in the education system (which will be considered in a later section), and has also led to further supplementary provision.

'School refusal', for example, has sparked off the introduction of a series of special schools aiming to offer a more intimate, supportive environment than do those in the regular system. Some children, who refuse not only the trip to school but even to emerge from their own rooms, have been a particular challenge. One of my doctoral students has chosen to focus his research on this group of children and in 2002 I visited the school in Tokyo where he is carrying out part of his fieldwork. Operating under the name 'free school', though this refers to the freedom of children not to attend rather than to a lack of cost, great pains are taken to make the place attractive and to provide encouragement to each individual who plucks up the courage to arrive. Numbers are small, as are the room sizes, and children who have made progress help those who are nervous. While we were there some 'graduates' of the school came back to play table tennis, and I learned of their success in proceeding back into normal life. The same organisation runs a series of schools to deal with children at different levels of ability to participate.

Another type of special facility that has been created in Japan is for the readjustment of children who spend even short periods abroad. In the early 1980s, when these were being set up, it was not only thought that these 'returnees' would find it difficult to re-enter the system, but that they might even threaten its tight order. Roger Goodman (1990) set out to examine the 'problems' such children were perceived to encounter, and found that, on the contrary, the facilities available to them were quite substantial and impressive. Places were even reserved for them in the best universities, and some parents actually started to send their children to schools abroad so that they might qualify. Parents of these returnee school children often occupy high-ranking positions, so they were well placed to lobby to turn the perceived disadvantage for their children into an advantage.

Goodman's analysis revealed as much about Japan's power structures and the way they operate as about the fate of the children, but his book addressed an important contemporary issue of Japan's attempts at 'internationalisation'. There was a clear division in attitudes to the outside world at the time between groups of people who valued the force for change these children represented, and others who were concerned about their loss of 'Japaneseness'. In the intervening years the number of Japanese who live abroad has increased exponentially, and early returnees have grown up and been able to use their skills to further the project that is now usually termed 'globalisation'. Moreover, increasing numbers of foreign teachers have also been recruited to teach English (and occasionally other languages) in Japanese schools, and these 'JETs' offer a living international dimension to more and more of the regular school system. From 2002, they started working in primary schools. McConnell's (2000) book is an interesting anthropological study of the JET programme.

This form of supplementary provision, and the subsequent long-term relationships with Japan that are very often pursued by former JET teachers, cannot help but contribute to the mature view of the outside world mentioned in Chapter 1. It is one thing to be taught in theory about a world outside the one you know – and the wider world becomes a focus from the final year of primary school – but it is quite another to have a regular teacher from somewhere in that outside world in your classroom. The JET teachers also live for one to three years in the most rural areas of Japan as well as in the cities, and their influence on the local community, especially amongst young people of their own age, may well also be something of an education in areas where formerly few non-Japanese lived.

In general, the numbers of 'newcomers' sending their children to school in Japan has also increased a great deal over the past two decades and most of them do not have English as their first language. The majority of foreign residents has for long been Korean, some of whom have been living in Japan for three or four generations, and they have apparently suffered considerable discrimination at school, though there are a few specialist Korean schools (Fukuoka 2000, see Chapter 6). However, there are also increasing numbers of Chinese, Brazilians and Filipinos, as well as smaller numbers from other countries, and for many, Japanese language is for a while a problem. There are international schools in the major cities, and even some Japanese families choose these, but they are expensive and they do not seek to integrate their charges into Japanese society or even necessarily to impart much Japanese language.

It is up to the regular Japanese schools to incorporate these foreign children then, and they will quite often create a special class to help them over their initial difficulties. In my own experience of watching a Japanese primary school deal with my two (foreign) sons, as well as the child of a family of some local ill-repute, the teachers were tireless in their attempts to help these children fit in. They insisted on treating them as individuals who should not be held responsible for the associations of their parents. Bullying and discrimination were sometimes a problem, but if noticed by the adults the issues were treated with great care and sensitivity, as also reported by Fukuoka for Korean children. A haven of escape for one of my sons was another interesting extra provision in Japanese schools, namely the nurse's office, and this has been reported to be playing an important role for middle school pupils with social difficulties (Fukuzawa and LeTendre 2001).

SCHOOL AND SOCIAL DIVISIONS

Rohlen suggested that Japanese schools 'pace society'. They teach rhythms and segmentation of time which 'complement . . . the working order of industry and modern organisation' (1983:168); 'shaping generations of disciplined workers for a technomeritocratic system that requires highly socialized individuals capable of performing reliably in a rigorous, hierarchical, and finely tuned organizational environment' (1983:209). His overwhelming image of high school classes is one of boredom – of children accumulating facts but having little opportunity to discuss them, of having views, but not able to express them, of possibly resenting the authority of teachers, but of learning not to challenge it (1983:246). In such an environment diligence is a highly prized quality and long-standing Japanese virtues of self-control, dedication and singularity of purpose are admired and rewarded.

Reports from ex-JET teachers that I have taught would suggest that this picture is one reserved only for the most academic of schools, however. Elsewhere considerable disruption is reported, and this has been another subject of interest to the media. The use of mobile phones in class is one complaint, another is a severe lapse in observance of a formerly quite strict dress code. It is only necessary to step on a train in Japan to see the way that uniforms are elaborated, especially by girls, and the variety in hair colour has been another source of virulent fashion. There have even been reports of high school girls selling their young bodies for pocket money. Rohlen also noted that it was in vocational schools, rather than academic ones, where disorderly conduct and delinquency were to be found. Although socioeconomic factors play a part, Rohlen suggested that a lack of purpose leaves a void of ambition, despite attempts to make these vocational schools more attractive.

This division reinforces the one going back to middle school between children whose parents are able to send them to classes after school, and those who are not. A further division arises as the children who do not attend begin to engage in other activities. For Kobe, Rohlen calls these the 'city' activities – going out with friends, riding motor bikes, visiting coffee shops, 'cruising' and 'dating'. All these are low-status activities for academically orientated high school students. Those who leave after middle school – when such activities were not allowed – also engage in them. Those who are involved have usually given up on the race for university entrance, and their parents are probably not pushing them either. Serious students return home after their classes, and late at night they are to be found at their desks. For students who lag behind Rohlen felt that there is no satisfactory place in the system. Perhaps the success of the egalitarian principle in the early stages of schooling makes the pill of hierarchical sorting more difficult for them to swallow.

In fact the two principles of equality and hierarchy vie for attention throughout the school career of Japanese children. Classmates are among the most equal relations that a Japanese person will encounter in his or her entire life, and many adults retain ties with their school or university friends through regular reunions, as we saw in the last chapter. On the other hand, relations between classes are strictly hierarchical, and club activities, which are held on school premises, begin to train children in the less formal aspects of close hierarchical relations. These clubs form something of an antidote to the uniformity of the system, as already mentioned, but interpersonal relations within them resemble those appropriate for seniors and juniors in various other walks of life. The relations between pupils and their teachers are also hierarchical, and some teachers who take part in club activities provide role models in areas of common interest.

These formal relations are rather different to those based on an ability to excel in exams, however, and this last form of hierarchical division may be reinforced by another sort of 'club'. Private classes (*juku*) may be much smaller than school ones and these have been likened to a form of education that existed in the Tokugawa period. One teacher of my acquaintance provides his charges with brightly coloured bags, arranges for them to stay overnight at the school together for special sessions, and takes them on trips, walking or skiing as the season dictates. Offering these activities is an attempt to address the criticism that children have little time left for informal play once they begin to prepare seriously for university or school entrance exams. A child's closest friendships may also be with members of his or her *juku*. As well as attending the same classes several times a week, they may also travel to and fro together and so they enjoy opportunities for informal play as well as the hard work.

UNIVERSITY AND JUNIOR COLLEGE

Once a place has been gained in a university, the quality of career that a young person can expect is relatively independent of the outcome of the degree. This relieves some of the pressure that preceded university entrance, and students can relax and enjoy their studies or their social life during this time. In anthropological terms this period can be interpreted as part of the transition from childhood to adulthood. Many of the characteristics described long ago by van Gennep (1977, see Chapter 8) of rites of initiation, which include ordeals, education and freedom from social constraint, are present here. Japanese university students have successfully negotiated the ordeals of the entrance examinations, they have filled themselves full of 'education' and they are at last allowed to develop a sense of freedom.

Their contemporaries in employment may take a parallel kind of freedom by having a series of short-term jobs, making no commitment to 'a career' and possibly expressing rebellion against adult society, symbolised, for example, in unconventional clothes and hairstyles. This is an example of the 'freeter' phenomenon mentioned in Chapter 2. Students used to get involved in political movements (Steinhoff 1984), and some of their most spectacular activities, such as those expressing opposition to Narita airport, were reported in the international press. More recently, however, students seem less and less interested in politics, and if the resources are available, international travel has become another means to dabble in freedom from the constraints of Japanese society. Nor may this freedom terminate with graduation, as it has become quite common to spend a period studying abroad before settling down. Indeed, such students may argue that this will better equip them for the globalised world, though their potential employers are apparently slower to agree with them.

Nearly half of the graduates from high school went on to university and junior college in Japan in 2002, and a further 27 per cent entered special training schools (*FFJ* 2002:159). There is a difference at this stage between the courses chosen by boys and by girls, however. Four-year degree courses are the most common ones embarked upon for boys, and in 2001, 63 per cent of university students were boys, although the proportion of girls is increasing year by year. Law and economics were the most popular subjects in 2002 (ibid.). On the other hand, the two-year junior college course is popular with girls, who accounted for nearly 90 per cent of enrolment in 2002, though again the proportion of boys is gradually increasing. Here, education and home economics are likely subjects of study, although McVeigh's (1997) book, *Life in a Japanese College* suggests in the subtitle that one of the main aims is '*learning to be ladylike*'. This amusing account discusses in detail the training in etiquette and other more subtle skills that are part and parcel of this allegedly academic course.

According to statistics, attendance at junior college peaked in 1993 and has been diminishing ever since, partly for demographic reasons, but clearly also partly because larger numbers of girls are choosing four-year courses. Until this stage, boys and girls move through the system in more or less equal numbers, girls often having the edge over boys for high school entrance, although attitudes have tended to be different. Boys are more likely to be striving towards entry into the best university they can manage, whereas girls are generally more relaxed. It is not seen as advantageous for girls to be more qualified than their prospective husbands and marriage is still the chief goal of many women. Nevertheless, if girls choose really to make the effort in higher education, there are few hurdles put in their way on the basis of gender, and an academic career is a definite possibility for a woman. In any case, the mothers of the next generation are probably among the highest qualified in the world.

A relatively recent development in higher education in Japan is the possibility of life-long learning. The University of the Air has been broadcasting since 1985, but the numbers of 'mature students' joining regular postgraduate courses has also been increasing in the past few years. These facilities will no doubt be a comfort to some of the people made redundant in the recession, and it seems at last to be possible to contemplate a complete change of career in mid-life in Japan. Within local communities public lectures are a popular pastime, and organisations like Onna Daigaku (women's university) offer regular courses in a variety of subjects for recreational purposes. Language classes are popular, particularly but not exclusively English, and in some regional areas classes have been set up to preserve local skills. In Hokkaido, for example, the Ainu language may be studied, and I visited a community centre where Ainu women were enthusiastically learning the carving and stitching that were practised by their forbears.

Figure 5.2 These Ainu women are learning skills in public classes that their mothers would have passed on to them in former times.

EDUCATIONAL REFORM

The Japanese education system provides a very high standard of average education, so that the achievements of Japanese children compare more than favourably with their contemporaries in other countries. However, various criticisms have been made of the system, and some parents have been encouraging rebellion against the stress they feel their children are put under. A few have simply sent their children abroad to gain a different set of skills. The pressures of the exam system have been blamed for a number of evils, and big business has been charged with compounding the problem by selecting graduates only from top universities. Demographic changes have relieved the pressure somewhat, and there also seems to be evidence of a more adventurous selection process by up-and-coming middle-sized companies, as well as by larger ones seeking a way out of economic stagnation.

From the point of view of the education system itself, the Prime Minister set up an advisory council for educational reform in 1984, and its first report was submitted in June 1985. It proposed a greater emphasis on individuality, creativity and choice, among other things, but it was also the subject of much controversy and debate. The variety of views expressed, together with the range of arguments put forward to support them, for some time seemed to militate against much action, although certain less controversial aspects of the report have gradually been implemented. In December 1998 the Ministry of Education announced a new curriculum for kindergartens, primary schools and junior high schools, implemented in 2002. It aims to make education 'less regimented and more nurturing of children's ability and willingness to solve problems by themselves'.

During visits to primary schools in 1994, I was told about innovations such as 'team teaching' and 'streaming' within classes. The teachers I met also used other English words to describe activities which they had been practising for many years, but which they said they had modified to take more into account than they felt they had previously done the individuality and creativity of their charges. They also emphasised the way that children could now choose between a range of options for the work they did: topics for essay writing, themes for poetry, subjects for their painting classes. In practice, as I looked around the schools I visited, they seemed little changed from the time in 1986–7 when my own children experienced the system, but these primary schools had impressed me at that time with the care and attention they gave to the individual needs of the pupils. It will be interesting to see what changes are heralded by the new curriculum of 2002.

CONCLUSION

Education has been an issue of great importance in Japan throughout the 'modern' period. In many ways the education system and even the examination entrance system have taken over roles that used to be played by the family, and the new nuclear family has slotted into a place within that system. Continuity is still an important principle underlying Japanese thinking, and where the family has lost its former role in that respect, education has taken over and opened up new avenues. It is within this system that people maintain the status that their families bequeath them, but also where they gain new status appropriate for the world they grow up to encounter. Changes of one sort or another have been rife in post-war Japan, and the education system strives to keep preparing new generations for new worlds. In the next chapter we will examine in detail sources and consequences of status within Japanese worlds.

REFERENCES AND FURTHER READING

Cummings, William K., *Education and Equality in Japan* (Princeton University Press, Princeton, NJ, 1980)

Dore, Ronald, *The Diploma Disease* (Allen & Unwin, London, 1976), chapter 3

—— *Education in Tokugawa Japan* (Athlone Press, London, 1984)

FFJ – Facts and Figures of Japan (Foreign Press Centre, Japan, 2002)

Fukuzawa, Rebecca Erwin and Gerald K. LeTendre, *Intense Years: How Japanese Adolescents Balance School, Family and Friends* (RoutledgeFalmer, New York and London, 2001)

Goodman, Roger, *Japan's 'International Youth': The Emergence of a New Class of Schoolchildren* (Clarendon Press, Oxford, 1990)

—— *Children of the Japanese State: The Changing Role of Child Protection Institutions in Contemporary Japan* (Clarendon Press, Oxford, 2000)

—— 'The Changing Perception and Status of Japan's Returnee Children (*Kikokushijo*)' in Roger Goodman *et al.* (eds), *Global Japan: The Experience of Japan's New Immigrant and Overseas Communities* (RoutledgeCurzon, London, 2003)

Hendry, Joy, 'St. Valentine and St. Nicholas in Japan: Some Less Academic Aspects of Japanese School Life', *Japan Forum*, 3, 2 (1991), pp. 313–23

Kobayashi, Tetsuya, *Schools, Society and Progress in Japan* (Pergamon Press, Oxford, 1976)

Lock, Margaret, 'A Nation at Risk: Interpretations of School Refusal in Japan', in M. Lock and D. Gordon (eds), *Biomedicine Examined* (Kluwer Academic Publishers, Dordrecht and Boston, 1988), pp. 377–414

McConnell, David L., *Importing Diversity: Inside Japan's JET Programme* (University of California Press, Berkeley, Los Angeles and London, 2000)

McVeigh, Brian, *Life in a Japanese Women's College: Learning to be Ladylike* (Routledge, London and New York, 1997)

—— *Wearing Ideology: State, Schooling and Self-Presentation in Japan* (Berg, Oxford, 2000)

Nagai, Michio, *Higher Education in Japan: Its Take-off and Crash* (University of Tokyo Press, Tokyo, 1971)

Ohki, Emiko, 'Pre-kindergarten "Education" is Flourishing in Tokyo', *Japan Education Journal*, 27 (1986), p. 10

Okano, Kaori and Motonori Tsuchiya, *Education in Contemporary Japan: Inequality and Diversity* (Cambridge University Press, Cambridge, 1999)

Passin, Herbert, *Society and Education in Japan* (Columbia University Press, New York, 1965)

Rohlen, Thomas P., *Japan's High Schools* (University of California Press, Berkeley, 1983)

Singleton, John, *Nichu: A Japanese School* (Holt, Rinehart & Winston, New York, 1967)

Steinhoff, Patricia G., 'Student Conflict', in Ellis S. Krauss *et al.* (eds), *Conflict in Japan* (University of Hawaii Press, Honolulu, 1984), pp. 174–213

White, Merry, *The Japanese Educational Challenge: A Commitment to Children* (The Free Press, New York, 1987)

—— *The Material Child: Coming of Age in Japan and America* (The Free Press, New York, 1993)

FILMS

The Games Teachers Play (1992 Hideyuki Hirayama)
Schools (*Gakkō* series) (Yōji Yamada)
Twenty-four Eyes (*Nijushi no Hitomi*) (1994 Keisuke Kinoshita)
Typhoon Club (*Taifū Club*) (1985 Shinji Somai)

6 Status, hierarchy and ethnic diversity

INTRODUCTION

Hierarchy is one of the most important principles of classification in any society, as anthropologists have shown, but it is important to recognise that the assumptions one brings to the subject from one's own background may need radical revision in a different cultural context. Louis Dumont (1980) has illustrated this clearly in his introduction to *Homo Hierarchicus*, a detailed study of the Indian caste system, where he points out that the emphasis on equality in modern Western society may blind its members and prejudice them against a proper understanding of his subject matter. He draws on the classic studies of Tocqueville and Talcott Parsons to show that hierarchy is an inevitable part of social life, but he goes on to emphasise that this hierarchy may be 'quite independent of natural inequalities or the distribution of power' (1980:20). This point is important to bear in mind in the case of Japan.

In the previous chapter we began to see some of the hierarchical differences that impinge on early life in Japanese society. First there were the straightforward differences of age. In the primary years of schooling these are the only ones given official support since other forms of inequality are played down and children move up through the system regardless of ability. Second, there are differences in skills, recognised informally between children themselves and often encouraged implicitly in contributing to collective endeavour, though at this stage speed at running probably plays as much of a part in forming relative status as a facility with figures. Gradually, however, academic skills become important as competitive examinations loom, and children find themselves divided physically by the school entrance they can attain. There is a third kind of difference, however, and this is based on a status acquired through birth and background, an *acquired status* that is different from the status *achieved* through individual effort, and this one may be a cause of discrimination, positive and negative.

In this chapter we will examine examples of all these sources of division, and some of their consequences in long-term influence as well as in daily life. We will thereby get an idea why school tests are taken so seriously. However, it is also important to remember the continuing parallel emphasis on equality that we have seen, at school and kindergarten, and in the community. In all three cases we saw the symbolic way in which membership involved relations of equality, as each person or house took a strict turn in carrying out duties or accepting privileges. Hierarchical relations exist throughout, and their sources will be discussed in the following pages, but the simultaneous expressions of equality should not be forgotten. Sociologists tend to call this subject 'stratification', but I avoid the term here because I feel its association with a kind of inflexible layering of society prevalent in European societies and their related manifestations in the New World may distract from a sound understanding of the situation in Japan.

Hierarchical ranking runs through Japanese life. It orders individuals, groups, institutions, material objects, even foods, but at any particular level there is always a certain flexibility based on that opposing principle of equality. Thus, in contrast to members of the outside world, Japanese people tend to regard themselves as equally Japanese despite very great differences within their own cultural milieu. Similarly, members of a particular company, when dealing with outsiders, will express equality amongst themselves as members of that company, though the divisions within it are clear-cut and strictly enforced. In these contexts, the *uchi/soto* distinction overrides hierarchical differences. It is clear then that we need to build some flexibility into our understanding of status difference.

This chapter will open with a description of various manifestations of hierarchy and status difference in modern Japan. It will move on to consider some of the historical foundations for them, and examples of continuing sources of acquired status differential including a fairly long section on ethnic diversity. It will then return to discussing more general principles underlying hierarchical difference, including gender, and a final section will be devoted to ways in which these can be manipulated. The reader will note that the socialisation discussed in Chapter 3 lays the ground well to prepare children to make their way as adults through this complicated social world.

EXPRESSIONS OF HIERARCHY IN MODERN JAPAN

There is no doubt that hierarchical differences affect interaction between Japanese people in their everyday lives. Indeed, in many situations it is difficult to know how to behave unless one can place the other people present in a hierarchical order in relation to oneself. This begins from the moment of greeting, for bowing is a good example of the expression of status differences. One bows more deeply to a superior than to an inferior, and one should stay down longer than one's superior. An amusing situation arises where the relation is unclear, for each side will try to stay down longer, on the assumption that it is better to err on the inferior side than on the superior one. The custom of exchanging name cards on meeting a new person helps to resolve such problems.

Speech in Japanese also varies depending on the relationship between the partners engaged in a conversation. The complicated system of speech levels, already mentioned in the discussion about *tatemae* and *honne*, makes it possible to show different degrees of respect or self-deprecation, and the choice of inappropriate levels can sound very offensive. It is even possible to be rudely over-polite. Verb endings vary and some common words, such as 'go', 'come' and 'speak', have completely different forms according to the degree of politeness being used and the location of their use. It is virtually impossible to have a conversation without making a decision about the appropriate level to use.

Terms of address also vary. The example of the family has already been given, where brothers and sisters are always distinguished according to whether they are older or younger, and this same model is transferred into wider relations between children. As a general principle in the house, inferior members address superior ones with a term of relationship, while superior ones may use personal names, and this same form of distinction is carried into the world at large. Within specific institutions, where members occupy named positions in the hierarchical scale, they will be addressed by these titles by more junior members, whom they will address by name. Interesting modifications to the language have occurred in Hawaiian Japanese, where, presumably in response to the American cultural milieu, English words like 'brother' and 'sister' have been adopted to replace some of the Japanese words which imply differences of status.

Again in Japan, on any formal occasion and a good number of less formal ones, seating in a room is decided according to an appropriate hierarchical order. In a traditional Japanese house, there is a *tokobashira*, or principal construction post, in the main reception room and on one side of this is a special raised alcove called a *tokonoma* (see Figure 6.1). In this space are placed various beautiful objects, usually a hanging scroll and a flower arrangement, as well as other objects of significance to the family. A similar arrangement is found in many of the rooms of Japanese restaurants and inns. This area marks the top of the room, and it is necessary for decisions to be made about how people will sit in relation to it. There are various rules which govern this procedure, and there may be differences of opinion about

Figure 6.1 The top seat in a Japanese room is in front of the *tokobashira*, or principal construction post, seen here between the *tokonoma* and a set of decorative shelves. (Photograph courtesy of Firas Naji.)

which should prevail. A show of modesty is usually in order, too, so that some shuffling may precede the final arrangement.

Another expression of hierarchical difference is to be found in the non-reciprocal exchange of gifts. Within a community, as described in Chapter 4, houses keep a record of the gifts they receive in order to maintain overall reciprocity with each other. Some houses receive a large number of gifts that they do not need to return, however, and these are associated with expressions of debt or goodwill in a hierarchical relationship. It is common in many societies for gifts to be used in symbolic ways such as this, and there is usually something intangible going in the other direction. Thus students take gifts to their teachers as an expression of gratitude for learning imparted. Shopkeepers and tradespeople present small gifts to their customers at certain times of the year as thanks for their continued support. The wrapping of this type of gift usually makes clear its purpose and value so that some people even keep a store of received gifts to present again when the appropriate moment arises.

HIERARCHY IN JAPANESE HISTORY

There have been clear differences of status in Japan since at least as far back as the Tomb period. Some of the environmental factors involved have already been discussed, and archaeological evidence remains to testify to the material ways in which these differences were marked. Since the emergence of a dominant imperial family, with an allegedly unbroken line of descent to the present day, there has always been some kind of nobility set apart from the common people, even if its role has gone through several changes. The imperial family illustrates a special case of the general principle that lines of demarcation are based on membership in a family or *ie*, a common means of distinction which may well go back further. It certainly seems likely that such acquired status has been important throughout the historical period, although it is important to remember that this is not always based on kin connections.

In varying degrees throughout Japanese history it has also been possible to achieve status by individual or cooperative effort. The early warring periods illustrate such competition for dominance between groups, competition that was repeated again and again at various times throughout the subsequent years. In the intervals, relatively stable periods have been marked by a greater emphasis on inherited status. The courtly Heian period is one such example, as is the 250-odd years of Tokugawa rule, during which Japan was virtually closed to the outside world. Within larger groups relations have been based on a combination of earned and inherited characteristics, each being recognised in different ways according to the group and to the time. Chance for mobility within the system has also been a variable factor.

In the two centuries immediately preceding the Meiji Restoration, Japanese society was divided into four clear classes. The samurai warriors were at the top, followed by farmers, artisans and merchants, in that order. Everyone was supposed to remain within his or her own class, continue the work of their forbears and marry within their own social category. Samurai warriors were empowered to maintain order by taking immediate retaliation against overt expressions of rebellion by using the swords they carried to decapitate the offender. Above the samurai, and associated with ritual duties that placed them closer to the gods than to human beings and their affairs, were members of the nobility, which included the imperial family. An excellent ethnography of the descendants of these families, entitled *Above the Clouds*, gives a clear and detailed account of the system and the extent of its continuity into the modern age (Lebra 1993).

At the other end of the scale were the 'Eta' or *burakumin* (people of certain communities), who were assigned defiling occupations, such as burying the dead and tanning the hides of animals – the former polluting from a Shintō viewpoint, the latter in a Buddhist order of things. These human beings were regarded as 'outcastes', literally 'non-people', closer to animals than to other humans. Another interesting study, *The Monkey as Mirror*, discusses the development of this class of 'special status' people in a long historical context (Ohnuki-Tierney 1987) and reveals changing attitudes to the top and bottom of the hierarchical system in Japan over the centuries. From a structural point of view, there are important similarities between the sacredness of the top and the pollution of the bottom of a social system as both are dangerous and therefore forbidden to ordinary humans, and this principle is hard to eradicate, as we shall see.

In fact, despite the rules, it was not impossible for individuals or families to cross these apparently rigid barriers. Sometimes this would be for economic need. The warriors, at the top of the human scale, placed very little value on material wealth, indeed they prided themselves on their frugality. Consequently they were often bad at managing the property they did own. Merchants, on the other hand, although they were officially at the bottom of the scale, were able to use their wealth to become effective landowners by helping families who fell into debt. It was not unheard of for a judicial marriage, which would benefit both sides, to be arranged between two such families. Priests and scholars also floated within the system to some extent, and there were itinerant travellers whose status was also unclearly defined. The anthropologist Jacob Raz (1992) has carried out interesting fieldwork with descendants of this last group. On the whole self-betterment was not encouraged, however, and people were expected to know their place, even within the four major divisions, and stay within it.

Although the system was abolished at the beginning of the Meiji period, its legacy was forcibly expressed by Ruth Benedict (1967) in her classic anthropological study of Japan, *The Chrysanthemum and the Sword*, written during the Second World War. In a chapter entitled 'Taking one's proper station', she discusses some of the hierarchical attitudes and assumptions with which the Japanese entered the war, tracing them back to the rigidity of the 'caste system' of the Tokugawa period. She, like Dumont (1980), points out an important distinction between the fixed position one occupies according to the rules of hierarchy, and the quite different degree of dominance or power that one may wield behind the scenes (Benedict 1967:39). The two are quite separate, and the latter gives no right to violate the former. This is an important aspect of Japanese hierarchy that has by no means disappeared.

There have been many changes, however, and during the modern period much new ideology was also imported to rival the older ideas. In the early days of Western contact, there was some considerable reinforcement of the system of nobility, and roles and titles were introduced to parallel those of the European aristocracy (Lebra 1993). Ideas of equality and individual freedom also thrived amongst intellectuals, though, and they came to influence many of the new institutions that were introduced. During the Meiji period, when class divisions were abolished, universal education was introduced throughout the country, and opportunities opened up at all levels in the new industries that were beginning to develop. Universal male suffrage was not introduced until 1925, but then it was applied to all men over 25.

After the Second World War a further forceful influx of ideology was introduced by the Allied Occupation. The new Constitution officially brought democracy to Japan, men and women over 20 were given the right to vote, and American ideas of equality and freedom flowed intoxicatingly through the defeated nation. As elsewhere in the industrialising world, a higher status could now be achieved legitimately through individual effort. A person's occupation was no longer expected to depend solely on the family position into which he or she was born or adopted, although this continued to play an influential part. It is now possible, at least in theory, for a Japanese child from any background to rise to a position of great eminence in society, given ability and perseverance, as we saw in Chapter 5.

MARGINALITY, ETHNICITY AND CONTINUING STATUS DIFFERENTIALS

Despite these greater opportunities for mobility, some aspects of a rigid hierarchical order do persist and, as we have seen in previous chapters, they tend to perpetuate themselves. In a society with such a rich fund of identity markers and such clear classification of inside and outside, there are bound to be people who find themselves situated at the margins. Sometimes this is the cause of discrimination, as members of most of the groups we shall discuss can surely verify, but it may also give people a particular power. A continuing problem is that if people who are discriminated against take political action, and gain benefits, they draw attention to themselves and may spark further discrimination. One strategy for such people has been to try and pass as regular Japanese, but recently there has been such awareness and support that many have been encouraged to take a pride in their marginal status.

We have already discussed the way the imperial family remains removed from everyday life above the top of the social scale, occupying an extremely valuable portion of land in central Tokyo and participating in tremendous ritual activities on appropriate occasions. Through educating their children together, and preferring marriage largely within the group, the wider nobility has also retained a distinctive status, so that when an imperial marriage crossed the boundary by involving a commoner it was possible to work out the lack of appropriate connections. Some members of this noble class carry out quite mundane jobs, but there are various small ways in which they distinguish themselves, through language, dress on certain occasions, and passing on an awareness of certain forms of behaviour. Their status also continues to be maintained by the recognition of the surrounding commoners (Lebra 1993).

Representatives of the 'outcaste' class, or *burakumin*, at the other extreme of the social scale, were officially declared *dōwa* – or literally 'same Japanese' – in 1871, but they have suffered from all kinds of discrimination. Despite the former association of pollution with their occupations, as described above, various political groups have worked hard to convince their fellow Japanese that they are no different from everyone else. Nevertheless, some of the districts where they live are well known and many 'regular Japanese' are still frightened of them and concerned not to 'pollute' their own blood-lines by marrying them. As recently as 1998 a scandal erupted when it transpired that there were companies still buying information about prospective employees that included the category of *dōwa*. This kind of prejudice and discrimination exacerbated the poverty that became one of the characteristics of the *buraku* communities, along with poor educational achievement (Davis 2000).

As long ago as 1969, a political movement called the Buraku Liberation League managed to secure a series of 'special measures' which included financial support from all levels of government, and accommodation and educational achievement have gradually improved. A splendid museum of human rights has also been built in a *buraku* area of Osaka. An unfortunate backlash against this kind of help came from other groups of poor people who argued, quite logically, that if the *burakumin* are no different from other Japanese then they should not receive any more help than any others. In fact in the past few years a policy has been adopted to try and overcome the discrimination altogether by dropping the 'special measures' law. Davis (2000) argues that the communities are not clearly defined these days anyway, but it is apparently still quite a powerful way to instil fear in a street brawl to be able to claim to be from a *buraku* district.

An excellent study that helps to explain both the fear and the power associated with outcaste status is a book by Jane-Marie Law (1997) about the puppeteers of Awaji Island in the Inland Sea of Japan. The puppets that form the focus of the book were originally held to be able to embody certain spiritual beings that had powerful but also dangerous qualities, and the people who manipulated them were avoided for their 'polluting' association with these deities. This was another example of an occupation that conferred outcaste status, then, and after the Meiji period, the puppeteers lost their role of mediating with the gods as well as their status. For a generation or two they tried to deny their past, as did members of other outcaste groups, but along with the nostalgic revival of traditional arts in Japan the puppets have become popular again. An interesting development that perhaps illustrates a greater acceptability of minority groups has been the revival of one of the ritually most powerful performances that associates the puppeteers with their former polluting status.

Three other minority groups in Japan have similar associations with the peripheries of a formerly strict social system, but this time based on geographical and ethnic boundaries. They are all people with their own clear distinctive cultural features, but during the course of Japanese history they have played different roles in defining the boundaries of Japanese national identity. As discussed in Chapter 1, the people of Ezo in the north and the Ryukyu Islands in the south had been colourful foreigners at the periphery of a Japan centralised on a Chinese model, and Korea was at that time another of these foreign peripheral groups. Later they all became part of a general Japanese expansion, if in slightly different ways, and during the first half of the twentieth century efforts were made to turn them all into Japanese citizens. Korea is now of course independent, but ethnic Koreans form the largest foreign minority in Japan and, along with the Ainu and the Okinawans, who are by nationality Japanese, suffer discrimination on the basis of their ethnic status.

A study of Koreans in Japan, including many descendants of those who came three or four generations ago before and during the colonisation of 1910 to 1945, is to be found in *Lives of Young Koreans in Japan*, by Yasunori Fukuoka (2000) and translated by Tom Gill. Based on a large number of personal histories, the book is a lively, wholly human account of the situation of young Koreans today, as well as a source of much information about the historical roots of their contemporary communities. It explains how conflicting ideas about ethnicity and continuity of kin have continued to separate them, for by retaining their Korean nationality they have been denied the full rights of Japanese citizens, even when born and entirely educated in Japan. Many achieve a kind of compromise by taking Japanese citizenship and adopting a Japanese name for school and other public activities while retaining their Korean name only for home, where Korean customs are preserved. One problem has been poverty, again, since many found it difficult to gain more than menial work, but other Koreans have thrived, especially in business, and this seems to help considerably with the improvement of their general social status. A film, *Osaka Story*, made by a partially Korean anthropologist brought up in Japan, is revealing of the problems of Korean Japanese both in Japan and back 'home' in Korea where resentment against Japan persists. The work of Sonia Ryang (1997, 2000) is a good source of further information about North Koreans in Japan.

The situation of the Ainu, who have occupied the north of Japan since pre-history, is rather different for they have a legitimate claim to be 'the first Japanese' and have been in touch with indigenous people in other parts of the world for support with this claim. Until the Meiji period, people in Hokkaido (then Ezo) and other northern islands lived by fishing and hunting in quite abundant forest lands, now referred to in the Ainu language as *Ainu moshir*, or 'calm land of human beings' (Hanazaki 1996). They may not all have been related, as we saw in Chapter 1, but people practised their own ritual and political life in relative freedom, and traded with their neighbours. During the Tokugawa period, the shogunate gave the Matsumae clan dominion over the northern areas, and they began to extract unequal shares of food and other goods, which they interpreted as tribute. The Ainu perceived this as exploitation and though they tried several times to rebel, they had not the might and continued to be suppressed.

Worse was to come, however, as in the Meiji period they were deemed 'former aborigines', and thus to be civilised along European lines, and they lost their lands and their right to make a living by hunting and fishing. They were given relatively infertile plots to cultivate and were assiduously educated to eradicate their cultural heritage and become Japanese. Some resistance was successful in the Taisho period (1912–26), after the Ainu had been put on display at the Great Britain–Japan Exhibition in London in 1910, but the Second World War put progress on hold and for many years the government line was that they had been assimilated. Discrimination in schools and employment was severe, and many Ainu tried to 'pass' as Japanese. Resistance continued, however, and 1972 saw the organisation of the Ainu Emancipation League, 1983 the beginning of a revival in Ainu language with the opening in Nibutani of the first of several schools, and in 1997, a new national law came into force positively to promote Ainu culture.

This has been a long, hard struggle, interspersed with periods of extreme discrimination, but the mood in 2002 when I visited some Ainu communities in Hokkaido was quite buoyant. In Shiraoi, for example, very close to the famous resort town of Noboribetsu, there is a well-stocked open-air museum of Ainu culture, and in Nibutani, the home of long-term activist and author, Shigeru Kayano, there are two. Nibutani is also one of the sites of resistance to dam construction, for one manifestation of discrimination was the allocation of Ainu lands and water as sources of power, and the community's loyalties were split. Enough local Ainu politicians supported the venture to make it possible and their reward was not only a splendid museum of Ainu culture, but also another to record the history of the Saru river. Richard Siddle's (1996) book, *Race, Resistance and the Ainu of Japan*, is a comprehensive account of the Ainu people and their resistance to Japanese oppression.

Okinawa is the other main region of Japan with its own distinctive history, and its own grievances with regard to the wider nation, but the Ryukyuan people are also quite mixed in their backgrounds and views of the world. On the main eponymous island of Okinawa, contemporary resentment is focused on the continuing presence of an American base, whereas other islands have benefited from an influx of tourist trade and development to their pleasant tropical beaches and coral reefs. The Second World War Battle of Okinawa left many scars, human and physical, and one-third of the civilian population died, either in the battle itself or in the devastating outbreak of malaria which thrived in the caves and gullies where people took refuge from the soldiers. The designation of Okinawa for American occupation until 1972 has moulded a completely different and somewhat negative view of outsiders to that found elsewhere in Japan.

This view of outsiders is sophisticated, however, for the location of the Ryukyu Islands made possible long-term trading relationships with China, Korea and South-east Asia, as well as Japan, during its period as a kingdom from 1429 until it was made forcibly into a Japanese prefecture in 1879. Like the Ainu, they have a distinctive language, but they also have a complicated recorded history and material cultural treasures, many of which are now stored in Shuri Castle in the capital city of Naha (see Figure 6.2). In general the groups of islands that make up Okinawa prefecture have a different feel to them. The architecture varies, becoming more Chinese in the far south, and the people too express local allegiances as well as allegiance to Okinawa generally (see for example, Røkkum 1998). Nevertheless, some call for Okinawa as a whole to be a free trade area, an area of self-reliance, and Okinawan intellectuals like to compare the archipelago with Polynesia, Micronesia and Melanesia, after the novelist Toshio's Shimao use of Yaponesia (Hanazaki 1996:129). Perhaps more than elsewhere, Okinawans have few doubts or fears about expressing their distinctive identity.

There are several other minorities whose status is based on ethnicity in Japan, some of completely different nationality, such as the Chinese and the Filipinos, and others who claim Japanese ancestry, such as those from Brazil and Peru. These foreign workers have settled in different ways, according to their own cultural differences, and Komai's (2001) study identifies a relative hierarchy in their treatment, especially in the labour market, where the former Japanese (*nikkeijin*) generally find better paid jobs than complete outsiders. Over time, he has found that immigrants from Iran, Bangladesh and Pakistan have moved up the scale towards the level of longer-term

Figure 6.2 Shuri Castle, the former home of the King of the Ryukyu Islands, is now a rich source of information about the distinctive culture it protected.

immigrants from China and Korea while those from Thailand and the Philippines (including women in the entertainment industry) remain the most poorly treated. An interesting anthropological study by Millie Creighton (1997) reviews the differential representation of foreigners in advertisements in terms of the extent of their status as relative insiders (*uchi*) and outsiders (*soto*).

Many studies are being made of the various neighbourhoods and other groups that have formed amongst foreign migrants to Japan, as well as of the treatment they are receiving from the wider society. Timothy Tsu's (1999) article, 'From Ethnic Group to "Gourmet Republic"' about the Chinese community in Kobe, is an interesting attempt to offset what he sees as an underrepresentation of the Chinese living in Japan. Another important example, by Nobue Suzuki (2000), examines the way that the Filipina wives with whom she worked in Tokyo and in the Philippines set out to rectify the idea commonly held in both places that all Filipina women who travel abroad are engaged in entertainment and the sex industry. Suzuki is somewhat critical of the 'sexist' way the women choose 'good feminine virtues' for their models, but the point is clearly made that such people need to overcome surrounding prejudice and define an 'affirmative space' for themselves and for their children to grow up in.

Tsuda's (2000) work on Brazilian Japanese makes the interesting point that people who felt they were acting Japanese in Brazil now find themselves acting Brazilian in Japan. They did not set out to behave like this, but because of their Japanese looks, they are not recognised as foreigners and Japanese they meet expect them to behave like any other Japanese. Many of them are second or third generations Brazilian Japanese, however, and they know little Japanese language and less about Japanese forms of etiquette. They argue that if they try to be Japanese they are given less leeway for strange behaviour than foreigners who look different, so the best plan is to resist the pressure to be Japanese and instead to emphasise their Brazilian-ness. In any case, there is something of a *caché* to be able to participate at festivals in the samba, for example, though they may not even be very good at it and would not have done it in Brazil! Takenaka (2000) found similar reactions among Japanese Peruvians.

Other groups of people who have marginal status of one sort or another change with time. In the Meiji period it was discovered that groups of Christians had remained practising since the sixteenth century, hidden behind a facade of Buddhism, and the Mayor of Nagasaki protested a few years ago that his grandfather had been tortured for revealing these beliefs. A somewhat fanciful but gripping novel by Liam Hearn (2002) is built around the shocking discrimination that such people experienced if they were discovered at the time when Christians were forcibly expelled from Japan (see Chapter 7). In contemporary Japan, religion is not usually a cause for special status or discrimination unless it interferes with other duties, such as the neighbourly shrine-cleaning mentioned in Chapter 4. However, a suspicion of new religious sects has arisen since shocking stories were revealed about the Aum group that released poisonous gas in the Tokyo underground.

James Valentine (1990, 1997) discusses the general significance of marginality in Japanese society, summarising several other categories of people who are regularly set apart, notably by the Japanese media. His own particular areas of interest have been with those marginalised on the basis of their sexuality and with people who suffer from disabilities, but his papers also place the Japanese case in the context of anthropological and sociological work on the subject. In a society that emphasises form and clear lines of demarcation between *uchi* and *soto*, people who fall between them are seen as threatening. One strategy is to try and adopt an appropriate *tatemae* for most situations, and many people spend much of their lives doing just that. Trying to 'pass' as a member of mainstream society brings a risk of discovery that might seem worse than coming clean, however, and the toll taken by the associated fear is well illustrated in a novel (and film) about a *burakumin* who tries to live as a regular school teacher (Shimazaki 1974).

Sexuality is a characteristic that is not necessarily revealed widely in Japanese society, and McClelland (2000) found that many of his male homosexual informants preferred to compartmentalise their lives to avoid their parents and workmates knowing about that part of their lives. Finding accommodation may be a problem, as reported by Lunsing (2001), because public housing especially is usually reserved for families, and a general pressure to marry has led to discrimination at work and at home against those who 'come out' and reveal their preference for living an openly gay lifestyle. Marriages of convenience used to be a kind of solution to this problem, but the recent increase in the numbers of people living alone has made it easier to be single and gay, though lesbians have for long been able to live together without attracting undue attention. In general, private homosexual relationships have been more acceptable in Japan than in many other countries for centuries, but these sexual practices were neither exclusive, nor did they necessarily determine a marginal lifestyle in public.

There is sometimes a power attached to the ambiguous or liminal, and people in marginal positions may benefit from their special status, as we saw in Chapter 5 for the returnee schoolchildren. In Japan, foreigners of one sort or another, like half Japanese, are often chosen to appear on television programmes, though their 'talents' may be treated with some fun (Miller 1995). Minority groups may be allocated funding for various projects, which is not always all that they need. However, I would like to suggest that the dawning of the new millennium is a good time for multiculturalism and for the indigenous people of the globe, and Japan is unlikely to be left out of this realignment of views.

BROADER PRINCIPLES OF HIERARCHICAL ORDER

Relativity

Apart from the more or less rigid divisions, then, what are the principles underlying modern expressions of hierarchical difference? One of the first things to note about Japanese hierarchy is that it is to some extent relative to the situation, so that in different situations different principles take precedence. As noted with *tatemae* behaviour, for example for homosexuals, a single individual may have different faces for different occasions. It is also possible for a hierarchical relationship between two individuals to be reversed in different arenas. This relativity makes possible the apparently contradictory idea outlined above that notions of equality are expressed under certain circumstances among groups or people ranked in other ways hierarchically.

A straightforward example of the relativity of expressions of hierarchy may be given in describing seating arrangements when entertaining. Guests (outsiders) will be placed above members of the group responsible for organising the occasion (insiders), and the latter may de-emphasise their own hierarchical distinctions in expressing deference to the guests. For example, at a formal family celebration guests may sit in hierarchical order round the outside of an arrangement of tables, while members of the inside group will circulate, regardless of their own distinctions, round the inside of the tables where they can greet each of the guests in turn. In another house, the same people will be ordered quite differently, and at a village or neighbourhood gathering, when there is no special seating order demanded by the occasion, everyone sits in age order, although the men will probably place themselves above the women. Except for this male/female divide, to which we will return, this arrangement expresses rather well the underlying equality of houses that we have already discussed.

Another example in quite a different context introduces the notion of the company or other institution as an inside group. This is no exaggeration of the concept and the word *uchi* is used to describe one's own company, school or other place of attachment and the other people who belong to it. In conversation with outsiders, as mentioned above, one is expected to use self-deprecatory speech forms not only for oneself, but also for all the other members of one's own inside group, however high-ranking their position. Within the group, clear-cut hierarchical distinctions may well still be rigidly maintained. The *uchi/soto* distinction, taught so carefully at the level of the house, also underlies the principles of relative ranking, and it would seem useful to continue by distinguishing between ranking within and ranking outside of such social groups.

Ranking within social groups

The principles of ranking within the most intimate *uchi* of the family were discussed earlier, and this model has been used again at an ideological level to explain hierarchical difference throughout society. Benevolence from a person in a superior role should, at least ideally, be reciprocated with deference and loyalty from a partner in an inferior role. Thus a young person may become attached in whatever walk of life to a senior, who will help in the early stages of his or her career. Gradually a debt is built up to the senior, and this may be likened to the one that a child has towards a parent, a debt that should be repaid with long-term loyalty and support. This type of relationship is sometimes described by the expression *oyabun/kobun* (parent-part/child-part), a phrase which has been translated as a relationship of patronage (Dore 1971).

R.P. Dore discussed this type of relationship long ago in his book *City Life in Japan*, and the following quotation illustrates the above principles in a practical arrangement within a company:

> A, who gets his job in the United Glass and Steel Corporation through the influence of B who was, perhaps, at the same High School with A's uncle, is thereafter marked as B's man. This not only means that B is the obvious man to ask to be his marriage go-between, the obvious man to go to for advice when he is in trouble over a girl, or the obvious man to ask for a loan, nor only that he takes it as a matter of course that he is expected to run personal errands for B, or even for B's wife. It means also that he will join the rank and file of the B group in its cold war against the X group and the Y group within the firm, and that his own chances of success will depend on the B group's maintaining its power.
>
> (Dore 1971:207)

There have been many changes since Dore was writing in the 1950s. For one thing, there was a generation of people dubbed 'the new human beings', who insisted on putting their family commitments before their company ones, at least at times. Then there has been a recession, and companies have sought innovative ways of improving their lot, not necessarily by continuing the 'tried and tested' methods of economic success. Indeed a friend of mine who works for a large multinational has found himself more in demand that he ever was before because his prior international experience is currently overriding more conservative links as the company seeks to survive. Major companies such as Nissan even appointed complete foreigners to lead them out of tricky situations when, for example, Renault bought out nearly half of their shares.

However, it would be foolhardy to ignore the principles that were important, and just as we learned from the old principles of the *ie* in Chapter 2, we will lay out some of the prior expectations here too. It might be less likely now that a man would join a large company through the influence of his uncle, though in smaller concerns this type of recruitment may well still be practised. Indeed, a shortage of employment has been another of the effects of the recession so those uncles may have their uses again. Good contacts are certainly still important in finding academic jobs.

The rival groups within a firm, mentioned at the end of Dore's quote, are also ranked informally within the larger group, but while the relationships between individuals within them are fairly fixed hierarchically, the relationships between groups may fluctuate. They are also subject to fission, particularly if a person at the top of the group dies or retires. Such factions (or *habatsu* as they are called in Japanese) are to be found in many other spheres such as political parties, self-defence forces, theatrical groups and underworld gangs.

This kind of organisational structure has also been strikingly described by Chie Nakane, a Japanese professor of social anthropology retired from Tokyo University. In her book, *Japanese Society* (1973), she isolates the *oyabun/kobun* type of relationship as the basic structural principle on which Japanese social organisation rests. She represents this 'vertical principle' diagrammatically as shown in Figure 6.3 (1973:43). In this case, B and C are both in an inferior relationship with respect to A, and she emphasises that their relationships with A are more important than their relationships with each other. The A/B relationship here corresponds to Dore's B/A relationship above. This 'inverted V', as she terms the shape, may be regarded as a building block for larger groups, where a leader A may have several *kobun* in the structural position of B and C, who in turn may have *kobun* of their own as shown in Figure 6.4 (1973:44).

As long as the leader, A, remains in the original position of being the ultimate *oyabun* of a group, relations within that group are effectively maintained, since A can rely on B and C, who can rely on D, E, F and G, who can in turn rely on their *kobun* to carry out any tasks required. Similarly, in the reverse direction, the *kobun* have close relationships with superiors to whom they turn for help and advice. New members can be recruited to the lower levels, and the same principle can work effectively throughout a large

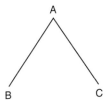

Figure 6.3 Nakane's basic model.

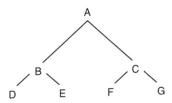

Figure 6.4 Nakane's elaborated model.

organisation. Examples can be found in many areas of Japanese life, she argues, and as well as those mentioned above as having factions, Nakane claims that this kind of structure also characterises new religious groups such as Sōka Gakkai, as well as establishments for teaching traditional Japanese arts.

Once A is removed, however, for whatever reason, Nakane points out that there is no clear way to decide who shall be the successor. The relationship between B and C is unspecified, since each is related individually to A, so it is at this point that fission may occur and two (or more) factions emerge. Subsequent relations between these factions may well be delicate, and a number of outcomes are possible. Within a large company, Nakane argues that the formal administrative organisation will usually preserve the overall group, even if efficiency is temporarily impaired. Elsewhere, this type of hierarchy may be the chief organisational principle and the headship perhaps a hereditary position, such as in *nō* theatrical groups and schools for flower arrangement and tea ceremony. In political parties, on the other hand, future leadership very often depends on relations between factions, and understanding these principles of organisation is essential to making sense of Japanese politics, as we shall see in Chapter 11.

Nakane also discusses the qualities that are required for leadership in such arrangements, and she argues that the ability to inspire loyalty is more important than personal merit. Indeed, such a system works rather well if the leader has some weaknesses that require reliance on subordinates, whom a good leader is also expected to know well and respect. These characteristics are important for leadership in other societies, and specific requirements of leadership in particular Japanese arenas will be discussed later, but it is important to distinguish between a long-term superiority of this kind, and superiority based directly on merit.

In varying degrees, people are accorded status or superiority according to their personal abilities, but in a structure like the one described above, it is difficult formally to move ahead of one's senior however distinguished one may become. As in school and kindergarten such a group takes collective responsibility for tasks assigned to it, and each member contributes to the best of his or her ability, allowing the group as a whole to receive any praise or criticism which may accrue. Thus talented members of the group are appreciated and respected for their abilities, but this respect is quite different from that based on length of service, and it is the latter which maintains the working cohesion of the group. Nakane gives a striking example of how Japanese scientific research teams carry out projects more efficiently if they have prior connections of this sort, even if they come new to a field, rather than if they are composed of experts who were previously unknown to one another.

Relations between groups

Nakane also applies her model to relations between groups. Just as *ie* are ranked within a community, she argues, other associations become ranked throughout the social structure. Thus companies, for example, are assigned positions in a hierarchy, and their members, whatever their rank, all share to a degree the status accorded their company in the outside world. This ranking is found particularly amongst companies in the same fields, and members of the company are, therefore, encouraged to work hard to improve the company's position, and so improve their own status outside. Interdependent companies, on the other hand, may develop long-term links not unlike those between human beings, sometimes even referred to as *oya/ko* relations. Some small companies may prefer to maintain several non-exclusive allegiances, but when times are hard these may also be the companies to go under.

Schools and universities, too, are ranked amongst themselves, as we saw in Chapter 5, and high-ranking schools supply high-ranking universities, who will in turn supply high-ranking companies. A particularly prestigious career is in the civil service, where ministries are also ranked, and most graduates entering the top ministries are from the top university, which is Tokyo. At this level it seems that even the faculties are ranked, and law takes pride of place, though medicine is another that confers a lot of status.

Status in the wider world and the influence of gender

An individual's overall status in the world outside his or her *uchi* groups clearly depends on a variety of factors, and may be manipulated according to the situation. In stable areas, where families have been living in close contact for generations, considerable weight is still attached to a depth of family background, and the position of one's *ie* in a long-standing hierarchical scale, such as a *dōzoku* system, or association with the ownership of land. In the more complex and changing society of urban areas, householders may derive most of their status from institutional attachments, and Nakane argues that companies and other occupational groups have taken over the function of the *ie* in this respect. As a result a family takes its position in society from the attachment of its head to an outside institution, which may demand the same total commitment of the individual as used to be accorded to the *ie*.

Nakane's model has been criticised for trying to be too all-embracing, among other things, and the generalisations she makes are sometimes very sweeping. The principle outlined is pervasive in Japanese society, however, and she drew on her experiences in India, Europe and the United States to compare its operation in practice with different hierarchical principles found elsewhere. She reiterates, for example, that the Japanese vertical principle differs from that underlying a caste or class system, and she examines some of the consequences of these differences. Hers is a useful book, but it needs to be borne in mind that it is a structural analysis, rather than a direct description of behaviour, and its manifestations in practice may be quite various. It is not intended to account for all Japanese behaviour everywhere, and the above analysis is generally more appropriate for the behaviour of men than of women, although women may become involved in such vertical relations as well.

In the circles of a Japanese housewife, however, it is less likely that people will be ranked so rigidly. For one thing, there are various criteria by which ranking is assessed and several conflicting influences may operate between the same people. On the one hand, a wife inherits her status from her husband's occupational position, especially in company housing, but on the other, she usually has various attributes of her own which play a part. For instance, a woman's educational and occupational background will influence her ranking among other women, as will her current activities. For example, in groups centred around a traditional hobby such as flower arranging or tea ceremony, there may be a ranking system not unlike that described above, and common interest groups such as the PTA or the Women's Group have office-holders among their ranks.

Since many of the groups housewives join are based on local allegiances, it is quite likely that the same women will meet in different arenas. Thus a woman who is a low-ranking pupil in one context may well hold a position of office in another. Sometimes women who have achieved teaching qualifications in different arts will exchange lessons. These examples illustrate the contextual nature of hierarchy discussed earlier, and in particular situations the vertical principle may well underlie formal interaction. However, since housewives in a neighbourhood are likely to meet in all sorts of situations, they need a more general way to communicate. Age is important again here, and women of within about ten years of each other are often reciprocal in their use of deferential language, or they drop the respect forms altogether, in either case implying a relationship of some equality.

As for relations between men and women, these have not been much discussed yet, largely because the principles above are basically independent of gender. Within specific contexts, such as the family, the office and the bar or (night) club, status is also divided along gender lines, and men and women play complementary roles. We have discussed the family in Chapter 2, and we will return to discuss gender roles in the office in Chapter 9 and in bars and nightclubs in Chapter 10. It is worth emphasising, however, that in all these situations the husband/wife relationship is a good example of the need to separate status and power, since a man is still almost always accorded more status than a woman in seating arrangements and so forth, though this may have little to do with their relative power. The book by Yuko Ogasawara (1998) discussed in Chapter 9 is an insightful study of gender politics within an office.

An interesting situation arose in the chain store where Louella Matsunaga (2000) carried out a research project twice over a crucial ten-year period of decline in fortune that led ultimately to the bankruptcy of the company. She spent both periods working with part-time women who had little status and did not earn much, but who were freer than the more 'permanent' employees to come and go at times to suit themselves and could thus combine their jobs with family commitments. They needed to defer, at least in principle, to the men and women around them who had been taken on as career employees, yet when the company needed to make redundancies to save costs, it was these women who were the last to go. They were of course cheaper than men who expected incrementally secured salaries and bonuses, but as it turned out the women's jobs dealing with the customers were absolutely indispensable.

STATUS MANIPULATION – WRAPPING

Within this system of Japanese hierarchy, how do individuals deal with the balance of achieved and acquired status in any system of ranking, and how do they exercise power at the same time as recognising formal status or authority? In this final section we will consider some of the strategies used to gain advantage in the more fluid matters of status distinction, and how these, if successful, allow a measure of power in interpersonal relations. Some of my own research has been directed to this end, and much of it was carried out with housewives, partly because of their relative freedom of status allocation, although the principles are quite applicable to interaction between men, too. I started out by looking at polite and respectful language in Japanese, but the subject opened out into other forms of presentation, and eventually I decided that the process was epitomised in the non-verbal signals transmitted by the beautiful wrapping which is used when presenting gifts in Japan (Hendry 1993).

Nevertheless, language is very important in determining relative status. People make judgements about one another depending on their ability to use polite forms appropriately, and it is said by some that this skill can only be acquired as a child, so that family background may have an indirect benefit. This characteristic of Japanese interaction is one that resembles the assumptions made about class in a European context. In the same way as in Europe, the skilful use of speech levels can go much further than this, however, and those who use them most effectively are able to manipulate others around them to comply with their expectations. A person who is most successful in this respect is one who is able to adjust his or her mode of speaking with clarity, but also with subtlety. In other words, the way something is said – the way it is wrapped in appropriate language – is as important, sometimes more important, than what is said.

My findings did not stop with language. In working with housewives, I noticed that the same principles apply to mode of dress, or 'wrapping' of the body, the way a room is prepared, or 'wrapping' of space, even the way time is organised, and, of course, the way gifts are presented. The wrapping represents the degree of formality and it expresses the system of etiquette, but it also offers opportunities for manipulation, not of the system, but through it. These principles are of course found in any society, but the Japanese advantage in dealing with members of many other societies where these things are taken for granted, is their relative awareness of the power of wrapping. Elsewhere there is often a propensity to disregard 'wrapping' as mere adornment and to seek to rip it off in an effort to reveal what lies beneath. In Japan this may well be a mistake.

In attempting to explain the way 'wrapping' is used to manipulate status and exercise power, I have made comparisons with other societies studied by anthropologists, mainly in the Pacific region. Their common feature is a reluctance to bring difference of opinion too far out into the open in continuing relationships, and various means are used to communicate at a more subtle, often ritualised level. The emphasis on harmony in Japanese relationships is indicative of this type of system. It doesn't mean that there are no disputes, or indeed, that everyone is living in an orderly, contented fashion. Not at all! It simply means that polite, harmonious interaction is an appropriate way to wrap one's communication, whether it be innocuously pleasant or severely barbed.

CONCLUSION

Clearly hierarchical differences are important in Japanese society, if somewhat complicated to describe. To summarise, it is necessary to remember the way in which any individual may be involved in a number of different hierarchical dyads in different situations and contexts. It is also important to distinguish between differences of status based on a position in some scale of seniority, and possibly quite independent distinctions of merit or power. It is also worth restating the complementary importance of equality as a

Japanese value. Even in measures of hierarchy, it has been shown that the possibilities are fairly distributed, and status comes eventually to those who serve long and well. Finally, skills to manipulate the system may be acquired and polished just as one may learn the skill to wrap a beautiful gift.

REFERENCES AND FURTHER READING

Allen, Matthew, *Identity and Resistance in Okinawa* (Rowman & Littlefield, Lanham, MD, 2002)

Benedict, Ruth, *The Chrysanthemum and the Sword* (Routledge & Kegan Paul, London, 1967)

Creighton, Millie, '*Soto* Others and *Uchi* Others: Imaging Racial Diversity, Imagining Homogeneous Japan', in Michael Weiner (ed.), *Japan's Minorities: The Illusion of Homogeneity* (Routledge, London and New York, 1997)

Dalby, Liza Crihfield, *Kimono Fashioning Culture* (Yale University Press, New Haven, 1993)

Davis, John H. Jr, 'Blurring the Boundaries of the *Buraku(min)*', in J.S. Eades, Tom Gill and Harumi Befu, *Globalization and Social Change in Contemporary Japan* (Trans-Pacific Press, Melbourne, 2000), pp. 110–22

Dore, R.P., *City Life in Japan* (University of California Press, Berkeley, 1971)

Dumont, Louis, *Homo Hierarchicus: The Caste System and its Implications* (University of Chicago Press, Chicago, 1980)

Fitzhugh, William W. and Chisato O. Dubreuil, *Ainu: Spirit of a Northern People* (Smithsonian Institute and University of Washington Press, Washington, 1999)

Fukuoka, Yasunori (trans. Tom Gill), *Life of Young Koreans in Japan* (Trans-Pacific Press, Melbourne, 2000)

Hanazaki, Kōhei, 'Ainu Moshir and Yaponesia: Ainu and Okinawan Identities in Contemporary Japan', in Donald Denoon, Mark Hudson, Gavin McCormack and Tessa Morris-Suzuki (eds), *Multicultural Japan: Paleolithic to Postmodern* (Cambridge University Press, Cambridge, 1996)

Hane, Mikiso, *Peasants, Rebels and Outcastes: The Underside of Modern Japan* (Pantheon Books, New York, 1982)

Hendry, Joy, *Wrapping Culture: Politeness, Presentation and Power in Japan and Other Societies* (Clarendon Press, Oxford, 1993)

Ishino, Iwao, 'The *Oyabun-kobun*: A Japanese Ritual Kinship Institution', *American Anthropologist*, 55 (1953), pp. 695–707

Komai, Hiroshi, *Foreign Migrants in Contemporary Japan* (Trans-Pacific Press, Melbourne, 2001)

Law, Jane Marie, *Puppets of Nostalgia: The Life, Death, and Rebirth of the Japanese Awaji Ningyō Tradition* (Princeton University Press, Princeton, NJ, 1997)

Lebra, Takie Sugiyama, *Japanese Patterns of Behavior* (University of Hawaii Press, Honolulu, 1976)

——*Above the Clouds: Status Culture of the Modern Japanese Nobility* (University of California Press, Berkeley, 1993)

Linger, Daniel Touro, *No One Home: Brazilian Selves Remade in Japan* (Stanford University Press, Stanford, CA, 2001)

Lunsing, Wim, *Beyond Common Sense: Sexuality and Gender in Contemporary Japan* (Kegan Paul, London, New York and Bahrain, 2001)

McLelland, Mark, *Male Homosexuality in Modern Japan: Cultural Myths and Social Realities* (Curzon, Richmond, Surrey, 2000)

Matsunaga, Louella, *The Changing Face of Japanese Retail: Working in a Chain Store* (Routledge, London and New York, 2000)

Miller, Laura, 'Crossing Ethnolinguistic Boundaries: A Preliminary Look at the *Gaijin Tarento* in Japan', in J.A. Lent (ed.), *Asian Popular Culture* (Westview Press, Boulder, CO, 1995)

Nakane, Chie, *Japanese Society* (Pelican, Harmondsworth, 1973)

Neary, Ian, *Political Protest and Social Control in Pre-War Japan: The Origins of Buraku Liberation* (Manchester University Press, Manchester, 1989)

Ohnuki-Tierney, Emiko, *Monkey as Mirror: Symbolic Transformations in Ritual and History* (Princeton University Press, Princeton, 1987)

Ota, Yoshinobu, 'Appropriating Media, Resisting Power: Representations of Hybrid Identities in Okinawan Popular Culture', in Richard G. Fox and Orin Starn (eds), *Between Resistance and Revolution: Cultural Politics and Social Protest* (Rutgers University Press, New Jersey and London, 1997)

Ouwehand, Cornelius, *Hateruma: Socio-religious Aspects of a South Ryukyuan Island Culture* (Brill, Leiden, 1985)

Raz, Jacob, *Aspects of Otherness in Japanese Culture* (Institute for the Study of Languages and Cultures of Asia and Africa, Tokyo, 1992)

Røkkum, Arne, *Goddesses, Priestesses and Sisters: Mind, Gender and Power in the Monarchic Tradition of the Ryukyus* (Scandinavian University Press, Oslo, 1998)

Ryang, Sonia, *North Koreans in Japan: Language, Knowledge and Identity* (Westview Press, Boulder, CO, 1997)

——(ed.), *Koreans in Japan: Critical Voices from the Margin* (Routledge, London, 2000)

Siddle, Richard, *Race, Resistance and the Ainu of Japan* (Routledge, London and New York, 1996)

Suzuki, Nobue, 'Between Two Shores: Transnational Projects and Filipina Wives in/from Japan', *Women's Studies International Forum*, 23, 4 (2000), pp. 431–44

Takenaka, Ayumi, 'Transnational Community and its Ethnic Consequences: The Return Migration and the Transformation of Ethnicity of Japanese Peruvians', *American Behaviorist Scientist*, 42, 9 (2000), pp. 1459–74

Tsu, Timothy, 'From Ethnic Group to "Gourmet Republic": The Changing Image of Kobe's Chinatown in Modern Japan', *Japanese Studies*, 19, 1 (1999), pp. 17–32

Tsuda, Takeyuki (Gaku), 'Acting Brazilian in Japan: Ethnic Resistance among Return Migrants', *Ethnology*, 39, 1 (2000), pp. 51–71

Valentine, James, 'On the Borderlines: The Significance of Marginality in Japanese Society', in Eyal Ben-Ari, Brian Moeran and James Valentine (eds), *Unwrapping Japan* (Manchester University Press, Manchester, 1990), pp. 36–57

——'Skirting and Suiting Stereotypes: Representations of Marginalized Sexualities in Japan', *Theory, Culture and Society*, 14, 3 (1997), pp. 57–85

——'Disabled Discourse: Hearing Accounts of Deafness Constructed through Japanese Television and Film', *Disability and Society*, 16, 5 (2001), pp. 707–27

Weiner, Michael (ed.), *Japan's Minorities: The Illusion of Homogeneity* (Routledge, London and New York, 1997)

White, Merry, *The Japanese Overseas: Can They Go Home Again?* (The Free Press, New York, 1988)

Yoshino, Roger and Murakoshi, Sueo, *The Invisible Visible Minority: Japan's Burakumin* (Buraku Kaiho Kenkyusho, Osaka, 1977)

RELATED NOVELS AND LIGHTER READING

Hearn, Liam, *Across the Nightingale Floor: Tales of the Otori* (Riverhead Books, Penguin Putnam, New York, 2002)

Honda Katsuichi (trans. Kyoko Selden), *Harakur, An Ainu Woman's Tale* (Cambridge University Press, Cambridge, 2000)

Keyso, Ruth Ann, *Women of Okinawa: Nine Voices from a Garrison Island* (Cornell University Press, Ithaca and London, 2000)

Molasky, Michael and Steve Rabson (eds), *Southern Exposure: Modern Japanese Literature from Okinawa* (Hawaii University Press, Honolulu, 2000)

Shimazaki Tōson, *The Broken Commandment* (Tokyo University Press, Tokyo, 1974)

FILMS

The Osaka Story (1994 Tōichi Nakata)

The Outcast (*Hakai*) (1962 Ichikawa Kon) (film of *The Broken Commandment* by Shimazaki Tōson)

Takie Sugiyama Lebra (talks about *Above the Clouds* – Asian Educational Media Service, 1998)

7 Religious influences

INTRODUCTION

In this chapter and the next we temporarily leave the world of Japanese institutions which may readily be compared with their counterparts elsewhere, and plunge into a very different cosmological system. At this stage the reader with some anthropological background will have a definite advantage, for religion in Japan may much more easily be compared with any number of indigenous religions around the world than with the great traditions which are discussed in 'religious studies' or 'comparative religion'. What should be included under the term 'religion' in Japan remains open to discussion. It has been described as 'a ritual system which pervades all institutions' (Fitzgerald 1993), and it has been argued that to the Japanese themselves even their language is endowed with sacred qualities (Miller 1977).

One of the problems is that Japan has been influenced by a great number of religious traditions. Another is that religion pervades many spheres that others might call secular and it cannot easily be separated from them. It is thus sometimes difficult to draw a line between the 'religious' and the 'secular', a problem not infrequently encountered by anthropologists and reflected in their writings. Also, the English language tends to distinguish between magic, science and religion in a way that reflects a European philosophical heritage, being based largely on developments arising out of the work of Newton and Descartes. It is, however, impossible to make such clear distinctions in other cultural contexts, as some Western scientists have realised (e.g. Capra 1983), and in Japanese government statistics 'religion' comes under an overall heading of Science, Technology and Culture.

The content of this chapter may, therefore, include areas which are not immediately recognisable as 'religious' from an outside point of view, and readers may be surprised to find references to books about medical anthropology in the reading list. On a global scale, however, explanations of misfortune, including illness, are frequently couched in supernatural terms, with supernatural remedies, and anthropological work on Japan would suggest that these are by no means absent here. Other aspects of Japanese epistemology will emerge in the pages that follow. The sections of this chapter consider influences that may be regarded as 'religious', separated according to the divisions of their leaders, but also in some of the mixed, or syncretic, forms found amongst the practitioners. Read in conjunction with Chapter 8, on ritual and the life cycle, a broad understanding may be gained of ideas that underpin 'worldviews' held in Japan.

Another problem for some readers in coming to terms with Japanese religion may relate to the question of belief. Many Japanese people claim to be non-religious, if asked directly. They have no strict allegiance to a particular religious organisation, and if asked whether they believe in a god or gods, they may well reply 'no', or 'only if I want something'. The same people may, however, *practise* a variety of activities that seem 'religious' in the course of their lives, and many even pray daily at shrines and altars to be found in their home and work place. Shintō and Buddhism, which are widely regarded as the two main religions of Japan, claimed in 2000 to have nearly 108 million and 95.4 million followers respectively. The total population of Japan is only 127 million, so clearly many people attend in some way to both.

Again, the problem seems to arise from a completely different understanding and expectation associated with the concepts of religion and belief. When religion is something quite distinct from the other affairs of life, one can talk about believing in it, or otherwise, and members of the world of Western philosophy are accustomed to this approach. Indeed, Japanese refer to members of particular sects or other religious groups as 'believers'. When religious ideas pervade all areas of society, as is the case in many traditional worlds, the use of the word 'belief' is less appropriate, because there is really much less opportunity for choice (see Needham 1972). Japan is an interesting case because Western philosophy is taught in Japanese schools, yet for many Japanese the world they know is based on an epistemology quite different from the one that they learn about in schoolbooks. Probably the best way of elucidating this is to present some of the evidence.

SHINTŌ

The most ancient and all-pervasive religious influence in Japan is that which has come to be known as Shintō. This is the name given to indigenous elements of Japanese religion that can be traced back to the pre-historical times described briefly in Chapter 1. Much of Shintō may have been imported, but it is Shintō that is associated with the mythology of Japan's creation and the supernatural ancestors of Japan's imperial line. It is Shintō that is associated with the very foundation of Japan's identity as a nation.

During the warring years leading up to and including the Second World War, Shintō doctrine, developed and propagated by a specially created state Shintō office, sought to inspire Japanese people with nationalistic fervour. This state Shintō was dismantled by the Allied Occupation as having been responsible for much of Japan's aggression and the post-war Constitution includes a clause separating religion from the state.

Some Japanese still refer to Shintō activities as superstition, but the disrepute into which it fell has failed to eradicate Shintō rites and festivals, as we saw in Chapter 4. Indeed, these have been expanding in the past couple of decades, and the funeral of the Shōwa Emperor, as well as the enthronement of the new one, were conducted with secular rites for the outside world, but also embodied the Shintō rites which were designed to follow ancient custom. A comprehensive study of the relationship between Shintō and state from the Meiji Restoration to the end of the Shōwa era is to be found in Hardacre (1989).

The word Shintō was chosen to correspond to the names of other religions, like Buddhism and Christianity, that were known in the outside world, and it translates literally as 'the way of the *kami*'. The character for 'the way' (pronounced *tō* or *dō*) is the same one used for arts and life-paths such as in jū*dō*, bushi*dō* (the samurai way) and sho*dō* (calligraphy). *Kami*, another reading of the character for *shin*, has been translated as 'gods', but it is also applied to natural objects regarded as sacred, such as trees, mountains, seas, birds and animals, as well as to some human beings, usually but not always after they have died. The mythological characters who appeared in Chapter 1 are *kami*, and their supposed descendant, the Emperor, was regarded as having divine qualities until the last incumbent formally renounced them during the Occupation.

One of the most evident manifestations of Shintō all over the country is to be found in the shrines which form the centre of the neighbourhood festivals described in Chapter 4. These buildings are maintained by the local people who in turn come under the protection of the particular deity who is remembered there. This *kami* is called the *ujigami*, the *kami* of the local *uji*, which in ancient times used to be a local unit of related families. These days, however, the relationship of common residence is enough to elicit protection, and members of a community are supposed to share the benefits and duties of this relationship. Annual festivals illustrate the strength of such support, as residents of all ages participate in the customary celebrations, and such events provide a good example of how 'religious' activity may be intermingled (or not) with the other interpretations mentioned in Chapter 4.

Other Shintō shrines are associated with deities with special powers, rather than with specific geographical areas. The larger ones have a resident priest or priests, sometimes aided by shrine maidens called *miko* – unmarried daughters of priests or parishioners – who also dance for the *kami*. Together, they take care of visitors, who may be very numerous at the most famous shrines. One such is the Izumo shrine in Shimane prefecture, where the deity is supposed to help cement marriages, so that it is visited almost constantly by young couples. There are shrines all over Japan where the deity is supposed to help with learning, and schoolchildren and parents visit these regularly. Others specialise in performing a safety rite for motor cars. The most famous and sacred shrine is the one at Ise, where the nation's founding ancestress, Amaterasu, is remembered, and this is the shrine that age-mate groups used to save up to visit at least once in their lives.

Shrines that are supposed to bring good business may be found tucked into the corners of factories and offices, on busy street corners, and also as part of larger shrines formally dedicated to some other purpose. A comprehensive study by Karen Smyers (1999) brings together a positive abundance of material on one such deity called Inari, very often referred to as the fox deity, for its representations take a variety of fox-like forms. It is also associated with a jewel, one of the early symbols of Japan mentioned in Chapter 1, and has a much longer connection with the production of rice than with contemporary business. However, Smyers suggests that the reason Inari worship is so popular in contemporary Japan is precisely because its chief symbols of fertility and growth also incorporate a primary meaning of change and shape-shifting, characteristics that have applied to Japan for a good many years.

People visit shrines for particular reasons, and they visit them at particular times, such as New Year, or for the age celebrations which will be described in the following chapter. They also visit them as tourists. In all cases, the behaviour is much the same. They enter the shrine compound, wash their hands and mouth, if there is a source of running water for the purpose, and approach the front of the shrine. Here they make a monetary offering, ring the bell to attract the attention of the deity, clap their hands and bow their heads in prayer. Afterwards it is customary to buy a charm or amulet for the Shintō shelf at home, or to write one's prayer on an appropriate receptacle at the shrine. On special occasions, one or more priests may perform a ritual, and this usually involves four main elements: offerings, purification, prayer and a ritual feast of some sort, even if it is only a drink of sake.

In general, Shintō is concerned with notions of pollution and purity, as can be seen from the ritual elements outlined above. The washing on entry to a shrine purifies a person from the pollution of the outside world, ritually marking the sacred inside of the shrine compound, just as the removal of shoes marks the inside of a house. A further 'inside' is found in the shrine building itself, although most visitors will not penetrate this far, except for special celebrations, and it is rather the area of the priests and their assistants. At the heart of the shrine very often a mirror reflects back the face of the worshipper, though there are some that contain a wrapped 'sacred body' (see Hendry 1996 for sacred powers of wrapping). For a special ritual, a further rite of purification initiates the proceedings, and this is accomplished by the shaking of a decorated staff over the participants. Local communities invite priests to carry out similar purification rituals annually for their shrines.

In the Shintō order of things, death, injury, disease, menstrual blood and childbirth are regarded as polluting. Thus the bereaved and women who have recently given birth are not supposed to enter a shrine compound for a definite pollution period. In the house of the deceased, a white sheet of paper may be hung up over the Shintō shelf to protect it from this pollution, and a warning notice should be displayed on the outer door of the house during the mourning period. Salt is regarded as a purifying agent, and it has been customary to present small packets of salt to guests at a funeral. In fact, in most houses Shintō is divorced entirely from dealing with the dead because at this time families turn to the other major religion, namely Buddhism. On the whole, Shintō ritual is associated with celebrations of life and its development, with the harvest and fertility, and with house-building and the community.

BUDDHISM

Buddhism, which was introduced into Japan around the sixth century AD, has developed a large number of Japanese sects and sub-sects. Their doctrines are now very different from the original Indian variety of Buddhism, as they are from the interpretations of the Chinese sages who transmitted the religion to Japan. Several times over the centuries efforts have been made to amalgamate Shintō ideas with Japanese Buddhism, for example by explaining *kami* as manifestations of Buddhas and Bodhisattvas, and most Japanese people can without conflict practise both Buddhist and Shintō rites. Sometimes these are even combined. Buddhist edifices are usually called temples, as opposed to Shintō shrines, with correspondingly different Japanese words, but there are places where both exist on the same site, and priests of either religion may officiate in the buildings of the other.

However, Buddhism has also maintained a separate identity, and this has not been tainted by the disrepute into which Shintō fell in the post-war years. Buddhism appears sufficiently self-contained to be described as a 'religion' or 'faith'. In the Chinese script it comprises two characters: one is the character for Buddha; the other, also used in Christianity and Confucianism, literally translates as 'teaching', and Buddhist texts and sutras give it a body of dogma which Shintō lacked until very recently. Many of the sects have doctrines of enlightenment, of escape from the constant cycle of reincarnation: one may strive to become either a Buddha, or by refraining from nirvana in order to help others, a Bodhisattva.

Ordinary people are often unaware of such doctrine, however. They refer to their recently deceased relatives as 'Buddhas' (*hotoke*) anyway, and turn to Buddhist priests for funerals and the memorial rites which they understand will bring their souls safely to a secure state as ancestors. Such memorials are held at regular intervals for up to 33 or even 60 years after death, when some people feel that their ancestors become converted into *kami*. There is an excellent if somewhat dated anthropological study of this aspect of Japanese religion by Robert Smith (1974), and a collection of essays which appeared shortly afterwards compares the attention paid to Japanese ancestors with that found in Africa and other parts of East Asia (Newell 1976). A newer study, by Hikaru Suzuki (2001), about urban funeral practices, is discussed in Chapter 8.

Japanese families with deceased relatives to remember usually have a Buddhist altar (*butsudan*) in the house, as described in Chapter 2, although here too there has been change in the size of the sum families are willing to spend on this sometimes extraordinarily elaborate item (Eades *et al.* 2000). They will also have affiliation with a particular Buddhist temple in the area, although they may not share this affiliation with their neighbours, as they do in the case of the local Shintō shrine. Buddhist affiliations tend to be on a household level, rather than a community one. The physical remains of the family ancestors may be buried in a graveyard associated with the temple, or they may be stored in urns in a purpose-built *nōkotsudō* somewhere in the vicinity of their residence. This is often the site of dancing at *Bon*, the annual summer festival when people travel all over Japan to visit the families of their ancestors.

Some families visit their temples to make offerings and to attend meetings at particular times of year, particularly the spring and autumn equinoxes and New Year, as well as the *Bon* summer festival, but many more receive the priest at their houses, and then only for funerals and memorial services. Members of newer Buddhist movements, such as Sōka Gakkai, attend their temples regularly, but for most Japanese families their original affiliations were established by their forbears during the Tokugawa period and they do not have any great personal commitment. At that time it was compulsory for everyone to be registered at a Buddhist temple, a system which dated back to the anti-Christian purges of the late sixteenth century.

The temples themselves are organised in a hierarchical way, with a chief temple for each of the main sects, usually in Nara or Kyoto, and branch main temples in the provincial capitals that service the smaller local temples. This system made it possible to register the whole population, and some temples still have their records of the local populace going back for two hundred years or more. Until the Second World War, the temples owned enough land to support them, but since the post-war land reform removed much of this source of income, their activities have had to diversify. A traditional occupation of Buddhist priests in the Tokugawa period was teaching, and many temples ran schools for the local children. Some priests now have teaching and other jobs in the wider community; others have set up youth hostels, courses for schoolchildren and kindergartens within the temple premises.

Like Shintō shrines, there are also Buddhist temples associated with special needs, and some of these have been developed as important sources of income in recent years. One example is that temples all over the country have become associated with people praying for a quick death so that they will not be a burden to their relatives. Another is of temples where mothers may pray for the souls of their aborted babies. This may involve the purchase of a small statue of the Buddha Jizō, and such temples may organise regular ritual activities for the bereaved parents. Abortion has been a common form of birth control in Japan, and women seem to be encouraged to attribute misfortune that may befall them later to the actions of the aggrieved souls whose lives they terminated – an interesting phenomenon since Buddhism is officially opposed to the taking of life. LaFleur specifically addresses this question in his book *Liquid Life* (1992).

In practice, the activity of a lay person visiting a Buddhist temple is not much different from that of one who visits a Shintō shrine. In front of the altar, hands are held together silently, rather than clapped, and there may well be images of the Buddhist figure being invoked. Purification is usually with the smoke of incense rather than with water, and the receptacle is not necessarily at the entrance to the temple, as is the water at a Shintō shrine. But a variety of amulets and talismans are usually on sale here too (see Figure 7.1), and it is again possible to have one's prayers written on an appropriate receptacle and hung in the buildings. It is also common to purchase a printed version of one's fortune to tie onto a convenient tree. A special rite would involve priests clothed rather differently from the Shintō ones, and the esoteric interpretation of events would be distinct. However,

Figure 7.1 A selection of protective charms and amulets like these are available at shrines and temples.

many of the ritual elements are directly comparable from the point of view of a lay participant.

One Buddhist sect which has become rather well known in the West, and which has particular functions with regard to modern Japanese companies, is Zen. This sect arose out of Chinese teachings like the rest, but it has flourished in Japan in association with indigenous aesthetic ideas, and it has become associated with Japanese arts, such as the tea ceremony and flower arrangement, which will be discussed in Chapter 10. An essential element of Zen is a practice known as *zazen*, which is literally 'sitting meditation', and which involves sitting, usually cross-legged, for long periods of time, during which one is supposed to remove oneself from all thoughts and bodily concerns. This kind of discipline is supposed to develop one's strength, or one's spirit (*seishin*), and Japanese companies have been reported to send their new employees for a period of *zazen* during their training (Rohlen 1974; Kondo 1990, referred to in Chapter 9).

FOLK RELIGION, TAOISM AND HEALING

Some religious figures in Japan make use of both Shintō and Buddhism, as well as drawing on ideas from Taoism. Taoism is rather like the Chinese equivalent of Shintō, in that it incorporates a variety of indigenous ideas about nature, so that it is not always possible to separate these various strands from each other. Such specialists may practise, among other things, geomancy, divination, healing and shamanism. They are usually consulted by individuals with particular requirements, for example seeking explanations of misfortune such as illness or loss, or seeking advice about auspicious times for important events such as weddings, house-building or funerals.

Such consultations are based on a largely Taoist view of the world in which time and space are not regarded as homogeneous. In other words, there are good and bad times to do certain things. The simplest example of this notion is the six-day calendar commonly used in Japan in which one day is regarded as good for all endeavour, another is likewise bad, and the others are good and bad at certain times and for certain events. The calendar used by specialists is much more complex, however, and takes into consideration a number of other factors. These include the division of time according to the Chinese zodiac, which allocates hours and days to a cycle of animals, in the same way as it allocates years. Time is also accorded one of the five elements, in its yin or yang aspect, so that the combination of factors on a particular day, at a particular time, will colour that occasion for any activity.

A similar set of notions about space, and particularly directions, involves the allocation of auspiciousness and inauspiciousness to spatial movements as well. These ideas are brought into play when a house is being designed, for example, and the direction it faces, as well as the design of the rooms, may well be decided in collaboration with a specialist in such lore. Similar discussions sometimes take place when journeys are planned, and the shrine visits made at New Year may be chosen according to directions which are thought to bring good luck for that year. A resort in the case of persistent misfortune is to examine the location of one's house or family graves, and a specialist may advise some considerable upheaval in order to alleviate the perceived problem.

The time (and place) of birth is supposed to affect the character and destiny of a person, as is their chosen name. Parents therefore often consult a specialist before deciding on a name. The issue turns on the number of strokes it takes to write the chosen characters, and a problem may be alleviated by keeping the pronunciation of a name, but choosing a different character to write it. Specialists are frequently consulted about the suitability of prospective marriages and the combination of names and birth signs is carefully considered. Sometimes inauspicious aspects of a union can be overcome by changing the name of one of the partners. Politicians are also wont to consult specialists about their chances, and they too have been known to change their names on the advice of such a person.

Illness is another reason for such consultations, and healing may take a variety of forms. In Kyushu, for example, I witnessed specialists chanting themselves into trances during which they claimed to be able to discern the cause of an illness by entering the body of an afflicted person, even if that person were absent. They could then make recommendations for removing the irritant, whatever it happened to be, and sometimes a rite of exorcism would be performed. If the cause of illness were attributed to some outside supernatural agent, then recommendations would be made about how to pacify the offended spirit, *kami* or ancestor. Certain shrines and temples are associated with healing, sometimes of particular complaints, and people flock to the more popular ones to purchase talismans and other aids to recovery. Again they may write the nature of their desire on a wooden tablet, or even just a piece of paper, and hang it up.

Illness in Japan may be explained in terms of some polluting force, and it is not uncommon for a healing process to be described as purification. The anthropologist Emiko Ohnuki-Tierney (1984) has discussed the medical roles of religion in Japan in the context of this kind of symbolism. As was mentioned in Chapter 2, she discusses the association of germs and disease with the 'dirt' of the 'outside' (*soto*) world as opposed to the 'clean' inside (*uchi*) of the home. She also carried out an investigation of deities and Buddhas associated with healing, and concluded that whether they be Shintō, Buddhist or Taoist, they are associated with marginality, or the boundary between inside and outside. This is the very area she associates with 'cultural germs' so that, as is commonly found in anthropological discussions of classification, the polluting and purifying forces fall between the important categories of society (cf. Douglas 1970, referred to in Chapter 3).

In my own research in Kyushu, I came to the conclusion that the specialists (known as *ogamiyasan*), who draw on Taoist ideas as well as those of Shintō and Buddhism, were consulted at times of change and therefore danger. Marriage, house-building and illness are all occasions when the usual order of things is threatened, and neighbours and relatives respond to these situations by making gifts, particularly of money. Disasters, such as fire or injury, meet with similar responses, both in the presentation of gifts, and in the consultation of specialists to divine possible causes. Law's study of puppeteers, discussed in Chapter 6, describes the way in pre-war days they used to make visits to houses at New Year to extract 'dangerous spirit forces'

Figure 7.2 Decorative masks depicting the bad spirits to be chased away may be worn by children and others at *Setsubun*. Some packets of beans are seen here too. (Photograph courtesy of Firas Naji.)

(1997:50). A continuing popular custom throughout Japan, held on a day in February (close to the Chinese New Year) known as *Setsubun*, is to throw beans symbolising bad spirits out of the house, so that good fortune can come in and take their place.

Ohnuki-Tierney points out that people usually consult regular bio-medical doctors as well as religious specialists when they are ill, and talismans purchased in a shrine or temple frequently adorn hospital rooms. Japan also has a range of practitioners of Chinese medicine, which are discussed in some detail in another anthropological monograph by Margaret Lock (1980). Again, the author puts the medical systems available into a context of Japanese and generally Eastern ideas about illness and its causes, and expectations about treatment and care. Lock's (2002) more recent study of attitudes to organ transplants in Japan and America helps to explain radical differences in ideas about the body and its relationship to the spirit world in Japan. A law was passed in 1997 legalising organ transplants with prior permission of the donor, but until the end of March 2002, only eighteen had taken place (*FFJ* 2002). Together these books also illustrate the relativity of the boundaries that exist in Western thought between magic, science and religion.

The attribution of illness to some outside polluting force, whether it be conceived of as germs or as some malevolent supernatural being, may be associated with the general concern with purity in Japanese religious and secular ritual. Visits to shrines and temples are often made for protective purposes, and houses may be purified if a source of pollution is suspected, perhaps through persistent disaster. On one such occasion, the specialist drew on the symbolic force of objects from Buddhist ritual for the deceased members of the house, and from Shintō ritual for the living members.

Roger Goodman's (1990) work discussed in Chapter 5 raised the ambiguity of attitudes towards 'returnee children' – on the one hand 'polluting' the educational system, dangerous beings in need of the purification provided by special classes and special schools – but also valued for their international experience. In Chapter 6 we saw similar attitudes to people in marginal positions in society. These attitudes resemble those more generally adopted towards an outsider or stranger, who may be seen as dangerous and polluting, or who may be a god bringing good fortune. The Japanese anthropologist, Teigo Yoshida (1981), has interpreted such attitudes in terms of anthropological theories about marginality and mediation between 'this world and the next'. The Brazilian Japanese, also discussed in Chapter 6, illustrated the way that marginality may be perceived as more dangerous than complete outsider status.

In the context of a strong Japanese sense of *uchi* about themselves as a nation, and the recent emphasis on the importance to Japan of globalisation, some parallels can be discerned between previous attitudes towards gods and contemporary ones towards foreigners. Thus the returnee children slot into a mediatory role between Japan and the outside world, and, as we saw in Chapter 1, a number of rural communities have sought to offset their marginal position in contemporary Japan by installing foreign country theme parks. In the same way that people visit shrines and temples to approach the spiritual world, they may now seek to approach the outside, often equally mysterious foreign world, by visiting representations of it in Japan. Most of the parks representing European countries – Holland, Germany, Spain, Russia and Switzerland – had churches in them, and some offered them for marriage services, thus reinforcing the idea of protection. This is a theme that will recur in Chapter 8.

CONFUCIANISM

The Confucian influence in Japan is of a rather different order to those discussed already. It has no priests and very few places of worship, but Confucian ideology has been called upon at various stages in Japanese history to support and justify codes of conduct and moral behaviour. Although in post-war Japan it has suffered something of the same fate as Shintō, in that it has been blamed as an undemocratic and feudalistic influence, it has also been credited with responsibility for some of Japan's success. Introduced into Japan at approximately the same time as Buddhism, it greatly influenced the legal system from the seventh century until the Meiji Civil Code.

The family system, for example, drew much of its strength from the Confucian idea that stable families, rightly governed, lead to a stable and happy state. According to Confucian precepts, an individual needs training in the virtues of benevolent action, loyalty and filial piety in order to participate properly in five basic relationships. These are those between ruler and subject, father and son, husband and wife, elder brother and younger brother, and friend and friend. Rulers, and superiors generally, need to learn to inspire loyalty through benevolence. The only dyad in the group in which relations are equal is that between friends.

In Chinese practice, Confucian ideals underpinned the whole of the system of government. In Japan, the ideals that supported indigenous notions were most enthusiastically drawn upon, whereas those that conflicted with them brought about much discussion at an intellectual level without necessarily making much impact in practice. In the Tokugawa period, samurai education was based upon Confucian texts, but there was plenty of argument, for example, about whether loyalty to a ruler should or should not take priority over filial piety in a situation of conflict. In the modern period the Japanese found a solution to the problem in the ingenious Shintō idea that all Japanese families are ultimately related as branches of the imperial line, so that loyalty to the Emperor could be seen as an extension of filial piety.

It is obviously a male-oriented scheme that conflicts with democratic ideals, and it is easily related to the system of hierarchical relations discussed in Chapter 6. However, it would seem that the Confucian influence, like others from outside Japan including democracy, has been modified to fit in with indigenous ideas, rather than being solely responsible for the Japanese ideology of hierarchy. It is a 'teaching', like Buddhism, so it is accorded status on that basis, but it is much more a moral or ethical system than a system of religious practice, and it has been drawn on to build and support the ethics of both Buddhism and Shintō.

CHRISTIANITY

The influence of Christianity in Japan has also been a diffuse one rather than a story of success in attracting followers. The first influx of missionaries in Japan began in 1549, when Francis Xavier and his followers secured a number of converts, but in 1640 Christians were banned by the Tokugawa regime, and some 37,000 were massacred brutally near Nagasaki. During the following two centuries all families were to be registered at a Buddhist temple, and except for a few 'hidden' communities in Kyushu (from one of which came the Nagasaki mayor mentioned in Chapter 6), Christianity was virtually eliminated from the country. Since the mid-nineteenth century, when missionaries were allowed into Japan again, converts have numbered less than 2 per cent of the population.

On the whole Japanese Christians tend to be individuals rather than whole families, and their children do not necessarily follow their example. It has become a 'personal religion', rather than an association of the continuing family, and some Christians are individuals who have moved for their employment away from their family and friends. One of the problems for Christianity in Japan is the exclusive nature of the religion. Other religious influences have always been readily accepted as long as they can be modified to fit in with the existing cosmology, and syncretism is an important facet of the Japanese worldview. Christianity in its Western form demands the rejection of other religious ideas and practices, so that Christians are discouraged from helping to care for their local Shintō shrine, or carrying out Buddhist rites for their ancestors. Although Christians themselves may accept such demands, members of their families and communities are less able to understand such a seemingly selfish religion, and sometimes Christians are ostracised for their behaviour. The anthropologist, David Lewis (1993), has published a study of Christianity in Japan.

There have been various movements to make Christianity more Japanese, and some churches have, for example, introduced memorial services for the ancestors of their parishioners which are held in the summer during the *Bon* festival. These and other efforts have had some limited success, but on the whole the major influence of Christianity has been in other directions. There are, for example, a number of Christian kindergartens, schools and universities, which have a good reputation for their educational achievements, and there are also hospitals, homes for the aged, day nurseries and institutions for the disabled, founded and administered by Christian organisations. Stevens (1997, referenced in Chapter 2) has several examples of these and of the influence of Christianity in encouraging the work of volunteers. Most towns have at least one Christian church in their midst, and it is quite common for couples to request a Christian wedding, even though they are not practising the faith.

There have been other less obvious influences that ultimately derive from the Christian tradition, one example of which may be associated with the practice of seeking Christian weddings. This is the modern use of the concept of 'love'. In pre-Meiji times, the Japanese word *ai* was used to apply to a love from a superior to an inferior, and there was another word that referred to simple physical attraction. Missionaries chose the first word *ai* to translate God's love for man, but they also used the word reciprocally to express man's love for God, and this levelling has spread to indicate the relations between lovers. Popular music has of course had a considerable influence on attitudes, and so have Western romantic literature and films, and the modern emphasis on 'love' as a basis for marriage is not necessarily directly related to Christian ideas. However, the deeper meaning that has become attached to the concept cannot easily be derived from any other source, and there is certainly a prevailing ideology now that marriage in Japan, too, may acceptably be based on mutual love.

'NEW RELIGIONS' AND 'NEW' NEW RELIGIONS

If Christianity has provided a 'personal religion', which may answer the needs of individuals cut off from their families by virtue of the demands of the modern, industrialised society, there are various competing religious organisations which have been even more successful in this respect. Collectively known as the 'new' religions, they comprise a number of religious movements which have developed over the past century or so, often drawing on Buddhist or Shintō traditions already much more acceptable to Japanese ways of viewing the world. Typically, they have a charismatic leader who attracts followers to some new, hopeful way of life, and in this respect, they may be compared with millenarian movements that have arisen in many parts of the world in times of great social change. Indeed, the phenomenon began to mushroom as the time approached for the recent new millennium.

The spate of 'new' new religions that appeared at that time tended to oppose themselves to an overabundance of materialism and scientific rationality within a world of frantic education and pressurised overwork, and seek instead the spiritual meaning that people thought had disappeared in the established religions. The approach of the millennium, and more specifically the prophecies of Nostradamus that the world would end in 1999, gave the movement an urgency found in other countries, too, but the most spectacular effort to call a halt to this disintegration came from a movement known as Aum Shinrikyō. On 20 March 1995, members of this group set out to release sarin gas in the Tokyo underground system during the busy rush-hour period on five trains converging towards the Japanese parliament, ministries and police headquarters. It was fortunate that no more than twelve people died, but thousands were injured, physically and emotionally. Ian Reader's (2000) book *Religion and Violence in Contemporary Japan* provides a detailed and convincing analysis of the rationale behind such an extraordinary attack.

This was a particularly violent case, however, and more generally new religions have been interpreted as providing a suitably traditional format for the changed circumstances of their adherents. Members join through their own personal volition, and this is in keeping with the post-war emphasis on individual rights, but in many cases they then establish long-term relationships of loyalty with a previous member of the group who will be expected to exercise the benevolence due in a traditional superior/inferior relationship. In time the new member will gather newer members, perhaps through having converted them, to whom he or she will in turn act as a benevolent superior. These close links provide security, and many of the converts are people who have been for some reason insecure before they joined the 'new' religion.

Apart from people who have moved away from their families and friends, and this now includes a large number outside Japan (see Clarke 2000), a common example is of people who join religious groups because of persistent illness or misfortune. In this case, they may try several groups until they find one that appears to be effective. Nor do the 'religious' groups reject 'scientific' approaches (see, for example, Picone 1998). An anthropological work by Winston Davis (1980) discusses this phenomenon in considerable detail in a study of a religious group called Mahikari Kyokai (see also Matsunaga 2000). His book also provides fascinating illustrations of the way Japanese cosmology blurs our distinctions between mystical and scientific explanation, and Davis chooses to use the word 'magic' rather than religion to describe the activities of the people he studied.

Unlike Christianity, most of these 'new' religious groups tolerate the participation of their members in other religious rites, so that there is less likelihood of alienating relatives and neighbours who expect cooperation in more traditional activities such as ancestor memorials or maintaining the local Shintō shrine. There is one very successful exception, however, and that is the group known as Sōka Gakkai, a modern manifestation of Nichiren Buddhism, which has also made converts in many countries other than Japan. The temples provide alternatives for all the Shintō rituals, and expect their members to destroy previous ancestral tablets when they join. It also formed the basis for a political party called the 'Clean Government' Party (*Kōmeitō*), which has had considerable success, particularly in local government. It claims to have several times as many followers in Japan as Christianity does, and even the most conservative estimate would suggest a multiple of more than three (Shimazono 1993:222). Important studies of these 'new' religions include Hardacre (1986) and Earhart (1983).

CONCLUSION

This chapter has presented some of the religious influences in Japan in a rather *ad hoc* manner. The form of presentation is not inappropriate, however, for religious activity for many Japanese people may be carried out in a similarly *ad hoc* way. An overriding conclusion must be that syncretism is a strong characteristic of the Japanese case. Nevertheless, there are various underlying themes which run through the sections, or which link up with other chapters of the book, and this is again appropriate in the light of the opening remarks of the chapter about the difficulties of distinguishing between 'religious' and 'secular' areas of Japanese society. A very accessible book offering further detail about religion in contemporary Japan is Reader (1991).

It should perhaps be added that there are Japanese people, particularly intellectuals, who claim to have no religious allegiances at all, who have turned rather to Marxism or even Maoism for a blueprint for life. Nevertheless, the majority of the population still turns to Shintō for life crises and to Buddhism for funerals. In the following chapter we turn to look in more detail at these and other rituals of the life cycle practised by members of Japanese society.

REFERENCES AND FURTHER READING

Bellah, Robert, *Tokugawa Religion: The Values of Pre-industrial Japan* (Free Press, Glencoe, IL 1957, reprint: Beacon Press, Boston, 1970)

Blacker, Carmen, *The Catalpa Bow: A Study of Shamanistic Practices in Japan* (George Allen & Unwin, London, 1975)

Bocking, Brian, *A Popular Dictionary of Shintō* (Curzon, Richmond, Surrey, 1996)

Capra, Fritjof, *The Tao of Physics* (Flamingo, London, 1983)

Clarke, Peter B., *Japanese New Religions in Global Perspective* (Curzon, Richmond, Surrey, 2000)

Davis, Winston, *Dōjō: Magic and Exorcism in Modern Japan* (Stanford University Press, Stanford, 1980)

——*Japanese Religion and Society: Paradigms of Structure and Change* (State University of New York Press, Albany, 1992)

Eades, Carla, Jerry Eades, Yuriko Nishiyama and Hiroko Yanase, 'Houses of

Everlasting Bliss: Globalization and the Production of Buddhist Altars in Hikone', in J.S. Eades, Tom Gill and Harumi Befu, *Globalization and Social Change in Contemporary Japan* (Trans-Pacific Press, Melbourne, 2000), pp. 159–79

Earhart, H. Byron, *The New Religions of Japan* (Michigan Papers in Japanese Studies no.9, Ann Arbor, 1983)

FFJ – Facts and Figures of Japan (Foreign Press Centre, Japan, 2002)

Fitzgerald, Timothy, 'Japanese Religion and the Ritual Order', *Religion*, 23 (1993), 315–41

Hardacre, Helen, *Lay Buddhism in Contemporary Japan* (Princeton University Press, Princeton, 1984)

—— *Kurozumikyō and the New Religions of Japan* (Princeton University Press, Princeton, 1986)

—— *Shintō and the State 1868–1988* (Princeton University Press, Princeton, 1989)

—— *Marketing the Menacing Fetus in Japan* (University of California Press, Berkeley, Los Angeles and London, 1997)

Hendry, Joy, 'The Sacred Power of Wrapping', in P.F. Kornicki and I.J. McMullen (eds), *Japanese Religion: Arrows to Heaven and Earth* (Cambridge University Press, Cambridge, 1996)

Ionescu, Sanda, '*Sōka Gakkai* in Germany: The Story of a Qualified Success', in Harumi Befu and Sylvie Guichard-Anguis, *Globalizing Japan: Ethnography of the Japanese Presence in Asia, Europe and America* (Routledge, London, 2001)

Kisala, Robert J. and Mark R. Mullins (eds), *Religion and Social Crisis in Japan: Understanding Japanese Society through the Aum Affair* (Palgrave, Basingstoke and New York, 2001)

Kornicki, P.F. and I.J. McMullen (eds), *Japanese Religion: Arrows to Heaven and Earth* (Cambridge University Press, Cambridge, 1996)

LaFleur, William R., *Liquid Life: Abortion and Buddhism in Japan* (Princeton University Press, Princeton, 1992)

Lewis, David, *The Unseen Face of Japan* (Monarch Books, Tunbridge Wells, 1993)

Lock, Margaret, *East Asian Medicine in Urban Japan* (University of California Press, Berkeley, 1980)

—— *Twice Dead: Organ Transplants and the Reinvention of Death* (University of California Press, Berkeley, Los Angeles and London, 2002)

Matsunaga, Louella, 'Spirit First, Mind Follows, Body Belongs: Notions of Health, Illness and Disease in Sukyō Mahikari UK', in Peter B. Clarke, *Japanese New Religions in Global Perspective* (Curzon, Richmond, Surrey, 2000), pp. 198–239

Miller, Roy Andrew, *The Japanese Language in Contemporary Japan* (American Enterprise Institute for Policy Research, Washington DC, 1977)

Miyake, Hitoshi, *Shūgendo: Essays on the Structure of Japanese Folk Religion* (Center for Japanese Studies, University of Michigan, Ann Arbor, 2001)

Mullins, Mark R., *Christianity Made in Japan* (University of Hawaii Press, Honolulu, 2000)

Mullins, Mark R., Shimazono Susumu and Paul L. Swanson (eds), *Religion and Society in Modern Japan* (Asian Humanities Press, Berkeley, CA, 1993)

Needham, Rodney, *Belief, Language and Experience* (Blackwell, Oxford, 1972)

Nelson, John K., *Enduring Identities: The Guise of Shinto in Contemporary Japan* (University of Hawaii Press, Honolulu, 1999)

Newell, William H. (ed.), *Ancestors* (Mouton, The Hague, 1976)

Ohnuki-Tierney, Emiko, *Illness and Culture in Contemporary Japan* (Cambridge University Press, Cambridge, 1984)

Picone, Mary, 'Science and Religious Movements in Japan: High-tech Healers and Computerized Cults', in Joy Hendry (ed.), *Interpreting Japanese Society* (Routledge, London and New York, 1998), pp. 222–8

Reader, Ian, *Religion in Contemporary Japan* (Macmillan, Basingstoke and University of Hawaii Press, Honolulu, 1991)

—— *Religious Violence in Contemporary Japan: The Case of Aum Shinrikyō* (Curzon, Richmond, Surrey, 2000)

Shimazono, Susumu, 'New Religious Movements: Introduction', in Mark R. Mullins, Shimazono Susumu and Paul L. Swanson (eds), *Religion and Society in Modern Japan* (Asian Humanities Press, Berkeley, CA, 1993), pp. 221–30

Smith, Robert, *Ancestor Worship in Contemporary Japan* (Stanford University Press, Stanford, 1974)

Smyers, Karen, *The Fox and the Jewel: Shared and Private Meanings in Contemporary Japanese Inari Worship* (University of Hawaii Press, Honolulu, 1999)

Tanabe, George J. Jr and Ian Reader, *Practically Religious: Worldly Benefits and the Common Religion of Japan* (University of Hawaii Press, Honolulu, 1998)

Yoshida, Teigo, 'The Stranger as God: The Place of the Outsider in Japanese Folk Religion', *Ethnology*, 20, 2 (1981), pp. 87–99

Yuasa, Michiko, *Japanese Religion* (Routledge, London, 2002)

RELATED NOVEL AND LIGHTER READING

Endo, Shūsaku, *Silence* (Kodansha International, Tokyo, 1982)

Murakami, Haruki, trans. Alfred Birnbaum and Philip Gabriel, *Underground: The Tokyo Gas Attack and the Japanese Psyche* (Harvill Press, London, 2001)

FILMS

The Birth of the Founder of Religion (*Kyōso Tanjō*) (1993 Toshihirō Tenma)

Fire Festival (*Himatsuri*) (1985 Mitsuō Yamagimachi)

Fancy Dance (1989 Masayuki Suo)

8   Ritual and the life cycle

INTRODUCTION

In many anthropological studies ritual and religion are closely related, although in complex societies there is often no particular connection between them, and the term 'ritual' may also refer to behaviour, like etiquette, which is decided by society and where individuals have little choice about its execution. In Japan there is much behaviour that falls into this category, and some of it has already been described and discussed in previous chapters. In this chapter the focus will be on ritual associated with the life cycle, and on the passage of Japanese people through various stages of life (and death), as celebrated by society. Having discussed some of the religious influences in Japan, we will be in a position to see how much part they play in this set of rites, and the various ways in which people are involved in religious practice.

Studies of rites associated with the life cycle are common in anthropological monographs of a particular people, for they aid an understanding of the system of classification underlying social interaction. These rites form a sub-group of the *rites de passage* identified by Arnold van Gennep (1977) as having many common characteristics in different societies. They often include, for example, distinct rites of separation from a previous state, rites of transition while the individuals are in a liminal in-between stage and rites of incorporation into the new state. The complete set of *rites de passage* also include rites of spatial transition, like those described in Chapter 3 accompanying moves between the inside and the outside of the house, and rites which celebrate the passage of time, like those associated with the New Year and other annual events.

The previous chapter focused on Japan's peculiar blend of religious influences, but the specific rituals covered in this chapter can easily be compared with rites of passage in many other parts of the world. Since the prime aim of this book is to elucidate Japan's systems of classification, however, an aim of this chapter will be to relate some of the events discussed to their wider context of social relations and their wider social significance. The rites will eventually be considered as a total system, in which marriage appears to play a pivotal role.

BIRTH AND CHILDHOOD

As in many societies, there is in Japan a great deal of ritual associated with the beginning of life. During a woman's pregnancy she will very likely observe a number of rituals, some of which have religious connections, but may also be given a 'scientific' basis. It should by now be evident that this combination arouses no sense of contradiction in Japan. One example is the use of a sash-type corset from the fifth month of pregnancy. This sash may be purchased from a shrine or a temple (e.g. Ohnuki-Tierney 1984:138), or more recently from a department store, and it may be signed with a character of good fortune by the prospective mother's gynaecologist, who is said to commend the use of such a garment as an aid to the ultimate recovery of the stomach muscles. Its acquisition may be celebrated by a public announcement of the expected birth, held on a Day of the Dog (according to the Chinese calendar), said to be in the hope that the child will be delivered as easily as dogs usually are. Mothers and grandmothers may also visit a variety of shrines and temples to pray and purchase amulets with this end in mind.

The birth itself usually takes place in hospital, but grandmothers, if not the parents themselves, may well take along amulets. It is said to be time to leave hospital when the baby casts off the remains of the umbilical cord, and this may well be carefully preserved in a box by the mother, perhaps to present to her child in due course when it leaves home to get married. The return home is often marked by a naming ceremony, when the child's name will be written out and hung up in the *butsudan* or some other prominent place. Members of the immediate family, including both sets of grandparents where possible, will gather to share a cup of sake to celebrate the safe arrival of their new member. This is referred to in many parts of Japan as the 'seventh night' celebration, although it may not take place exactly that number of days after the birth. I have written in more detail about these rites elsewhere (Hendry 1981, 1986).

In some parts of Japan, the mother and baby are regarded as polluted after the birth, for a period that varies regionally. It is around 30 to 33 days, sometimes longer for girl babies than for boys, explained by my informants in Kyushu as due to the natural association of girls with the pollution of menstruation and childbirth. During this time neither the mother nor the child should enter a Shintō shrine, but the mother is also expected to rest while her body recovers, and refrain from housework, exercise and even reading and watching television. Usually at the end of this period, although it may be later, the baby is taken for its first visit to the local Shintō shrine. Members of Sōka Gakkai have a parallel rite in their own temples. Typically, the child is dressed in a special kimono, which may well be a present from one set of grandparents. Relatives, particularly grandmothers, and even neighbours, may witness this event, or share in it by being given rice cooked with red beans, or specially prepared rice-cakes.

These two rites give the child a social existence as a member of an extended family and of a community, and the period of pollution can be interpreted both for the mother and the child as a period of transition in van Gennep's terms. Indeed, the mother's initial rite of donning the sash may be seen as her rite of separation from normal life, just as the visit to the shrine may be seen as a rite of incorporation for her back into normal life. For the baby, attention to the umbilical cord ritually marks a separation from the pre-birth state, and again, the visit to the shrine, usually to the community's protective deity, marks incorporation into social life. These rites have parallels in most societies, not least with the christening and a more ancient churching rite of Christian communities. The period of pollution and special care is also common, sometimes explained as due to the danger that a baby's new soul will slip away.

Another event accorded some importance during the first year of life is the first celebration of Girls' Day (on 3 March) for girls, and Boys' Day (on 5 May) for boys. For girls, tiers of shelves are set up for the display of splendid figures from the imperial court of the Heian period, together with sets of tiny accessories such as palanquins and tableware. To celebrate the birth of a boy, huge carp made out of cloth are hung out over the roof of the house (see Figure 8.1) for about a month before the day itself, and inside are set up warrior armour and helmets, arrows and dolls depicting fierce heroes. In either case, when the day arrives, the child is dressed in some suitable finery, possibly the same garments used to visit the shrine or temple, and relatives will gather to eat and drink in celebration of the new addition to their midst.

There is considerable symbolism attached to these events. The first child of each sex in a family is usually given the most attention, and the main guests from the wedding, including the go-between, are invited so the family gathering can also be interpreted as a celebration of the cementing of the marriage, symbolised in the birth of a child. The displays are set up year after year, however, and although this is basically a secular ritual, the objects are treated with a certain amount of reverence. The two themes, the rich splendour of the Heian court and the brave ferocity of the samurai armour, would also seem to serve an important symbolic role. They represent two

Figure 8.1 Huge cloth carp flying over houses celebrating the birth of a new baby boy symbolise courage in adversity and other qualities thought appropriate for men to acquire.

major periods in Japan's history, as well as two areas of dominant value, namely cultural treasure and military training, both of which have numerous sub-symbols, often also represented in contributory parts of the display.

As these objects are set up, and discussed with children, year after year, the children learn important values of their national heritage, and grow into the roles expected of members of such a nation. The carp, for example, symbolise courage in adversity because they swim upstream against the current and can even leap up waterfalls. It is said to be a quality boys should have, but, as we have already seen, children of both sexes in Japan are expected to work hard throughout their childhood years, and strive for goals which may prove to be quite beyond their reach. In later life, both men and women in Japan are praised for qualities of endurance and persistence, even in the face of failure.

The display for Girls' Day features a lord and lady with a retinue of servants and attendants, but the most important symbolic element here is that they are all attired for a wedding. In the more expensive versions there are elaborate depictions of the betrothal gifts, carefully prepared and wrapped, and accompanied by vehicles for their transport from one aristocratic house to another. There are also tiny models of the ceremonial food to be presented and consumed. Other elements of these displays represent other important values, and stories are often told about characters associated with them, renewing for adults and children alike familiar themes of their heritage, and emphasising for girls that marriage should be amongst their (if not the) chief goals in life.

Subsequent rites formally mark the progress of a child through various stages of development. A hundred days after birth there is a small ritual of 'first eating', associated in theory if not necessarily precisely in practice, with weaning. A child's first cut baby hair may be made into a brush for calligraphy. The first birthday is sometimes the occasion for a ritual associated with the child's first walking steps. Children of 3, 5 and 7 years are dressed up in smart clothes, often traditional Japanese garments, and taken

Figure 8.2 Children of 3, 5 and 7 years dress up in traditional costume to pray for good fortune in shrines all over Japan in November.

to a Shintō shrine on 15 November each year, when they take part in a rite for their protection and future good fortune. They may also be given gifts by their neighbours, a glossy photograph usually records the occasion and in some areas a party is held. This event seems to be an amalgamation of previous rites associated with the first wearing of various traditional Japanese garments, and it still provokes some considerable display of finery, especially for girls.

All these practices vary somewhat regionally, and the Japanese anthropologist Takao Sofue suggested long ago that social interaction with relatives and/or neighbours is a stronger motive for holding them than the 'supernatural effect' (Sofue 1965:159). The combination of social and supernatural is familiar from Chapter 4, when the community importance of Shintō festivals was described, and it will recur in Chapter 10. The Shintō ritual marks these occasions with an appropriate set of symbolic associations, but the exchange of gifts and parties provides a good opportunity for families to express their longer-standing relationships. Some of my own informants spent so long one 15 November dressing their daughters, at the hairdresser and in the photographic studio, that they left no time for the shrine before they had to arrive at the restaurant they had booked for the occasion. However, they did make an excursion to the shrine a few days after the event.

ENTRY INTO ADULTHOOD

From the time children enter school, in their seventh year, their life-cycle celebrations not surprisingly become geared to the education system. They celebrate graduation from kindergarten, entrance to school, graduation from primary school, entry into middle school . . . and so on. The next public occasion is when they officially 'come of age', on 15 January after their twentieth birthday. They will now be legally responsible for their own behaviour, and they may vote in local and national elections. Again, they dress up, some of the girls wearing very valuable kimonos, to attend a civic ceremony in their hometown. Typically, they listen to speeches about the upright citizens they are expected to become, and reply with poems and essays about the adulthood that stands before them.

In recent years, it is said that some youths – perhaps the 'freeters' and 'parasite singles' we spoke of in Chapter 2 – are not taking this rite seriously enough, and some cities have offered alternatives such as *karaoke* competitions and, notoriously in 2002, a visit to Disneyland! Legally, the young people become adults at this stage so a worry expressed in the press is that too many young people in Japan are postponing the acceptance of responsibility. In practice, this status was never really complete until the next rite – of marriage – had taken place, but as we also saw in Chapter 2, this too may be postponed, or even dispensed with altogether. In the next section we will see some of the reasons why this has also become a concern.

MARRIAGE

Marriage has for long been one of the most important events in the life of an individual in Japan, especially for a working member of a continuing family. Until their wedding has taken place, young people of both sexes have enjoyed considerable freedom of action, and their families have been quite tolerant of unusual lifestyles, travel, even career changes, as long as they settle down when they reach the age considered appropriate. This was for some time around 24 for girls and 27 for boys – indeed, unmarried women were compared with Christmas cakes, with the implication that they were no good after the twenty-fifth (Brinton 1992). However, these ages have been rising gradually, and in 2002, the average age of first marriage was nearly 29 for boys and 27 for girls. A newer expression replaces Christmas cakes with *toshikoshisoba* – a dish of noodles drunk to see out the year on the thirty-first. Young people thus glean a few more years before members of their family get too worried, but the idea of a cut-off age is still taken rather seriously.

For boys, marriage may also make an implicit statement about staying in the family business, or making a permanent commitment to a place of employment. For girls, it is more likely to spell change, for although most will work until they marry, unless they can find a spouse and/or mother-in-law to support them, they are still often expected to give up their job to take care of the home. In the case of a family business, a new wife would be expected to contribute to her husband's family concern, and the recession made this expectation economically important as well, to save cost. This situation would also apply to a man if he were to be adopted into his future wife's family business. However, during the period of greatest economic success, some women convinced even business families to let them make their own careers.

The means by which spouses are chosen are various, and this matter has undergone an interesting series of changes in the modern period. In the old Tokugawa villages, young people chose one another on the basis of mutual attraction, and groups of them would organise activities together as an opportunity to spend time away from their families. With increased mobility in the Meiji period, marriages were made over longer distances, and the samurai custom of arranged marriages spread throughout society. People in all walks of life saw it as important to make a selection appropriate for the continuing house, and adults sought the help of a go-between who knew both parties well. As Western influence spread, however, the notion of 'love' marriages began to appeal to young people, and after the Second World War, marriage based on the mutual consent of the individuals became part of the new Constitution. Back in the village where I worked, parents no longer feel it appropriate to interfere.

Elsewhere, both types of marriage persist, however, and it is not always possible to classify a particular marriage as 'love' or 'arranged', although statistics are collected as if it were. Some people meet and decide to marry, though they may not call their relationship one of love; others claim to have fallen in love after a meeting arranged by a go-between. It is this meeting, called a *miai*, which has characterised an 'arranged' marriage, and some couples even ask a senior to stage-manage a *miai* so that their old-fashioned parents will feel happy about the union. In fact, arranged meetings have themselves undergone considerable change to give individuals more say in the choice, and people see them as a convenient way to meet prospective partners. In the Meiji period, when marriage was more of an alliance between houses, young people had to be content with a mere glimpse of each other as they passed as if by chance, in a public place such as the theatre, a shrine or a restaurant. Later, a private meeting would be arranged, with an opportunity to talk, and eventually the couple would even be left alone for a few minutes.

Nowadays, such a meeting is followed by 'dates', and the young people are much freer to refuse a suggestion than they were in the past. They have also devised methods of their own to meet prospective partners, and one such arrangement, called a *konpa*, short for the English 'companion', involves groups of four or five boys going out together with the same number of girls to see how they all get along. A couple of other practices have drawn in newer technology, and meetings through the Internet are supposed to be one possibility, if a little risky. One of my students wrote an interesting dissertation about a practice known as *nanpa*, which he translated as 'cruising'. Apparently it involves boys out and about on the city streets seeking to meet girls, who are undoubtedly engaged in a similar activity, and the crucial step is to exchange mobile phone numbers. These liaisons are much more likely to lead to casual sex than to marriage, he thought, however (Sawkins 2001).

Marriages based purely on 'love' were for long regarded with suspicion, for the meaning of the word used in this context for 'love' (*ren'ai*) has only recently begun to take on some of the long-term associations it has inherited from Christianity. Before that it was very much an expression of physical attraction, and as such was associated with weakness, or extra-marital affairs, to be separated therefore from the serious business of marriage, which was concerned with nobler sentiments such as duty and filial piety. It is still customary for parents sometimes to investigate the background of the potential spouses of their children, and detectives may even be hired for this purpose. It is also quite usual for a religious specialist to be consulted about compatibility, name combinations and the auspiciousness or otherwise of the proposed wedding day.

The mediatory role of the go-between is a common one in Japan in general, and many other arrangements are made in this way in a society that tries to avoid direct negotiation between strangers. There are, in fact, several aspects to this role. First of all, the go-between can bring together people totally unknown to one another and make a formal introduction. Second, he or she can act as a liaison between the two families, providing information for each about the other, and once a marriage is agreed, transmitting and coordinating their wishes about the details. The go-between can also break the bad news and avoid loss of face if the negotiations fall through. At the wedding itself, there is a ceremonial role to be played, particularly in introducing the two families to each other, and a successful superior may be asked to do this, even in a marriage otherwise arranged by the couple. Finally, there is the role of guarantor, and the go-between may be called upon to mediate again if the marriage breaks down.

Particularly in stable, continuing communities, marriage represents the amalgamation, to some extent, of two separate *uchi* groups and the person or couple who successfully brings this about is ideally a member of an *uchi* group of both sides. Thus a relative, neighbour or work superior is an ideal person. In practice, there are some people who are more successful at it than others, and some for whom it becomes part of their business, like one I met who was also the owner of a bridal-wear shop. In many other areas of Japanese society, negotiations between strangers are ideally carried out through an intermediary who has *uchi* connections, such as a shared old school, or a common interest in some leisure activity. Perhaps for reasons such as these, marriages arranged by a go-between are still made, although love matches have been popular in Japan since the late 1940s.

Over the years there has been great variety in the type of ceremony chosen for the wedding itself. There may be a religious ceremony, but this is not compulsory, and a wedding can just be a public gathering, as long as it is registered legally. Hotels and 'wedding palaces' are very popular, typically providing the whole event as a package. This includes a ceremony, Shintō or Christian ones being popular, dress hire and hairdressers, a reception with a master of ceremonies, photographs, gifts and perhaps even the honeymoon booking. Edwards (1989) provides a detailed description of one such place, where he was employed during fieldwork, and he analyses the elements of the ceremony as a window to understanding Japanese attitudes to gender and the person. Another fascinating study focuses on the commercial aspects of the wedding industry, again from the back-stage, and this time the author, Ofra Goldstein-Gidoni (1997), worked as a dresser.

Churches are sometimes chosen, too, as mentioned in Chapter 7, and several of the foreign country theme parks offer a package with a reception in one of their on-site hotels. In Huis ten Bosch, a famous Dutch example, there is a replica of the Hotel Amsterdam available for a serious price, for this, like its namesake, has made the grade as one of the 'leading hotels of the world'. Members of Sōka Gakkai, on the other hand, have created their own Buddhist service. In large country houses, weddings used to be held in front of the ancestors at the *butsudan*, with several receptions to accommodate all the guests who needed to be entertained, and some supplementary parties are still held in this venue. Some couples even choose to take their whole wedding party on a package deal to Guam, Hawaii or even Australia for their nuptial celebrations, and these are said to be less expensive, even including the air fares, than holding the same event in an upmarket urban wedding hall.

The crux of the wedding, however it is celebrated, is a sharing of cups of sake between the bride and groom, and afterwards between each of them and the other's parents. The two families then drink together. Symbolically, the couple is joined together, but they join each other's families, too, and the two families become linked through them, as these families will call on each other for aid and ceremonial companionship in the future. The bride usually wears a headdress that is said to symbolise the hiding of horns of jealousy, and her white undergarment is supposed to represent the clean slate she brings to her new life. It is also common for brides to change their clothes during the reception and a likely outfit these days is a ball gown or the white dress of Christian weddings. Goldstein-Gidoni argues that these dresses create an idea of Japanese and Western tradition that may bear only passing resemblance to their original models.

A modern ceremony also includes an exchange of rings and a series of 'mini-dramas' which also happen to make excellent photographs. One such is the cutting of a multi-layered though often empty model wedding cake, and while the bride and groom pose, dry ice shrouds them in a romantic mist. Another involves a formal toast, followed by a series of speeches, and a third the distribution of a series of candles, which are then lit ceremoniously by the bride and groom who tour the tables to much applause. According to Edwards, the speeches lay out the expectations of this important occasion, and the candle ceremony expresses the future association (or dependence) the bride and groom hope they will continue to have with their friends and relatives. Finally, the bride and groom present bouquets of flowers to each other's parents, apparently as an expression of thanks for having raised their partner until that day.

An exchange of betrothal gifts usually precedes the actual wedding ceremony, and it is also common for girls (or *yōshi* – adopted sons-in-law) to take a large trousseau with them when they marry. The objects used on all these occasions have much symbolic association, largely concerned with long life, happiness and fecundity for the couple. Common symbols used in all manner of ways are the turtle and the crane, both representing long life, and an old man and woman known as Takasago. The betrothal gifts typically include expensive kimonos, or a large sum of money, which equals (and may exceed) the expenses of the trousseau. This is likely to comprise items for the future home, such as furniture, electrical equipment, clothes and even vehicles. Families may see these gifts for a daughter, or son going to be adopted into another family, as the settlement of their share of the inheritance.

The occasion is also an unrivalled opportunity for display, and since wedding guests usually include all of one's important acquaintances, it gives families an excellent chance to demonstrate their material wealth to the world at large. Particularly in times of change, such an event makes possible the confirmation of aspirations to a status higher than the one held by one's parents, and little expense is spared. Indeed, many families save for years for the weddings of their children and the total average cost at the peak of the bubble period, including engagement ring, nuptials and honeymoon, was estimated to be just over 8.3 million yen (more than £55,000 by the current rate of exchange). In more ways than one, marriage represents the redefinition and confirmation of status, for the families, as well as for the individuals becoming linked.

YEARS OF CALAMITY (*YAKUDOSHI*)

The only individual ceremonial occasions during the middle part of adult life are those associated with certain years of age when people are thought to be particularly vulnerable to illness or other misfortune. The major ages involved are 33 for women and 41 or 42 for men, although there are a number of less important years as well, and the preceding and following years should also be treated with some caution. Traditionally, Japanese people counted themselves a year older from 1 January, starting with the age of 1 at birth, and this method is still used for *yakudoshi*. Thus, a New Year visit to a shrine is an appropriate time to purchase a protective amulet, or even ask for a rite of protection to be performed by a Shintō priest, and certain shrines are said to specialise in this activity. In some areas a party is held, and appropriate gifts will be given.

Several anthropologists have mentioned these 'years of calamity', but the most comprehensive discussions are to be found in Norbeck (1955) and Lewis (1998). Both discuss the various reasons given for taking care at these times, and Lewis tries to estimate the number of people in the city where he worked who actually participate in the observances. He asserts that attempts to obtain statistics are unreliable because people who have yet to reach their major *yakudoshi* may say they will do nothing, but change their minds when the time comes. Nevertheless, he finds that more than half of his sample admits to paying some kind of attention to these supposedly calamitous years, and several of his informants did pay attention after saying that they would not. One of my close associates, on the contrary, set off with his age-mates to visit a shrine for protective amulets and ended up enjoying quite a different occasion of much drinking and jollification!

Lewis also notes an interesting tendency for people to cite 'scientific' explanations for *yakudoshi* observances referring, for example, to changes in the body which are supposed to take place at these times. Other explanations are concerned with the Chinese calendar, as discussed in Chapter 7, and with homonyms where words for the most serious ages also have inauspicious alternative meanings. *Sanzan* is a pronunciation for 33, for example, and this can also mean 'difficult' or 'troublesome', and *shini*, a way of saying 42, can also mean 'to death' (Lewis 1998:198). The 'scientific' ideas seem to be most acceptable, although events attributed to a lack of care during *yakudoshi* include disasters like the death of relatives, which could not possibly be explained in such a way. Lewis sees notions of years of calamity as structurally compatible with ideas of pollution and purity, and with a Japanese cultural emphasis on age. He also sees them as a pre-cursor for the kind of expectation of calamity that underpinned the violence of the Aum Shinrikyō sarin gas attack in Tokyo in 1995. They certainly help the collective blur between science and religion in a Japanese view.

A process recognised as part of the middle years of adult life, discussed in detail in a fascinating book by Margaret Lock (1993), is not marked by any ritual at all. This is what is commonly called the menopause in the English language, but Lock entitles her book *Encounters with Aging: Mythologies of Menopause in Japan and America*, deliberately to prioritise a general ageing process over the word that is predominantly associated with women in English-speaking societies. Comparing ideas of the process in Japan and America throws up a number of culturally specific expectations – for example, hot flushes are only rather recently found in Japan, where customarily an aching neck is blamed on ageing. The study also illustrates the idea more prevalent in Japan that men are affected as well as women.

RETIREMENT AND OLD AGE

According to the Chinese calendar, the precise combination of animal and element which characterises any particular year returns only once every sixty years, and another life-cycle celebration recognises this by marking the return of the year of a person's birth at 60. There are various ways in which this occasion may be celebrated. For academics, for example, *festschrift* may be published. Within the family, gifts may be given and a party held. The protagonists may dress in red garments, said to symbolise a return to dependence, this time on one's children rather than on one's parents, since red is a colour usually reserved for children. In some areas this is therefore also said to be the time to pass on the household to the next generation, though most people would probably claim to be too active to want to put this idea into practice. It is not uncommon for another visit to a shrine to be made, however, and this year is also a *yakudoshi* for men.

During the later years of life, there are again a number of celebrations for those who reach specific ages. The ages of 77 and 88 are often chosen, and the names of the celebrations are formed out of a rearrangement of the strokes of the characters used to write those numbers. A similar process applies for the ninety-ninth birthday. The anthropologist Thomas Crump (1998) discusses the way that the names of these celebrations are made up, and cites the process as an example of the many creative symbolic ways the Japanese use their originally Chinese script. He argues that the attributing of a mystical quality to the use of numbers resembles the ideas of the Pythagoreans, something we have largely lost in our Platonic scientific worldview (Crump 1998:42). The use of stroke-counting methods for choosing names is another example of this idea.

DEATH AND MEMORIAL CELEBRATIONS

A Buddhist priest usually carries out the rituals associated with death in Japan. There are secular ceremonies, and there are Shintō rites for exclusively Shintō families, the Emperor and members of the imperial family, but by far the most common arrangement is to turn to Buddhism. The body is prepared, perhaps with the help of close relatives, and dressed in a white garment, as at birth and marriage, but fastened the opposite way from usual. Many of the activities associated with death, funerals and memorials make use of this symbolism of reversal, and generally this class of ceremonial can be opposed to that used on happy occasions during life. It is customary, for example, to erect large wreaths outside the house of the deceased, these only distinguishable from the ones seen in front of new shops and business ventures because the colours of mourning are blue, yellow and green, rather than the red, orange and purple of celebration. On the evening after the death, it is customary for friends, neighbours and other associates to call on the bereaved family and express their condolences. The closest neighbours may help to prepare the house for these visits, erecting drapes and other equipment, which often belong to the community, to convert the main room of the house into an altar, decorated also with lanterns given by close relatives. These same neighbours also take over many other practical tasks, allowing the family to mourn, and greet their visitors. If the house is too small, the family may request the services of a local temple, where they receive visits, and often sit up all night with the body, which they then accompany to the crematorium the following day.

The funeral itself is then held back in the home of the deceased, or in the temple, the urn of ashes taking the central place. A Buddhist priest will officiate, and his chanting is often relayed by loudspeaker out of the house to the people who are unable to fit inside. All the various associates of the deceased will attend, and burning incense is passed round so that each can add a pinch to the fire as a token of farewell. The close neighbours serve tea and snacks and keep a record of who attends and how much money they give (so that the family can eventually reciprocate accordingly). They also hand out a card of acknowledgement from the chief mourners, sometimes accompanied by a handkerchief and/or a small packet of salt, which is to purify the visitors from the pollution of death. It is also said to repel the soul of the deceased, which may be reluctant to go on its journey into the afterlife and could 'stick' to a living person.

A recent study by anthropologist Hikaru Suzuki (2001), who carried out fieldwork in an urban funeral parlour, provides a wealth of information about the highly commercial 'funeral ceremonies' that have come to replace for city dwellers the old Japanese 'funeral rites' organised in and by the local community. This shift, she argues, reflects a move away from death as a source of pollution requiring quite long-term ritual attention to a much more rapid and pragmatic dispatch of the deceased, whose life is nevertheless appropriately celebrated. This, in turn, reflects the removal of vast swathes of the population from continuing families in communities equipped to deal internally with all life's passages, to the much less well-informed urban neighbourhoods, where these important events require the service of professionals to be carried out effectively. Her monograph leads us right into the daily life of the men and women who take care of death in Japan, we travel with them as they attend their calls, and we witness all the activities they are called upon to carry out, even when the deaths have been 'unnatural'.

In other parts of the country, however, the family of the deceased is still regarded as polluted at this time, and like a recent mother, they are wary of entering a Shintō shrine. It is customary to paste up a white sheet of paper over the Shintō god-shelf in the house, and most families also put up a notice on their front door to indicate that they are under pollution restrictions. These include dietary prohibitions on meat and fish. Further rites should be held for the soul of the dead every seven days for a total of 49 days, when the pollution period officially comes to an end. In practice the rites at the end of one week, when a posthumous name is given, one month – on the same date as the death – and 49 days, are those most strictly observed, and a Buddhist priest usually visits the house on each of these occasions.

Further memorials of a similar nature are held after 100 days, after one year, and again after 3, 7, 13, 25, 33 and 50 or 60 years, the timing of the final memorial depending on the Buddhist sect and the region. Robert Smith (1974), to whom we referred in Chapter 7, discussed these rites in some detail. Essentially they are said to be for the care of the soul. Typically, relatives of the deceased gather in the house where the ancestral tablets are held, a Buddhist priest comes and chants before the *butsudan* and special vegetarian food is served. A visit may also be made to the graveyard or the mausoleum where the remains are kept. In some areas the last of these rites becomes a celebration with food usually reserved for happy occasions, since the deceased is then said to have become a *kami*. After this, the individual ancestral tablet should be destroyed, and the deceased should join the general ranks of 'ancestors' of the house, which are remembered annually at the summer *Bon* festival.

Memorials for the dead are not confined to household practice, nor is the idea of the merging of an individual into a wider collectivity. Two articles in an interesting collection on *Ceremony and Ritual in Japan*, edited by van Bremen and Martinez (1995) provide analyses of these practices in a company and a community. Nakamaki (1995) discusses monuments and memorial rites for deceased members of a number of Japanese companies, and analyses the practice as an expression of association for members of the company analogous to that of pre-modern organisations. Stefánsson (1995) examines examples of rites that express a collective concern for spirits of the dead in a community and again suggests that these may relate back to ancient collective concerns to avoid upsetting the powerful spirits of the dead.

Monuments to those who die in the course of war are well known everywhere, and these may express memory at a national level. The Yasukuni shrine for the war dead in Tokyo is the object of criticism as a site of right-wing political activity, but it also serves to lay to rest the souls of those who lost their lives. Van Bremen (1998) reports on rites in the north of Japan to arrange ghost marriages for young men who died before they could gain this important aspect of adulthood as an aid to their peaceful repose. At a memorial museum in Chiran, the site of the take-off of many of the fateful *kamikaze* pilots, individual photographs and life histories of all the pilots are displayed alongside other memorabilia. The park is planted with avenues of cherry trees known for a blossom that is beautiful, but ephemeral. Year by year, it comes again, however, and while the loss of this generation of young men was heart-breaking for their relatives, the symbolism places their lives in a long-term context of continuity. Emiko Ohnuki-Tierney (2002) has devoted a whole volume to this difficult subject.

SYNCRETIC ASPECTS OF LIFE-CYCLE CEREMONIES

From the point of view of ordinary people taking part in ceremonies of life and death, some quite striking parallels and oppositions emerge. Considering the series of rites that are celebrated following birth and death, we find that they fall at approximately the same intervals. In both cases a rite is held after seven days, after a month, after 100 days and after one year. The length of the pollution period is different, but the same term is used for its lifting, and in both cases it is said to be associated with a concern for the soul, in the baby's case that it should become securely attached, in the case of the dead, that it should be firmly separated.

The annual ceremonies are not dissimilar either. For a child they occur after 3, 5 and 7 years, and an older rite of attaining adulthood which used to take place at 13 is still remembered in some areas. There is a *yakudoshi* for men at 25, and the major one for women is 33. Several of these years therefore correspond quite well with the memorial rites after death at 3, 7, 13, 25 and 33, and in some areas these actually continue until 60, which would correspond with the 'return of the calendar' celebration of official retirement. Progress through life thus has a parallel with the supposed progress of the soul through the afterlife until it becomes a fully-fledged ancestor and/or *kami*.

These rites are clearly distinguished from each other, however, in various symbolic ways. The food served is a good example. It has been mentioned that vegetarian food is prepared for memorials, but there are also special foods of celebration, which are used on happy occasions. These include red beans, spring lobster and sea bream, the last because its name, *tai*, is part of *omedetai*, the Japanese word for 'congratulations'. Gifts are also presented in different wrappings. For all events of celebration, including others not necessarily associated with the life cycle, the envelope or paper is imprinted with a representation of a small piece of abalone, originally to indicate to the recipient that the donor was not polluted (which would prohibit the use of fish or shellfish), and brightly coloured strings or markings. For a memorial gift, the colours will be the black, blues or greens of mourning, and the motif a lotus flower. Parcels are wrapped differently, too (see, for example, Matsunaga 1998).

Where events are associated with some religious activity, the rites that accompany a person through life are usually associated with Shintō, whereas the memorials tend to be Buddhist. Neither the Shintō nor the Buddhist priest would be likely to present the situation in quite the way it has been presented here, as each religion, and indeed each sect, has its own view of life and death. However, from the point of view of the lay participant, it is not unreasonable to emphasise this opposition, even if all activities do not necessarily conform completely. It is interesting to note, also, that sickness, when the normal course of life is threatened, provokes recourse to the middle area of shamanistic and divinatory activity, which may be any combination of Shintō, Buddhism or Taoism.

I developed this opposition further in my book (Hendry 1981) on marriage in Japan, where I also pointed out that Shintō is associated with the community as a whole, in that community festivals are usually celebrated in connection with the local shrine, and Buddhism is more a concern of the continuing family, remembered at the Buddhist altar in the house. I have also argued there that marriage and its associated ritual tends to mediate between these oppositions in various ways, bringing family and community together to celebrate, involving attentions to the *butsudan*, as a bride leaves her own family to join a new one, as well as to the Shintō shrine which she visits in her new community. Marriage is also appropriately associated with the middle area of divinatory activity, since specialists are consulted about compatibility and suitable dates for the various rituals.

The argument is too long to do justice to here, and in any case, the situation may be different in urban areas, but the pivotal role that marriage seemed to play ceremonially is still reflected in the important place it has in the life cycle, for both men and women. It allows its participants to make long-term statements about their own lives, and it finally confers full adult status on them, as they officially set up a new family of their own. It also provides an opportunity for the wider families involved to make visible adjustments to their own status, and to demonstrate to the world that they have done their duty by their children. We have also seen how the role of mediation in marriage and divorce can be related to the importance of mediation in other areas of social, economic and political life. Small wonder, then, that the drop in the marriage rate has sparked off such concern in contemporary Japan.

CONCLUSION

The previous chapter focused on Japan's various religious influences in turn, but by looking at a set of specific rituals in this chapter, we have been able to reveal the coherent way in which they intermesh indigenously. This chapter also helps to place Japan in a wider context since many of the rituals described here are directly comparable with those found elsewhere in the world. The principles of rites of passage are very widely applicable, and Japan is certainly no exception, as reference to van Gennep (1977) rapidly reveals.

REFERENCES AND FURTHER READING

Brinton, Mary, 'Christmas Cakes and Wedding Cakes: the Social Organisation of Japanese Women's Lifecourse', in T.S. Lebra (ed.), *Japanese Social Organisation* (University of Hawaii Press, Honolulu, 1992), pp. 79–107

Crump, T., *The Japanese Numbers Game* (Routledge, London, 1992)

——'The Pythagorean View of Time and Space in Japan', in Joy Hendry (ed.), *Interpreting Japanese Society: Anthropological Approaches* (Routledge, London and New York, 1998), pp. 42–56

Edwards, Walter, *Modern Japan through its Weddings: Gender, Person and Society in Ritual Perspective* (Stanford University Press, Stanford, 1989)

Feuss, Harald, *Testing a Spouse: Japan the Country of Divorce 1600–2000* (Stanford University Press, Stanford, 2003)

Goldstein-Gidoni, Ofra, *Packaged Japaneseness, Weddings, Business and Brides* (Curzon, Richmond, Surrey, 1997)

Hendry, Joy, *Marriage in Changing Japan* (Croom Helm, London, 1981)

——*Becoming Japanese* (Manchester University Press, Manchester, 1986)

Jeremy, Michael and M.E. Robinson, *Ceremony and Symbolism in the Japanese Home* (Manchester University Press, Manchester, 1989)

Lewis, David, 'Years of Calamity: *Yakudoshi* Observances in Urban Japan', in Joy Hendry (ed.), *Interpreting Japanese Society: Anthropological Approaches* (Routledge, London and New York, 1998), pp. 196–212

Lock, Margaret, *Encounters with Aging: Mythologies of Menopause in Japan and America* (University of California Press, Berkeley, Los Angeles and London, 1993)

Martinez, D.P. and Jan van Bremen (eds), *Ceremony and Ritual in Japan* (Routledge, London and New York, 1994)

Matsunaga, Kazuto, 'The Importance of the Left Hand in Two Types of Ritual Activity in Japanese Villages', in Joy Hendry (ed.), *Interpreting Japanese Society: Anthropological Approaches* (Routledge, London and New York, 1998), pp. 182–93

Nakamaki, Hirochika, 'Memorial Monuments and Memorial Services of Japanese Companies', in Jan van Bremen and D.P. Martinez (eds), *Ceremony and Ritual in*

Japan: Religious Practices in an Industrialized Society (Routledge, London and New York, 1995), pp. 146–58

Norbeck, Edward, '*Yakudoshi:* A Japanese Complex of Supernaturalistic Beliefs', *Southwestern Journal of Anthropology*, XI (1955), pp. 105–20

Ohnuki-Tierney, Emiko, *Illness and Culture in Contemporary Japan* (Cambridge University Press, Cambridge, 1984)

——— *Kamikaze, Cherry Blossoms, Nationalisms: The Militarization of Aesthetics in Japanese History* (University of Chicago Press, Chicago, 2002)

Sawkins, Philip, 'Playful Attraction: Examining the Nature of Japanese "Cruising"', MA dissertation, Oxford Brookes University, 2001, and www.reconstruction.ws

Smith, Robert, *Ancestor Worship in Contemporary Japan* (Stanford University Press, Stanford, 1974)

Sofue, Takao, 'Childhood Ceremonies in Japan', *Ethnology*, 4 (1965), pp. 148–64

Stefánsson, Halldór, 'On Structural Duality in Japanese Conceptions of Death', in Jan van Bremen and D.P. Martinez (eds), *Ceremony and Ritual in Japan: Religious Practices in an Industrialized Society* (Routledge, London and New York, 1995), pp. 83–107

Suzuki, Hikaru, *The Price of Death: The Funeral Industry in Contemporary Japan* (Stanford University Press, Stanford, CA, 2001

van Bremen, Jan, 'Death Rites in Japan in the Twentieth Century', in Joy Hendry (ed.), *Interpreting Japanese Society: Anthropological Approaches* (Routledge, London and New York, 1998), pp. 131–44

van Bremen, Jan and D.P. Martinez (eds), *Ceremony and Ritual in Japan: Religious Practices in an Industrialized Society* (Routledge, London and New York, 1995)

van Gennep, Arnold, *The Rites of Passage* (Routledge & Kegan Paul, London and Henley, 1977)

RELATED NOVEL

Tanizaki, Junichiro, *The Makioka Sisters* (Picador, London, 1979)

FILMS

The Funeral (*Osōshiki*) (1984 Jūzo Itami)

The Inferno (*Jigoku*) (1960 Nobuo Nakagawa)

The Makioka Sisters (*Sasame Yuki*) (1983 Kon Ichikawa)

Margaret Lock (talks about *Encounters with Aging* – Asian Educational Media Service, 1998)

9 Careers and continuity

Opportunities for working life

INTRODUCTION

Having talked rather generally about a variety of influences on Japanese life, we come in this chapter (and to some extent in the next) to consider specific possibilities for the mundane business of making a living. In previous chapters the scene has been set with discussions of hierarchy and the influence of education, the importance of securing a good job on graduation from school or university and the reluctance of an increasing number of young people to settle to a long-term career. In the last chapter it was mentioned that marriage is another crucial time for making a definite commitment to a future occupation, and for women, it is a time for important decisions about whether to combine a career with marriage, or to make marriage itself a career. Again, we saw the age of marriage being postponed and an increasing number of people refusing marriage and child-rearing altogether, but we also saw that the possibilities for returning to education have increased.

This chapter will examine various opportunities for work in contemporary Japan. It will open with a consideration of different types of employment and their characteristics, especially as described from the inside by anthropologists who participated, and some statistics will be adduced to give an idea of how the population is distributed between the different arenas described. It will go on to discuss the role of unions, and attention will also be paid to social security provision. There will be some discussion throughout of male/female differences in expectations, practice and opportunities for careers, and a final section will draw together the general choices for women. In the next chapter some alternative occupations for women will be represented in both leisure-time pursuits and employment in the entertainment industry.

To some extent, then, this chapter looks at life courses for men and women separately, because this still represents the way that life is organised for most people in Japan. An Equal Employment Opportunity Law (EEOL) did come into effect in April 1986, and immediately 'prohibited discrimination against women in vocational training, fringe benefits, retirement and dismissal' (Lam 1992:89). With regard to recruitment, job assignment and promotion, however, the first law only 'urged employers to "endeavour" to treat women equally with men' (ibid.), and it was not until an amendment implemented in 1999 that discrimination was prohibited in these areas as well. In December 1996, the Japanese government put forward a Plan for Gender Equality 2000, aiming to promote a gender-equal society by the year 2000 (*Japan Access*). This chapter will present the actual situation found by researchers at the time of their research and try to give some idea of the practice of this 'equality'.

COMPANY AND PUBLIC EMPLOYMENT

A common view that has been presented of Japanese work life is that of a company employee, especially the white-collar worker known in Japanese as a 'salaryman'. Several anthropological studies were carried out in large companies or banks, and the picture they present is now rather familiar as business people around the world have sought to learn the secrets of Japan's economic success. Their findings will be summarised here, and several specific examples are included in the reading list at the end of the chapter (e.g. Abegglen and Stalk 1985; Clark 1979; Dore 1973; Rohlen 1974), but it will be noted that they were all published some time ago. A good introductory summary of the different value of their representations, and how things have changed since, is to be found in Matsunaga's (2000) study, to which we will return after presenting their evidence. Some interesting recent analysis of the masculine model that the 'salaryman' came to embody is to be found in Dasgupta (2000) and Roberson and Suzuki (2002). Moeran's (1996) study of a Tokyo advertising agency still found men in all but one of the 'important positions'.

One of the chief characteristics of large Japanese companies that has been emphasised is that they tend to take over more of their employees' lives than companies elsewhere are wont to do. They prefer to recruit direct from school or university, and they provide training courses that inculcate company loyalty through songs and slogans as well as preparing employees for the particular tasks they must perform. Indeed, they seek to foster company loyalty before specific skills, for employees might be asked to turn their hands to quite different occupations during the course of their working lives, and flexibility is crucial, especially in times of change. In this way, large companies have been able to offer considerable security of employment, and since pay increases with years of service, as well as with seniority of work, it has been common for men to stay in the same company all their lives. As we saw in Chapter 8, company employees might well also be remembered after their deaths.

Companies also provide many services and benefits to their 'regular' employees. Pensions, health care and bonuses are commonplace, but they often offer accommodation too. There are likely to be dormitories for unmarried workers, apartments for families and even larger houses for senior employees, although many choose to purchase their own homes eventually. Company sports facilities are also often available, as are hobby clubs, and there may even be holiday sites in some attractive locations by the sea or in the mountains. In return for all this, employees are expected to work hard and often late, to take few holidays and to spend much of their 'leisure' time with colleagues, drinking in the local bars, playing sports together, or going on office trips and outings with them.

The work group can thus become another very close *uchi* group, and relations in many ways resemble those that were learned in the first such group in kindergarten. There is an emphasis, for example, on maintaining harmonious relations, as the title of Rohlen's (1974) book, *For Harmony and Strength* – the company motto where he worked – implied. There is also considerable peer pressure to comply with the expectations of the wider group, and the principles of reciprocity and cooperation underlie much of the daily interaction between colleagues. Members of the company are encouraged to share responsibility for it, and to take pride in being a small cog in an important big wheel. Like school life, company life is almost the whole life, and as mothers encourage children to look forward to attending kindergarten, many bright school-children are geared towards seeking employment in a large company like this.

Again, the individual is not neglected in this large group because long-term personal relations are established between peers joining at the same time, on the one hand, and between seniors and juniors, as described in Chapter 6, on the other. One inside group is of the former, and much social life will probably be spent with one's contemporaries, but these people are also one's rivals for promotion (see Keita 1980 for some fictitious depictions), and even closer relations may be established with specific superiors, and eventually inferiors. These are the personal relations of loyalty and benevolence on the senior/junior (*senpai/kohai*) or parent/child model (*oyabun/kobun*). Superiors concern themselves with the home life of their inferiors, taking trouble to offer help in times of need, perhaps making the occasional loan, acting as ceremonial go-between at their weddings, or even seeking a possible spouse if necessary. In return, the inferior is expected to give absolute loyalty to the superior, and be available for support any time the occasion should arise.

These relations were discussed in detail in Chapter 6, where the family was invoked as a model for company interaction, both for the hierarchical links and for the way the individual is expected to put the wider *uchi* group before personal life. To a considerable extent, too, neighbourhood relations are replaced as people look to the company for recreation, support at life-cycle celebrations and maybe even political activity. Like the community's 'circulating notice-board', there is a system of circulating ideas and proposals, which in theory gives everyone a chance to participate in decisions, although the seniority system clearly affects the practical influence any specific employee may have in this respect. Nevertheless, the idea is to give everyone a chance to express their views, and there is a balance here not unlike that in the traditional community between security and comfort on the one hand, and demands and obligations on the other.

Ideally, employees develop within such a framework throughout their working lives, and see their own interests as coinciding with those of the company. According to Rohlen's exposition of the official view, 'devotion to duty, perfected through greater self-discipline . . . leads to . . . an improved state of personal freedom and a sense of joy focussed on fulfillment in one's work' (1974:52). There are echoes of Zen Buddhism here, as Rohlen points out, and this is part of a general Japanese concern with the development and strengthening of the 'spirit' (*seishin*). This reliance on spiritual strength was regarded as partly responsible for defeat in the Second World War, but here it has been re-channelled into peaceful, productive effort, and is therefore seen in a positive light.

Clark (1979) investigated in more detail some of the ways in which reality departed from this idealised model of company relations. For example, there has in any company always been a degree of labour mobility, and he devoted a chapter to discussing this topic. His findings were consistent with the notion presented above that people are freer to change jobs before they marry, and he also found more fluidity among employees taken in after high school graduation than among those who completed university. There are also categories of part-time and temporary workers who are treated by big companies quite differently from the permanent employees, particularly at the 'blue-collar' end of the spectrum. Another ethnography that successfully probed and penetrated the ideology of a large enterprise is Noguchi's (1990) book about the National Railways discussed in Chapter 2. He portrays the meaning of belonging to such a huge concern trying to act as a 'family' from the points of view of people at several different points in the structure. During the uncertainty that surrounded the process of privatisation in the mid-1980s, there were a number of suicides, which hardly expresses a feeling of security.

Matsunaga (2000) discusses the differences between the conditions for 'regular' and 'part-time' (*paato* in Japanese) employees, generally, and specifically in the retail sector, pointing out that part-time workers may still work 30 hours or more per week though they do not get benefits such as pension, sick-pay and job security. In practice most part-time workers are women willing to forgo the perks associated with 'regular' employment in order to conserve a few extra hours to care for their families and the freedom to leave work at the agreed time rather than feeling obliged, as regulars might, to stay on or go drinking afterwards. The number of part-timers is greater in the retail sector than in any other, but part-timers have increased across the board, especially during the years of recession, for these provide companies with a greater degree of flexibility. Between 1990 and 2001 the proportion in the total employment structure grew from 16.3 to 23 per cent (*FFJ* 2002: 84).

Contract workers and temporary employees grew from 3.9 to 4.2 per cent of the total in the same period, but it is a little difficult to be accurate about these figures because of the way the system works. These offer even more flexibility to companies, and they include various categories of employee, none of whom have much security. They include the 'freeters' we discussed in Chapter 2, and the very word is said to be made up of 'free' and *arbeiter*, a long-standing German–Japanese word adopted for the type of temporary employment students might choose. They include seasonal work taken up by people unable to use their land in the long snowy winters of the north, and the harsh plight of one such group was described with poignant clarity by the journalist, Kamata Satoshi (1983), who posed as a seasonal worker for six months to experience at first hand the life of an automobile factory. They include many of the foreign migrants discussed in Chapter 6, and they also include the work gangs, recruited on the streets of cities, some of whose stories are told in Tom Gill's (2001) fascinating ethnography *Men of Uncertainty*, mentioned in Chapter 2 for the makeshift homes they create.

Several ethnographies have been published about the lives of women in Japanese companies, and these together give an excellent idea of the situation at different positions in the overall framework. Glenda Roberts (1994) worked in a lingerie factory with a group of 'blue-collar' women who struggled sometimes, but mostly managed to maintain both their homes and the benefits of *Staying on the Line* and being 'regular' employees, though their expectations were different from those of men. Matsunaga's (2000) study examines these differences as well as those between 'regular', 'paato' and 'arbeito' employees in a chain store. Jeannie Lo's (1990) book is about women working in a large manufacturing company and portrays the different expectations on the factory floor, in the office and in the company dormitories, where boys were given an automatic washing machine while girls had to rush to and fro with a twin-tub arrangement.

Ogasawara's (1998) book is a detailed analysis of a group well known in studies of consumption behaviour for their relatively large disposable income, but apparently few prospects for promotion, namely the 'office ladies', or simply OL. The term refers to women who work alongside the white-collar 'salarymen', though the latter group does include a small percentage of women. The OLs include graduates of four-year universities, as well as two-year 'junior colleges' and high school leavers, but they carry out 'simple, repetitive, clerical work without any expert knowledge or management responsibility' (Ogasawara 1998:27). Ogasawara examines why women in such an apparently subordinate situation do not seek better conditions, and supplies a rich and detailed ethnographic account of the way the clever use of things such as gossip and gift exchange empowers them with control and influence over the men with whom they work. The study concludes that the advantageous accommodation of OLs to their unequal situation paradoxically perpetuates it, but that it gives them a 'leverage that may not be available to women in societies committed to a more egalitarian policy' (1998:166).

We will return to gender differences later in this chapter, when we will evaluate recent changes for women, but it should be noted that since the first set of ethnographies were written a phenomenon known as 'my-homism' found some men also refusing always to stay late at work. These *shinjinrui*, or 'new species' of salarymen, sought to create a family life for themselves separate from the workplace, and the ground they have gained opens a path for women too as both can spend more time in child-rearing. Company employees who spend periods working abroad where their non-Japanese colleagues spend less time at work than they are used to in Japan are often stimulated to pay more attention to leisure and/or home-oriented activities. However, they are not unlikely to revert to old patterns once they return to Japan. Along with the broader effects of 'internationalisation' on large Japanese companies, Mitch Sedgwick has discussed the experience of Japanese managers working in Thailand (1999) and France (2000).

SMALL AND MEDIUM ENTERPRISES

After all this discussion of the famous big Japanese companies, we turn now briefly to address the differences in the situation of the majority of Japanese employees who work not in large corporations, but in small and medium enterprises with a maximum of 300 employees. Of the total number of manufacturing firms alone, 99.5 per cent fall into this category, and they accounted for 87 per cent of people employed in manufacturing in 2001. Of these enterprises over 90 per cent employed fewer than 20 people and over 60 per cent employed 4 or less accounting for 42.2 per cent and 14 per cent of the total number of employees respectively (*Enterprise and Establishment Census* 2001).

There are two excellent ethnographies of work in this sector. Kondo's (1990) analysis of a sweet-making factory has already been discussed in Chapter 3, and we will consider it again below. The other is an engaging account of the 'working-class' lives of men and women who are employed by a company the author calls Shintani Metals. James Roberson (1998) set out precisely to offset the prior emphasis on large companies, 'salarymen' and the company-as-community, to work with 'blue-collar' workers in a smaller enterprise, and to find out as much as he could about their lives outside as well as inside the firm. He places his findings within an abundance of prior publication about Japanese work, and the book is highly recommended. These two ethnographies illuminate the lives of both men and women in the factories where they worked and sometimes the relationships between them as well.

A large number of people are employed in smaller enterprises such as these that are entirely unable to provide the extra benefits and facilities described above. These smaller organisations are also much more vulnerable than the larger ones to changes in the economic climate, bankruptcy is not uncommon and they are not really in a position to guarantee long-term employment in the way that large corporations are. Efforts are made to protect employees, however, and Roberson discusses some of the responses to the bursting of Japan's economic bubble in the early 1990s, both at Shintani and in other small enterprises. Whittaker (1997), another useful, more statistical source on this subject, discusses the extent to which the restructuring of smaller companies has protected them against being laid off by large corporations to whom many of them had acted on a long-term basis as suppliers and sub-contractors.

For employees of these small enterprises, there are few of the material benefits large companies can provide, but there may well be a more real sense of shared 'family' enterprise among them because of the smaller scale. The employer will usually know all the employees well, they will exchange gifts at important times like weddings and funerals and they will know and respect intimate details of each other's lives. Perhaps more than within large companies, it is likely that employment will be gained in the first place through recommendation or introduction. Here, too, mediation is often used to bring together a person seeking employment and a prospective employer, and in the early days of industrialisation this type of arrangement was common in larger enterprises too. Typically, a young person seeking employment in a city would go to a relative who was already established there and ask for help. Indeed, some city dwellers say they stopped visiting their home village because they were constantly pestered by such hopefuls. Nowadays, most firms recruit from school and university graduates, but a final year student may prefer a company with a connection to a completely unknown one, and Roberson found a large number of Shintani employees still came from the prefecture of the man who established the company forty years previously.

Kondo's (1990) ethnography of a small family confectionery business illustrates the relations which characterise this type of firm, and she also sets out to examine what the family ideology achieves in practice. She was, as expected, introduced to the firm through the mediation of a mutual friend, in fact her landlady, and this connection ensured her loyalty to her (benevolent) employer (Kondo 1990:202). She describes the various efforts made by the owners to keep the family flavour of the company as it grew, through personal care of the younger employees from out of town, to outings and celebratory meals. She also examines the extent to which these ploys are successful on the factory floor, and the reciprocal use of the notion of 'company as family' with its 'multiplicity of meanings' and uses, which she describes as 'laced with contradiction, irony and compromise' (1990:218).

FAMILY OCCUPATIONS

Family employment has already been mentioned in Chapter 2 as a continuing tradition in some occupations, and it is by no means uncommon even in today's industrialised world. A variety of activities are pursued as family enterprises, although it is becoming more and more common than it used to be for individual members of such families to go out and work elsewhere. Formerly the pattern was for every member of a family to contribute as they could to the common enterprise, and they shared the benefits, as they needed them, no one receiving an individual salary. Nowadays there is a move in some families towards dividing up the tasks clearly between the individual members and paying each one a regular fixed sum, although it is probably not uncommon for people to stand in for one another when necessary.

The kinds of occupation which are carried out as family concerns are those which entail the passing on of a particular skill, or those which make use of family land or property. Thus, the potters studied by Moeran (1984) and discussed in Chapter 4, are a good example on both counts, for they pass on their potting skills to their sons, but they also need access to local land for their raw materials. Success in marketing the pots to tourists no doubt encourages the younger generation to remain in the family business, as does the success with chrysanthemums in Kyushu, where I worked, and with family inns near the ski resort, described by Okpyo Moon (1998, 1989, discussed respectively in Chapters 2 and 4). Elsewhere, a traditional occupation may be pursued only by the older generation in a family, while the younger members go out to some other work elsewhere.

D.P. Martinez (2003) has described such a situation for families in Mie prefecture who dive for shellfish, and these again characterise the principles of family cooperation. Women usually dive, using masks but no artificial breathing apparatus. Sometimes they dive from the shore, but to get out deeper they go out with their husbands in boats, weight themselves to make the descent to the seabed faster and rely on their menfolk to haul them back up before their breath runs out. The men's job is incidentally less arduous, but the whole venture is only successful with the cooperation of both members of the party. Usually several families dive at once, so there is an element of neighbourly support here too. Many daughters these days prefer to seek employment elsewhere, however, and the tourism industry has opened up new occupations for men too, but once they have children they might turn again to diving, it seems.

Small shops are often run as family concerns, and sometimes, particular members of the family will again have specific roles within the enterprise. One store may provide a delivery service, operated by one of the sons, and shops that provide gas cylinders for domestic use and undertake to change them when they run out perhaps allocate the responsibility to a young, strong member of the family. Farmers, too, tend to divide up their roles these days, and rice and more traditional crops may be the responsibility of the older couple, while innovations involving new machinery will fall to the younger couple. It is the case in some areas that the men of farming families will go off to find piece-work during the slack season, leaving the women to cope with the household. In others, younger members of farming families hold down full-time jobs and only work on the land at weekends and in crucial seasons such as when seedlings are planted out and the harvest. In many of these cases, neighbourhood cooperation and the local agricultural cooperative may play an important part in the smooth running of their economic as well as social lives.

Doctors were mentioned in Chapter 2 as another example of a profession that may be run as a family concern. There are many small, private clinics and hospitals, and these are not infrequently run by a father and his son or sons. In the more traditional arrangement, one son, usually the eldest, would be chosen to succeed, but a pair of brothers with different specialities can be a good team in a small local clinic, and if either of them should marry a doctor, she too can be incorporated into the practice. Otherwise, wives, or even daughters, may help with the administration, or perhaps work as nurses or assistants in the hospital. In one hospital I visited in 2002, the family that founded it had no doctors to take the chief medical role at that time, but various members of the family were involved in administrative capacities, and doctors were being trained in the next generation. A senior family member expressed the hope that the law requiring a head of hospital to be medically trained might change in the near future.

In these examples, the principles continue to some extent of employing any member of the family who happens to be available for a task in hand and some individuals may spend time away and then return to the home

Figure 9.1 These statues, which stand in front of Tateyama hospital, depict physically the family line which has headed the establishment since it was founded.

enterprise. This custom provides some degree of flexibility both for the family enterprise, which may have busy and slack periods, and also for the labour market in general which can thereby more easily accommodate fluctuating demands.

LABOUR UNIONS

Labour unions in Japan are usually organised first by the enterprise to which their members belong, and only second by industry. Thus all the permanent members of a particular enterprise comprise one union, regardless of their skills, and there are no outsiders in the group. There are then nationwide federations of unions for a particular industry, which superficially resemble those found in Western countries, but these are composed rather loosely of the many small autonomous unions, over which they have little authority, as opposed to being the national unions with local branches which are found elsewhere. Ultimately, members of unions put their own enterprises before the union as a whole, and these factors have worked against the development in Japan of a working-class consciousness of the type found in Britain and other European countries (though see Roberson 1998:13ff. for a discussion of his use of 'working class' in Japan).

Christena Turner's (1995) study of *Japanese Workers in Protest* quotes union leaders at local and national levels complaining about the lack of consciousness of a labour movement in Japan. They describe 'the average Japanese worker' as egotistical and selfish, interested only in issues that have a direct bearing on their own lives, and lacking a sense of social responsibility (1995:176). On the side of the workers, Turner identifies a sense of powerlessness, associated with feelings of personal insecurity, about speaking out in meetings with intimidating formal procedures and leaders who are perceived to go ahead and do their own thing whatever the comments from the rank and file. This is probably related to a mobility within companies, and the ease with which union leaders can be promoted to management positions – perhaps because they have shown potential for leadership – or because their superiors feel they will then cause less trouble for the enterprise as a whole.

Negotiations and demonstrations typically take place within one enterprise, and often enough at predictable times. Workers are very susceptible to arguments about the damage excessive action could do to the firm and therefore to their own interests, and their usually fairly reasonable demands are likely to be met. The way in which large companies recruit general employees, whom they then train for particular jobs, is partly responsible for this system, for there is consequently little attachment amongst workers to others who share their speciality. It seems such workers would prefer to be retrained with different skills rather than lose their jobs, if such a choice arose, and there are consequently few craft unions to object to the practice. Matsunaga (2000) reported quite an active union in the retail company where she worked, especially as financial problems brought the threat of redundancy closer. The union first fought to protect the jobs of their members, and then tried to ensure good severance pay when they did lose them.

There are, of course, historical factors that may be cited to account for this system, and Martin Collick (1981) has summarised these succinctly. In the early days of industrialisation, at the turn of the twentieth century, the expanding industries were seeking incentives to encourage workers to move from their rural family occupations to work for them, and the all-embracing Japanese firm developed in this way to take care of the needs of their uprooted employees. Long service incentives were further developed to keep the employees in times of labour shortage, and these included the deliberate inculcation of a sense of company loyalty. The family model was used to depict the factory, and the employer took on the aspect of a benevolent (though authoritarian) father to whom loyalty was therefore expected. The model was familiar, and it has worked against an excessive amount of protest from employees who perceive themselves as dependent on their company's largesse.

One of the effects of such a system is that there is little encouragement for employees of smaller firms to organise themselves into unions, even though by international standards their wages and conditions of work may compare quite unfavourably with those of bigger enterprises. There is instead a high value placed on good relations amongst co-workers, whatever their status, and the security of family-type relations has been regarded as contributing more to the quality of life than an increase in salary necessarily would. Roberson (1998) describes the formal Workers' Friendship Association at Shintani Metals that was created a few years after the company was. Its role was to organise social events and outings, to compensate individual workers for personal and family illness or injury and to send acknowledgements of other life events such as marriage and births. He reported some attempt at unionisation in the wake of a 'downsizing' exercise during the early part of the recession (1998:53), and it was unclear at that time whether this might replace the earlier 'friendly' association.

In general, figures have shown a steady decline in total union participation, however, from 34.4 per cent in 1975 to 20.7 per cent in 2001, although the rate is different in different branches of industry (*FFJ* 2002:88). There has also been a drastic decrease in labour disputes over the same period, from 7,574 in 1975 to 305 in 2000, and it would seem that general insecurity in the employment situation has dampened activity considerably. One explanation links this with the increase in the number of part-time workers who do not usually join a union, so that those apparently vulnerable to unequal treatment are underrepresented, though as reported in Chapter 6, Matsunaga's (2000) work in a failing company found these were the last to go. Gill (2001) also suggests that the various unions for day labourers and other temporary workers are more active during good times than bad (2001:32), though he comments that the one local to his field site in Kotobuki-cho operated as much like a charity as a union (2001:76).

Public employees are organised on a different basis and some of their unions have been much more antagonistic than the enterprise ones. Teachers, for example, are organised on a national basis. They have limited rights to negotiate, and much of their action has been highly political, expressing dissatisfaction with the rigidity of the centralised system. A book by Robert Aspinall (2001) is a good source on this subject. The employees of National Railways were in a similar position before it was privatised. Since public employees are ultimately employed by the government, their unions provide forums for the expression of left-wing dissatisfactions which may have only a passing relationship to the specific issues they use as vehicles at any one time.

SOCIAL SECURITY PROVISIONS

It will probably have become evident that security is a major concern of Japanese people at various levels of society. In Chapter 4 we discussed the combination of security and obligation that characterises membership in a close community, and we commented earlier in this chapter on the all-embracing nature of the large Japanese firm. For smaller firms in Japan, and particularly for family enterprises, the community is often still providing a fair degree of security of this type. Families themselves are also often to be found taking care of their unemployed and their ageing members. The face-to-face *uchi* group is where people seek their closest ties, and it is where people turn first in times of need. Even when people must be admitted to hospital, they try whenever possible to take a relative with them to attend to their most personal requirements, and there is generally something of an aversion to putting oneself entirely in the hands of strangers.

It is probably not surprising then that although a national social security system exists in Japan, and it has been continually developing its services throughout the post-war period of economic expansion, in some respects it still operates rather as a last resort when all else fails. Indeed, even some of the day labourers discussed by Gill in *Men of Uncertainty* preferred to avoid welfare payments, claiming they would 'sooner die on the street than take money from the state' (2001:167). Others are happy to take advantage of the system in place, however, since those who take the trouble to register can claim a daily payment when there is no work, once a certain number of days have been logged. The situation is more difficult for many foreign workers, however, for their immigration status may well be illegal. The district of Yokohama where Gill did his main research was also that studied by Carolyn Stevens (1997), referred to in Chapter 2. She has described in detail the advice and welfare facilities available in the *Seikatsukan* or 'Livelihood Building', as well as from volunteer groups based in the area that include groups specific to various nationalities of foreign workers.

The overall system is administered at a local level, but one of the problems has been that a multiplicity of public and private schemes are available for social insurance, health coverage and pension plans, so that administration has been complicated and sometimes difficult for the most needy beneficiaries to understand. Since 1961, a universal system has been in place for pensions and health insurance, and it was revised in the 1990s to take account of the decline in the birth rate, the ageing population and 'women's advance in to the work force' (*FFJ* 2002:143). A 'basic pension' plan has been introduced, but to offset the declining number of contributors to the system, the age of retirement is being raised from 60 to 65 (*FFJ* 2002:145). However, new 'Gold Plans' for the elderly include home-helpers, home-visit nursing care and the day-care centres we discussed in Chapter 2.

Another part of the 1990s reforms has been an attempt to encourage parents to have more children again. The Angel Plan for child-rearing support, first implemented in 1994 and revised in 1997, aims at increasing the numbers of nurseries, day-care facilities and after school clubs, among other things. An interesting change here is that in 1981 when I was carrying out research on child-rearing, these facilities were all presented as back-up for children whose parents could not care for them, whereas now they are offered as an aid to the parents. Glenda Roberts (2002) analyses this plan including detailed discussion of the reasons behind it, the various forms of its implementation by different ministries and an assessment of its effectiveness. An interesting aspect is the way it encourages fathers to take a greater part in the rearing of their offspring, although there has been something of a backlash from corporations against this idea. In any case, a chief aim of the programme is to help *both* parents to balance child-rearing and work.

Roberts's study is in a very useful collection that examines the way that social policy both creates and reflects the relationship between the individual, the changing family, the community and the state in contemporary Japan. Edited by Roger Goodman (2002), the book addresses facilities for people at different stages of life, from the babies of the Angel Plan, through day-care centres for old and young together in a chapter by Thang mentioned in Chapter 2, to 150 years of changes in policies associated with death (Tsuji 2002). Goodman's own chapter is about child abuse, a problem until recently denied to exist in Japan, but that has caused much media interest now its existence has been identified. Goodman (2000) also has an excellent book on child welfare in Japan, discussed briefly in Chapter 2.

Further detail about the types of old people's homes and their lifestyle are to be found in Kinoshita and Kiefer (1993) and Bethel (1992), and a summary of the facilities for those with mental and physical handicaps in Stevens (1997), all cited in Chapter 2.

WOMEN'S CAREERS

Since the Plan for Gender Equality has passed its target year of 2000, the whole of this chapter should in theory be applicable to men and women alike, and I have tried to give an idea in each section of gender differences as they have been reported. There has been much written about women in Japan, and some of this work has been cited, but it is difficult to generalise about half of any population and I would like to look further at some examples of different situations. There has been considerable scepticism expressed about the Equal Employment Opportunity Law (EEOL), which we will discuss shortly, but the fall in the birth rate does seem to have made a strong impression in policy-making circles, and efforts previously reported as nominal may now at last have more teeth. Factors such as these will affect the decisions made by individual women, which are also important to consider if we are to get a good overall picture of the situation for them.

In large companies we saw that women are of course employed, but in several different capacities. The EEOL since 1986 has obliged employers to treat men and women alike, at least in advertising and starting pay, but according to Lam (1993) some interview the women who apply only after the male applicants have been exhausted, and many companies created a two-track system. This obliges recruits to make an irreversible choice between regular, clerical work with low pay and little chance of training and advancement, and a managerial track which involves undertaking to accept mobility, in other words to transfer to another location if the company should require it. This was seen as a loophole for companies on the assumption that most women would hope eventually to marry, and would therefore be reluctant to choose the managerial track since such a commitment could cause possible difficulties in their future family life.

Some women throw caution to the wind and, if offered, they accept the management track anyway, but they then also come under the same pressure as men to put in long hours and go drinking after work. These women, if they marry, are more likely than their men to be the ones who decide to sacrifice their career if a posting comes up in a distant location, and they also need to decide how to deal with their child-bearing capacity. Sasagawa's (2002, see Chapter 1) study, mentioned in Chapters 2 and 4, would suggest that while a middle generation of *shinjinrui* (or 'new species') women did try to juggle having children with quite high-powered jobs, her younger informants are tending to make the decision to do only one of the two options. Thus we find highly educated mothers engaged in largely voluntary neighbourhood activities and numbers of single women and childless couples increasing as more and more of them decide to stay on at work rather than having children.

Many women do continue to opt for the less prestigious tasks in large companies, however, and their options depend on the level of education they have achieved. Graduates of two-year junior colleges or vocational schools may become OLs, or 'office ladies', though as Ogasawara (1998) showed, they may not feel as powerless as they have formerly been portrayed. They usually expect to leave on marriage, or at least when they become pregnant, although if they fail to marry or do not have children, their opportunities for advancement have on the whole been somewhat limited. Jeannie Lo's (1990) book about women in the Brother Company portrayed very clearly the situation for a woman in a regular office career who failed to find a marriage partner – though she worked for the same company for many years, there was virtually no possibility for promotion. Indeed, according to an earlier report by anthropologist James McLendon (1983) of women in a large trading company, the main intention of women who join large prestigious companies is to find a good husband.

Graduates of high school and junior high school would be more likely to find themselves on the factory floor, and Lo reported a similar situation for them, though if they could find a 'regular' position in a company like the one described by Roberts (1994), they might have better prospects. If conditions were right, they could also return to work after giving birth and thereby build up a pension and an incremental salary, however small. Another popular option is to take time off for a period during childbirth and the early years of child care, and then return as a *paato* in order to preserve the ability to manage the home at the same time as bringing in some cash. The retail trade has been a good source of female employment, as described by Matsunaga (2000) above, and by the mid-1990s it had nearly three times as many part-timers as the manufacturing industries (2000:19). Here the relationships between women in varying types of jobs were sometimes tricky because of age and experience differences, but as the company where Matsunaga worked went bust, the part-timers were no more insecure than anyone else.

In medium and particularly small enterprises, women may have similar intentions to those described above for large companies, but they may also find themselves treated rather better. They may start by carrying out more menial tasks than the men with whom they work, but the closer inter-personal relations may make it possible for women to exercise their abilities more fully. There may also be more opportunity for them to leave for a few child-bearing years and then return to a similar job. Roberson (1998) found all sorts of different sets of circumstances among the women at Shintani Metals, for example, and the case of women with part-time status also provoked some considerable discussion by Kondo (1990) for the small confectionery firm she described.

In fact, women accounted for 40 per cent of the Japanese workforce in 2001, and the graph of women's workforce participation by age shows a clear 'M' curve, rising even a little higher in the post-child-bearing years than it does in the younger ones. The peak participation ages are 20 to 24, when 72 per cent of all women were either in the labour force or seeking work, and 45 to 49, when it was similarly 72.7 per cent. Even at the lowest point, during the child-rearing ages of 30 to 34, there were 58.8 per cent of women out at work in 2001 (*FFJ* 2002:88–9). The proportion of married women in the workforce at this age rose from 40.1 per cent in 1975, when the lowest point was 32.1 per cent at ages 24 to 29, to 45.2 per cent in 1997 when 25 to 29 was still lower at 42.9 per cent. For the 45 to 49 age group, the percentage of married women rose from 59.1 to 70.4 per cent during the same period (*The Japanese Family in Transition* 1998:25).

If we turn to the women who are not counted as in the workforce, these figures are somewhat misleading, for married women are also often to be found gainfully employed in their homes. In a family enterprise all members of the family are expected to participate, regardless of their gender, but it should also be noted that some women take piece-work into the home while they are caring for small children. This is often a rather poorly paid occupation, and there is probably an element of exploitation here, but women find it convenient to be able to pick up and put down their work as they are able. Some, such as dressmakers and cosmetic saleswomen, make a career of such work, and a slightly fictionalised case of the latter is described in some detail in *Letters from Sachiko* (Trager 1984). In other cases women of the house are carrying on a family occupation while the men go out to more lucrative employment elsewhere. Sometimes these are locally noted crafts such as fan-, doll- or lantern-making, and the women thereby also keep such local specialities available.

In family occupations, women usually play an important part, although this will obviously vary from one family to another. In my own research in Kyushu I asked a number of families about who made important decisions and who took care of the money, and the answers were rather varied. The decisions were often said to be made after family discussion, a pattern comparable to company practice, but some said that men had the last word. In direct observation of such discussions, I noticed that women often appeared to allow men to make the final decision, but they were rather skilful at manipulating the situation. The family purse was sometimes taken care of by men and sometimes by women, and in urban areas this seems commonly to be a woman's role. Women are almost always responsible for cooking, cleaning and washing, although grandmothers and even grandfathers quite often find themselves looking after small children for a substantial part of the day.

In the farming families of my acquaintance, it was generally younger men who operated the machines such as tractors, planters and combine harvesters, while women were left to deal by hand with the spaces in their small fields that the machines could not reach. Elsewhere, however, women have been left to attend to the farm work without the men of the family, who commute to work in nearby towns, and they have proved quite capable of taking advantage of modern machinery. Women have always played a vital role in the diving families described by Martinez (2003), but tasks are generally divided at least ideally on the basis of gender in many traditional occupations. In a fishing community described by Arne Kalland (1981), taboos surrounding women until quite recently excluded them entirely from the boats. A glance at any of the anthropological monographs on Japanese communities will illustrate further these patterns of female employment in the family.

It must also be pointed out, however, that there is still quite strong pressure on women to marry in Japanese society, and unless they are the eldest in a family with no sons, they have also been expected to leave home and take up the occupation of their new family. In modern families, there is no longer necessarily a family occupation to pursue, but women are generally expected to be the ones to fit into the new situation which is why companies expected so few to commit themselves to a managerial track. Perhaps these pressures are related to the situation mentioned in Chapter 2 where more and more young women are postponing marriage, taking up short-term 'freeter' positions and spending their income in a flurry of consumption by living at home and becoming what the sociologist Masahiro Yamada (1999) called 'parasite singles'.

Another contributing factor is perhaps that women in Japan, once committed, do usually take very seriously the roles of wife and mother, and many would at least like to be at home during the early child-rearing years if circumstances allowed it. Indeed, some mothers regard the business of rearing children as a profession in itself, and there are men too who feel that their wives should dedicate themselves entirely to the home. In the late 1980s I spent some time doing research with a group of housewives in a provincial seaside town south of Tokyo and several of them, although highly educated, had chosen the 'profession' of housewife for their career while their children needed them. They explained that this gave them much more control over their own lives than trying to continue working outside the home, and they occupied themselves when their children were at school or kindergarten by attending classes and other activities, most of which could help them run a better home. Sasagawa's (2002) findings at the turn of the twenty-first century, within commuting distance of Tokyo, were rather similar, though perhaps emphasising rather the fulfilment of the woman herself (see above).

On the other hand, some women embark upon a career that they want to continue, and if they choose to marry, they will need to find a husband and preferably mother or mother-in-law who will cooperate. Particularly for professional women, it is becoming more and more acceptable to do this as they may well lose their chances of promotion if they break off to have children. This is easier in some professions than in others, and teachers, nurses and kindergarten teachers have managed to continue working for some time. Women lecturing at university, in medicine and in law, have also been better able to combine a career with marriage than their counterparts who enter the world of big business, but the recent support for child care could change this too.

A number of firsts for women have been reported in the past few years. In 1986, my own bank in Tateyama had the first woman manager (see Figure 9.2), who then proceeded to climb through the ranks at head office. In 1997, Tomoko Otake became the first woman pilot to fly for a domestic airline (*Japan Access*), and in 2000, Fusae Ota became the first female governor (of Osaka). We will see in Chapter 11 that there have also been several new female politicians.

Whatever their situation, women in Japan tend to think rather carefully about the kind of lifestyle they would like to have, and the best way to achieve their ambitions. For some, the ideal of being a full-time housewife, married to the employee of a prestigious company, sounds attractive and they prepare by pursuing just enough education, and then seeking short-term employment in an appropriate company. Others prefer to train for their own achievements and independence, in whatever walk of life, and they follow their various ambitions, though the recession and rising unemployment is working against guaranteed success. For this reason, too, others seem to prefer to drift in and out of temporary work, possibly even delaying leaving home. As for the decision about whether to marry and have children, this also seems to be more of a choice these days, and the

Figure 9.2 A local branch manager looks over the work of some of her subordinates in a provincial bank. This woman was Japan's first female branch manager, appointed autumn 1986.

subsequent falling birth rate may finally be pushing people in positions of power to put some more bite into those schemes for equality.

CONCLUSION

This chapter has presented some of the opportunities available for the working lives of men and women in Japan. It has by no means been comprehensive, but it has, I hope, been somewhat representative. The next chapter deals with arts, entertainment and leisure, and of course, for those involved in creating them, they may offer alternative ways of making a living. It should particularly demonstrate some of the possibilities for women that have not even been touched on in this chapter.

REFERENCES AND FURTHER READING

Abegglen, J.C. and G. Stalk Jr, *Kaisha: The Japanese Corporation* (Tuttle, Tokyo, 1985)
Aspinall, Robert, *Teachers' Unions and the Politics of Education in Japan* (State University of New York Press, Albany, 2001)

Clark, Rodney, *The Japanese Company* (Yale University Press, New Haven, 1979)

Collick, Martin, 'A Different Society', in Howard Smith (ed.), *Inside Japan* (British Broadcasting Association, London, 1981)

Dasgupta, Romit, 'Performing Masculinities? The "Salaryman" at Work and Play', *Japanese Studies*, 20, 2 (2000), pp. 189–200

Dore, R.P., *British Factory, Japanese Factory* (University of California Press, Berkeley, 1973)

Enterprise and Establishment Census 2001 (http://www.stat.go.jp/english/data/jigyou/a003.xls)

FFJ – Facts and Figures of Japan (Foreign Press Centre, Japan, 2002)

Gill, Tom, *Men of Uncertainty: The Social Organization of Day Laborers in Contemporary Japan* (State University of New York Press, New York, 2001)

Goodman, Roger (ed.), *Family and Social Policy in Japan: Anthropological Approaches* (Cambridge University Press, Cambridge, 2002)

Imamura, Anne E., *Urban Japanese Housewives* (University of Hawaii Press, Honolulu, 1987)

Japan Access, Japanese Ministry of Foreign Affairs (Kodansha International, Tokyo, 2000)

Japanese Family in Transition, About Japan Series no. 19 (Foreign Press Center, Japan, 1998)

Kalland, Arne, *Shingu: A Study of a Japanese Fishing Community* (Scandinavian Institute of Asian Studies Monograph Series no. 44, Curzon Press, London, 1981)

Kondo, Dorinne, *Crafting Selves: Power, Gender, and Discourses of Identity in a Japanese Workplace* (University of Chicago Press, Chicago and London, 1990)

Lam, Alice, *Women and Japanese Management: Discrimination and Reform* (Routledge, London, 1992)

—— 'Equal Employment Opportunities for Japanese Women: Changing Company Practice', in Janet Hunter (ed.), *Japanese Women Working* (Routledge, London, 1993)

Lebra, Takie Sugiyama, *Japanese Women: Constraint and Fulfillment* (University of Hawaii Press, Honolulu, 1984)

Lo, Jeannie, *Office Ladies, Factory Women: Life and Work at a Japanese Company* (M.E. Sharpe, New York, 1990)

McLendon, James, 'The Office: Way Station or Blind Alley', in David Plath (ed.), *Work and Lifecourse in Japan* (State University of New York Press, Albany, 1983)

Martinez, D.P., *Making and Becoming: Identity and Ritual in a Japanese Diving Village* (University of Hawaii Press, Honolulu, 2003)

Matsunaga, Louella, *The Changing Face of Japanese Retail: Working in a Chain Store* (Routledge, London, 2000)

Moeran, Brian, *A Japanese Advertising Agency: An Anthropology of Media and Markets* (Curzon, Richmond, Surrey, 1996)

Noguchi, Paul H. *Delayed Departures, Overdue Arrivals: Industrial Familialism and the Japanese National Railways* (University of Hawaii Press, Honolulu, 1990)

Ogasawara, Yuko, *Office Ladies and Salaried Men: Power, Gender and Work in Japanese Companies* (University of California Press, Berkeley, Los Angeles and London, 1998)

Plath, David (ed.), *Work and Lifecourse in Japan* (State University of New York Press, Albany, 1983)

Roberson, James, *Japanese Working Class Lives: An Ethnographic Study of Factory Workers* (Routledge, London, 1998)

Roberson, James E. and Nobue Suzuki, *Men and Masculinities in Contemporary Japan: Dislocating the Salaryman Doxa* (Routledge, London, 2002)

Roberts, Glenda, *Staying on the Line: Blue Collar Women in Contemporary Japan* (University of Hawaii Press, Honolulu, 1994)

——'Pinning Hopes on Angels: Reflections from an Aging Japan's Urban Landscape', in Roger Goodman (ed.), *Family and Social Policy in Japan: Anthropological Approaches* (Cambridge University Press, Cambridge, 2002)

Rohlen, Thomas P., *For Harmony and Strength: Japanese White-collar Organization in Anthropological Perspective* (University of California Press, Berkeley, 1974)

Saso, Mary, *Women in the Japanese Workplace* (Hilary Shipman, London, 1990)

Sedgwick, Mitchell W., 'Do Japanese Business Practices Travel Well? Managerial Technology Transfer to Thailand', in D.J. Encarnation (ed.), *Japanese Multinationals in Asia: Regional Operations in Comparative Perspective* (Oxford University Press, Oxford, 1999)

——'The Globalizations of Japanese Managers', in J.S. Eades, Tom Gill and Harumi Befu, *Globalization and Social Change in Contemporary Japan* (Trans-Pacific Press, Melbourne, 2000), pp. 41–54

Sellek, Yoko, *Migrant Labour in Japan* (Palgrave, Basingstoke, 2001)

Shimada, Haruo, *Japan's "Guest Workers": Issues and Public Policies* (University of Tokyo Press, Tokyo, 1994)

Social Science Japan Journal, special issue on 'Atypical' and 'Irregular' Labour in Contemporary Japan, 4, 2 (2001)

Tsuji, Yohko, 'Death Policies in Japan: The State, the Family, and the Individual', in Roger Goodman (ed.), *Family and Social Policy in Japan: Anthropological Approaches* (Cambridge University Press, Cambridge, 2002)

Turner, Christena L., *Japanese Workers in Protest: An Ethnography of Consciousness and Experience* (University of California Press, Berkeley, Los Angeles and London, 1995)

Whittaker, D.H., *Small Firms in the Japanese Economy* (Cambridge University Press, Cambridge, 1997)

Yamada, Masahiro, *Parasito Shinguru no Jidai (The Age of Parasite Singles)* (Chikuma Shobo, Tokyo, 1999)

RELATED NOVELS AND LIGHTER READING

Kamata, Satoshi, *Japan in the Passing Lane: An Insider's Account of Life in a Japanese Auto Factory*, trans. Tatsuro Akimoto (Allen & Unwin, London, 1983)

Keita, Genji, *The Lucky One* (and other humorous stories), trans. Hugh Cortazzi (The Japan Times, Tokyo, 1980)

Trager, James, *Letters from Sachiko: A Japanese Woman's View of Life in the Land of the Economic Miracle* (Abacus, London, 1984)

FILMS

Dirty Money Islands (*Kinyuufusyoku Retto*) (1999 Masato Harada)
Group Demotion (*Shūdan Sasen*) (1990 Shūnichi Kajima)
High and Low (*Tengoku to Jigoku*) (1962 Akira Kurosawa)
The Time of the Barley Harvest (*Bakushū*) (1951 Yasujirō Ozu)

10 Arts, entertainment and leisure

INTRODUCTION

Art and entertainment may be related to society in a variety of ways, and this chapter covers a broad range of examples, from glimpses of the court theatre of the distant past through to the 'global' music scene of contemporary Tokyo. As well as gaining an idea of arts for their own sake, one may also seek through art to understand something about the social and political organisation of the people producing it, and one may look for the symbolic meaning with which their work is imbued, whether it is there intentionally or not. In many cases, one may also seek to understand a people's religious and philosophical ideas through the art that represents them, and through collective ideas about what constitutes art, and how it should be produced. One may also learn of the place that arts and their accomplishment hold in the lives of practitioners, and in this case, the seriousness accorded to practices elsewhere associated with leisure and play.

There are many and various arts and entertainments in Japan, and it is not possible here to discuss them all individually. An abundant literature in Western languages enables a reader to pursue an interest in a particular Japanese art, and references are provided at the end of this chapter. In modern times, many arts have become an important medium for the expression of Japan's identity. They provide an attraction for visitors to the country, as well as a comfort to Japanese who feel swamped by outside influence, and they have for some time been exported to vastly different cultural areas. At the same time, Japan's artists have made an important contribution to international artistic fields, such as music, fashion and film-making, and these contributions may be related to international society as well as to their Japanese origins.

This chapter will open with a brief consideration of arts in historical perspective, concentrating particularly on the social organisation of the artists themselves, and the changes that have occurred in the arrangements through time. There will then be two sections on specific ways in which ordinary people are involved with arts and entertainment, the first being somewhat more concerned with the world of women than men, the second with men than women, although in the latter case the artists and entertainers are usually women. Finally, there will be a section on a leisure activity popular with all Japanese people, regardless of gender or socio-economic affiliations.

HISTORY AND SOCIAL ORGANISATION WITHIN THE ARTS

The arts, in many material forms, can provide us with tangible evidence of Japanese history, and we can examine them for an expression of the various influences that Japan has experienced over the centuries (e.g. Hall and Beardsley 1965: chapter 6). Some of the most striking examples are those associated with religion, such as the architecture of shrines and temples, the gardens in which they stand and the statues and paintings with which they are adorned. Some of the most prized modern articles of Japanese art, such as swords, kimonos and ceramics, were articles in daily use in former times, and Japanese paintings, literature and drama fill in some of the details of daily and ceremonial life of the times concerned. In this section, however, the concern will be rather with the place of artists in society, relations between them and the changes these have undergone in recent times.

In pre-modern Japan, specific arts tended to be associated with groups of people who inhabited particular positions in Japanese society. Artistic skills and knowledge were transmitted from one generation to another through family lines and through hierarchically organised groups that could usually be penetrated only by means of personal introduction and recommendation. Typically, such a group would be headed by a master, known as the *iemoto*, literally family source or origin of the *ie*, and he would pass on his position to a son, or someone specially adopted for the purpose. The principle is, of course, the same one that operated throughout Japanese society, and families associated with some artistic forms still exemplify this *iemoto* system today.

In an article entitled 'Organisation and Authority in the Traditional Arts', P.G. O'Neill (1984) has succinctly summarised the historical basis for this system and the principles which characterise it, using examples particularly from the performing arts. According to him, the first known groups of this kind were families engaged in ancient court music and dances known as *gagaku*, which date back to at least the early eighth century and probably combine the Chinese influence of the time with the earlier *kagura* shrine performances mentioned in Chapter 1. During the flourishing court culture of the Heian period, many artistic pursuits became popular, and houses developed their own specialities in broad areas such as poetry, perfume-smelling, culinary arts and horseback archery. The ensuing medieval period witnessed the more formal establishment of lines which have persisted until the present day in, for example, flower arranging, *nō* drama and music for its accompaniment.

Nō was patronised throughout the Tokugawa period by the military leaders, who supported and formalised the *iemoto* system, and a fascinating analysis of the political and even military context of its development in the time of Toyotomi Hideyoshi is to be found in Steven Brown's (2001) *Theatricalities of Power*. A similar structure was used in the prolific schools of military skills, such as unarmed combat and swordsmanship, which are also regarded as art forms, and in the entertainments of the townspeople which include *kabuki* and puppet theatre as well as various forms of popular music, dancing and singing. The skills of games and pastimes such as Japanese chess and *go* were passed on in this way, too, as were arts such as painting, calligraphy, gardening and the tea ceremony. Despite the long historical span and the wide range of activities, O'Neill identifies five characteristics, some or all of which he says were shared by these artistic lines.

First, there is the principle of hereditary succession to the headship, already mentioned above. Second, the transmission of skills and secrets of the art is usually accomplished through demonstration and minute imitation, rather than by explanation and formal teaching. This form of learning is appropriate for the stylised, ritual forms that characterise much Japanese art even today. The third and fourth points run together. Most groups developed a 'permit' system which pupils were granted as they improved, and which eventually granted them the status of teachers (or leaders), so that there developed a hierarchical, pyramid-shaped organisation. Communication within the group would go up the hierarchy step by step, and the final point is that each member would, or should, develop a strong sense of loyalty and obligation to his immediate teacher, and through him to the *iemoto* and the whole school or house.

These patterns are, of course, familiar from previous chapters, and indeed 'schools of art' exemplify Nakane's inverted V model, with the most experienced members remaining forever superior to their pupils, who usually remain loyal to them. As Nakane described, however, factions tend to occur when a master dies, leaving more than one contender for the ultimate superior position, and the different 'schools' within particular artistic fields usually represent splits of this kind which occurred when the succession was not clearly established. Less exalted artisan families passed on their skills in this way, too, and indeed, the principles are essentially those of the *ie* system described in Chapter 2. Anthropological comment on the system is to be found in Smith (1998) and Cox (2002), who provides a fascinating and much more detailed analysis of the way the system continues to work in contemporary Japan, particularly in the case of the tea ceremony and one specific martial art.

As Japan entered the modern period, the former military patrons of the arts lost their wealth and power, and the whole economic base of the system went through considerable change. Theatrical performers and their supporting musicians have now come to depend on their appeal to the general public, and many of the other arts are supported by amateur pupils who pay to study them (see the next section). The *iemoto* system has survived better in some arts than in others, and O'Neill (1984:643) suggests that one of the factors affecting this is whether or not the art is a creative or developing one. If the emphasis is on the preservation of tradition, as has now become the case in *nō* and the tea ceremony, the *iemoto* system tends to be maintained, although factions may still develop and lead to divisions within groups. If the art is more open to innovation, like flower arranging, dance and painting, it lends itself to the setting up of new lines, particularly where there is an abundance of paying pupils. There is even a new art of British tea ceremony that has been set up by practitioners who claim to have studied the art in places like The Ritz Hotel in London.

The *iemoto* system has come under fire from time to time, especially in the post-war period. It has been described as 'feudal' and artistically inhibiting, and an abundance of new forms of art and artistic cooperation have been tried out, influenced by many different countries. Some of these have made an impact, but the hierarchical structure of continuity dies hard, as has been shown in previous chapters, and many innovative Japanese artists have had to make their names abroad before they could be accepted in Japan. These include the conductor Seiji Ozawa, film-maker Akira Kurosawa, architect Kisho Kurokawa and designer Issey Miyake, to say nothing of John Lennon's wife, the mischievous Yoko Ono. Like Ono, the artist Yayoi Kusama travelled to New York in the early 1960s, where she made a name for herself that later became known in Europe as well. Now she lives in Japan, but she has set up her studio in a mental hospital. Other Japanese artists respected abroad, such as the photographer Nobuyoshi Araki, have experienced considerable disapproval in Japan.

It is not possible to discuss all the artistic movements of the past few decades in Japan, but a glance at a few publications should give a flavour for some of the trends, as well as directing the reader to areas of particular interest. In the world of theatre, for example, Brian Powell (2002) has argued that modern theatrical groups have now just about come full circle back to techniques which were Japanese before the influx of Western influence. The 'new theatre' groups which arose in reaction to the ritualised style of *kabuki* and *nō* have in turn become the target of reaction by 'underground' groups, which have made a considerable impression in the outside world by drawing on some of the traditional techniques the first groups were rejecting. He ends his book on *Japan's Modern Theatre* praising *kabuki* actors for their success not only in maintaining their theatrical skills, but bringing them to the world at large.

There is an interesting anthropological study of the all-female revue theatre, *Takarazuka*, founded in 1914 as a respectable school for theatrical accomplishment, in contrast to a former association of female performers with itinerant prostitution. Most theatre groups until that time, at least since the seventeenth century, had been exclusively male, and some actors in, for example, *kabuki* theatre would specialise in cultivating the art of female roles in order to present complete stories. Likewise, in *Takarazuka*, the girls must make the important decision during the course of their early training whether they will become male or female players in their performances, and that decision affects much of their subsequent behaviour off stage as well as on. Jennifer Robertson's (1998) study, subtitled *Sexual Politics and Popular Culture in Modern Japan*, examines the consequences of this androgynous behaviour for the lives of the revue artists and their fans, and places the whole in the broader context of Japanese attitudes to sex, gender and sexuality.

Another interesting anthropological paper is Valentine's (1998) discussion of dance in Japan. He identifies various spatial and temporal characteristics of Japan's various forms of dance, which he relates to other arts and the wider social structure, and shows how these influenced even American dances performed by young people at Harajuku in Tokyo and another Western genre known as *modan dansu*. He notes also that spatial patterns reproduce patterns of hierarchy amongst the dancers, and he again claims to detect Japanese traditional patterns in the Western dance forms. Resentment against the *iemoto* system in the dance world was illustrated in 1980 when the dancer Hanayagi Genshu stabbed in the neck the leader of the most renowned school of dance as a protest against the system and the monopoly its families have over dance teaching and performing in Japan. She served eight months in prison.

In the literary world, aspiring writers used to need to attach themselves to a successful member of their profession to advise them and help them to publish their work. Thus, the house of a famous writer would often also become the meeting place of a literary circle, again organised hierarchically, although the initial attachment was more likely to be through introduction and merit, rather than kin relationship. Before the Second World War, it was said that writers had to endure '10 years of hardship' because they were not allowed to publish ahead of their superiors, but since the post-war boom in commercial publishing, a young writer may become famous and successful overnight. Yoshimoto Banana is a good recent case in point. Irena Powell (1983) documented changes in the post-war literary world in a book entitled *Writers and Society in Modern Japan*. The older system is portrayed in Ishiguro's novel, *An Artist of the Floating World* (1985).

Another set of artistic skills that have been employed in a way that departs radically from the old system in post-war Japan have been those required to create the immensely popular *manga* comic strips and *anime* cartoon films. Both of these Japanese words are known by aficionados in other parts of the world, partly for the extraordinary variety of the stories they tell, and partly because they take the media so far beyond the lowbrow reputation they have in many European countries. Large quantities of *manga* are consumed by adults in all walks of life in Japan, as well as by children learning to read. Companies that produce them seek artists through open competitions in their own publications so that anyone whose work appeals to them can achieve success. Sharon Kinsella's (2000) book, *Adult Manga*, provides details of the production process as well as skilfully analysing the way *manga* have been used over the years as a medium for all sorts of political purposes.

Maria-Dolores Rodriguez del Alisal (2002), however, reports the comment of the well-known *anime* artist, Miyazaki Hayao, after screening applications from young people wishing to join his Studio Ghibli, that most lack 'a positive inner attitude to their work'. He concluded that most of them are 'just looking for fast results and effortless quick promotion' (2002:89). Miyazaki's work has been extremely successful, but his creations are the result of long hours of 'physical extenuation', and in a speech at the release ceremony of one of his best known productions, *Mononoke Hime*, he reported on the hard nature of the work and the endurance of his team (ibid.). Rodriguez del Alisal's chapter is about the playful elements of Miyazaki's work, however, set in the wider context of Japanese ideas about a creativity that involved the strong personal commitment and dedication that was all part of the old training that came through the *ie* system.

It is perhaps as a reaction to the apparent disintegration of the older system that some of the artisan crafts, initially made for daily use and often still produced by families which operate along the old *ie* lines, have become highly prized as *objets d'art*. Brian Moeran (1997) has discussed this folk craft movement in his book about the potting community where he worked, and talks of such objects inspiring a 'nostalgia' for the past, something he compares with a similar movement in industrialising Europe. Indeed, he analyses the way that European interest in Japanese 'folk arts' affected the local situation. Contemporary potters I met in the early part of the twenty-first century were creating objects of great individual taste and beauty, though one artist in Okinawa had spent five years working in a tourist village before he established and built up a reputation and a clientele of his own. Potting may also be taken up as a hobby, rather like the accomplishments that form the subject matter of the next section.

In a world in which much of the old order has been replaced by Western-inspired institutions, art is nevertheless a form that enables a people to maintain some continuity and, as will be illustrated again in the next section, this continuity may involve more than the preservation of objects. In a Japanese context, artists may themselves be categorised as 'living national treasures', and the practice of passing on highly valued skills from one generation to the next is an alternative means of conservation epitomised in the regular reconstruction of the Ise shrine and its contents. A number of examples of actual learning mechanisms in a variety of different fields are to be found in a book entitled *Learning in Likely Places: Varieties of Apprenticeship in Japan* (Singleton 1998).

ACCOMPLISHMENTS AND 'POPULAR CULTURE'

Many members of modern Japanese society come into contact with 'the arts' in their own study of some particular accomplishment. It was mentioned in Chapter 5 that small children go to classes in non-academic subjects, such as music and *kendō*, and women have also been in the habit of studying accomplishments such as the tea ceremony and flower arranging in preparation for marriage. Such study is by no means limited to these two categories, however, and the pursuit of accomplishments is a common leisure activity for Japanese men and women of all ages. Some take things more seriously than others, and those who devote themselves for years to a particular art may gradually accumulate the skills and abilities to become a teacher and master (or mistress). Others may attend a number of different classes during their lifetimes, or even at one time, as in the case of the girls preparing for marriage.

There are quite a number of arts that may be studied in this way and many of them express fundamental Japanese values, even if they were originally imported from elsewhere. Many are described as 'paths' or 'ways', using the second Chinese character of Shintō, referred to in Chapter 7, and sometimes pronounced *dō*. The examples given there were *bushidō* (the samurai way), *judō* and *shodō* (calligraphy). It can be seen that the system of classification includes 'ways' which would not necessarily always be called 'arts' in an international view, but for Japanese language users they share qualities which bring them together. An outsider would perhaps class the first as a career, the second as a sport, and only the third as an art in a more limited sense. An understanding of their shared qualities reveals some of the principles that underlie Japanese thinking more generally.

First of all, these are accomplishments that require a good deal of dedication and training. There is an underlying assumption that anyone could, with enough application, succeed in the pursuit of these arts. This assumption has already been met in the education chapter. Second, the method of learning is based largely on imitation and repetition, as mentioned above by O'Neill (1984) and discussed in detail in Rupert Cox's (2002) book. Much of the movement involved is ritualised, clearly decided, and a pupil strives to achieve perfection in conforming to expectations. Many hours are passed in repetitive routine. Perseverance and even suffering are an integral part of the process. It is only after many years of training and advancement that a pupil may begin to introduce originality into his or her work, but it is certainly not precluded from the process, despite the emphasis on copying as the method of learning. Many examples may be found in a volume on this subject edited by Rupert Cox (2003) and referenced in Chapter 1.

Another good example of the principles involved is to be found in the old process of acquiring the skills of carpentry, described with exquisite care to detail in Bill Coaldrake's (1990) book, *The Way of the Carpenter*. A decade's apprenticeship involved several years of 'miscellaneous chores around the workshop' during which time the carpenter's tools used to be forbidden to the trainee. Nor was any instruction given. The learning was based on observation and the experience acquired by being steeped in the work as it happened. By the time the apprentice was allowed to tackle a job he would have watched his master and more advanced trainees until he was 'overcome with an overwhelming desire to use the tools himself' (1990:8). A similar process is described by Hori (1994) for the monks of the Rinzai Zen Monastery. These days, with mechanisation, the process has been speeded up a little, but it still takes five or six years to learn the skills of carpentry, and they are still acquired through observation.

Third, one of the characteristics of all these pursuits is that they enable the participants to develop spiritual strength, or *seishin*, and the development of *seishin*, in turn, helps them to improve their skills. In this sense, these 'arts' are 'paths' or 'ways' through life, and they are thought to have value for helping ordinary people to cope with the demands and realities of everyday life. Taken to their limits, these 'ways' may absorb the whole person, as in the case of *bushidō* for the samurai class of the Edo period or for the master of a particular pursuit. One of the aims is to reach a stage when one knows so well the movements required that one can transcend all thought about them, an idea familiar from Zen Buddhism, which has certainly influenced many of these pursuits. Some of the spirit associated with the pursuit of these accomplishments is invoked in the training methods adopted by big corporations that included sending their new employees out for a period of *zazen*.

An interesting anthropological analysis that illustrates all these ideas, and places them in a detailed symbolic structure, is an article by Dorinne Kondo (1985) on 'the way of tea'. The author points out that this highly ritualised version of host/guest interaction also embodies the importance of *tatemae*, the formal graces required to maintain harmonious interaction. During the various stages of the 'ideal typical' version of the ceremony which she chooses to describe, the participants are led increasingly from the mundane world through physical and symbolic space to a totally ritual climax, and back again. Various other arts form part of the process, as the guests move through gardens, into a particular form of architecture, and admire a scroll, a flower arrangement and the pots in which the tea is served. An elaborate form of the ceremony may also include a light meal, introducing the art of cooking as well. Everything follows a formal, ritualised style, and as Kondo explains, 'it is by becoming one with the rules that the possibility of transcendence lies' (1985:302). A more comprehensive ethnographic account of Japanese tea ritual, which also puts it into an historical context, is to be found in a book by another anthropologist, Jennifer Anderson (1991), but Cox (2002) illustrates a lighter way that groups of friends might practise the same ritual.

As their children grow older and require less of their attention, full-time housewives may devote more and more of themselves to the development of personal skills such as calligraphy, painting or music – the Japanese stringed instrument, the *koto*, is particularly popular, for example. In some urban neighbourhoods women will give classes to each other in the arts in which they have become most adept, and for some, these pastimes eventually become careers. It should be noted, however, that housewifely accomplishments are by no means limited to traditional pursuits, and knitting, sewing and tennis classes were popular amongst the mothers with whom I worked, though they did impart some of the Japanese principles to their study. Knitting and sewing have specific stitches and, like ballet, are pursuits introduced from the West with plenty of form to be emulated. Tennis, too, though I have to admit that I had never before appreciated the importance of the placement of my little finger in returning a volley at the net.

An amusing article by an Italian anthropologist who did fieldwork in a university club for the practice of 'soccer' well illustrates the way that some of the principles of learning a Japanese accomplishment have been introduced into even this most global of games. Entitled 'When the Goal is Not a Goal', Simone Dalla Chiesa's (2002) chapter is a wonderful account of his

Figure 10.1 This ballet teacher illustrates the principle of teaching by helping
the child to absorb (the accomplishment) into her body.

frustrated efforts to inject a little Italian enthusiasm into a game which had
become the epitome of the 'repetitive routine, perseverance and even suffering' of the longer standing arts mentioned above (see Horne and Manzenreiter 2002 for a collection about soccer in Japan). William Kelly (1998) has
likewise applied an American eye to the Japanese version of baseball, a
sophisticated analysis of the importance of taking into consideration the
history and context of the introduction of the game as well as its local
popularity. 'Baseball in modern Japan has nationalized and pacified
patriotic sentiments', he goes so far as to assert, and it has 'massified and
mediated popular leisure' (1998:108).

Apart from the professionals, baseball is largely practised by children and
students in Japan, however. Grown men, like their female counterparts, go

for any number of other accomplishments such as *kyudō*, a traditional form of non-combative archery, tennis, one of the many other martial arts, or perhaps something more sedentary like *haiku* writing, ink painting or calligraphy. At regular festivals of arts held all over the country, an opportunity is made for displays of these various accomplishments and huge halls are filled with the work of local residents. These may include miniature gardens, *bonsai* and even attractive tree roots, mounted on stands for display. They also include collections, such as coins and stamps (see Frewer's (2002) work referenced in Chapter 1). Even *karaoke*, a popular pastime in bars and clubs, has been seriously formalised into a subject of preparatory study (William H. Kelly 2002).

Previously aristocratic arts have permeated the wider social structure, just as mundane products of the artisan class have been elevated to the ranks of art, and underlying principles of artistic endeavour are applied in the mundane life of the company employee. In fact, an elite activity for Japanese managers, especially those who are sent abroad for a spell, is the practice of golf, and according to Ben-Ari, the acquisition of enough skill to carry off a good game is part of a 'long-term strategy for life' (1998:139). According to his research, golf is a good test of character, a good game through which to create relationships, and for juniors on the managerial track of large Japanese firms, an essential part of the socialisation process towards becoming suitably qualified senior executives. Ben-Ari's research was carried out in Singapore, largely with men, but this game does not exclude women, so its role may be unaffected by recent developments.

GEISHA AND THE WATER TRADE (*MIZU SHŌBAI*)

To turn to what may at first seem a rather different aspect of Japanese entertainment, well known particularly amongst male visitors to Japan, is the nightlife they are pressed to enjoy. Typically this involves drinking and possibly eating, but invariably accompanied by attractive women who keep topping up their drinks, lighting their cigarettes and generally trying to make them feel relaxed and happy. The size and lavishness of the establishment is variable, as are the duties of the attendant women. It may be a swish nightclub with music and cabaret provided publicly, or in private rooms with artists who perform only for a particular party, and some of the attendant women may subsequently be available for more personal services. It may also be a tiny establishment with a few seats and a single owner/barmaid, whose chief role is to listen like a mother to the trials and tribulations of her treasured customers.

Many Japanese men have regular bars of this latter sort, and they visit them frequently, often in preference to returning home in the evenings. The barkeeper is addressed as *mama-san*, where *san* is a polite term of address, and *mama* is indeed a word also used for mothers. There have been several attempts at psychological explanation for this phenomenon, relating it to the way in which Japanese mothers indulge their small children, especially boys, but apart from any direct psychological effect, a long-term emphasis on mother/child relations over the conjugal one probably has a part to play. At larger establishments, too, there is a *mama-san*, who is in charge of the other women, sometimes referred to as 'big sisters'. These larger places are usually chosen when groups of friends or workmates go out together, the more plush and expensive places being selected when guests are to be entertained at the company's expense.

An interesting ethnographic account of a hostess bar by Anne Allison (1994) explains that 'playing' together in this fashion is one of the ways in which company colleagues cement their own social relations and consolidate relations with potential customers. A successful evening of relaxing entertainment, facilitated by the presence of attentive, beautiful women, is an accepted way of gaining a contract, and companies are willing to allocate a considerable part of their budgets to ventures of this sort, just as they pay the dues to a golf club. That the Japanese government approved of the activity was to be seen in the fact that expenses such as these were at least for a period tax deductible. It may be thought that the economic slump of the late twentieth century, together with the greater number of women beginning to rise through company ranks, may eventually put paid to some of these activities, but let us look further.

Before any generalisations are made on the basis of the male/female dichotomy, it should be pointed out that women who visit bars and nightclubs in Japan are also accorded attention and service, and they are not necessarily stigmatised for frequenting them as they might be elsewhere. There are even 'host clubs', which employ men to serve their female patrons, dance with them and provide them with sexual services if that is what they require. The principles of these establishments include the idea of treating customers like guests and helping them to relax and enjoy themselves so they can feel good about being together. There are also specialist bars for gay men and women, and Wim Lunsing (2002) has written about the world they create for their customers, again not to everyone's liking, but providing appropriate places of relaxation for many.

Many of these bars and nightclubs are to be found clustered together in narrow streets around the main stations in Japanese cities, and it is common for commuters to call in for a few drinks on their way home. Members of the same workplace may move together to a bar after work, and it is reported that it is possible to be much more frank with one's workmates when drinking together than it is in the formal atmosphere of the office or factory. An article in English describing these amusement areas (Linhart 1998) borrows the phrase of a Japanese sociologist in the subtitle: 'zones of evaporation between work and home'. He summarises the activities available, including gambling, *karaoke* and the buying of women, and he provides a brief historical setting, but he also argues that these entertainment areas provide relief from the stresses of the workplace in a society where the family is less well equipped to do this.

Linhart, together with Sabine Früstück (1998), has edited a whole volume about leisure activities in Japan, with chapters on several of these sources of 'stress-relief'. One is an interesting account of gambling activities by Japanese anthropologist Nagashima Nobuhiro (1998) who places contemporary attitudes to horse-racing and other forms of 'gamble racing' in a proper historical context. Attitudes introduced from Britain associating the aristocracy with horse-racing helped to give that particular form of gambling a respectable edge, and gambling has for centuries been popular in Japan, as elsewhere. However, much of it not only received official disapproval, but also became associated with the criminal underworld. Another ubiquitous form of gambling is to be found in *pachinko* parlours, and a chapter by Wolfram Manzenreiter (1998) in the same book provides a detailed account of this incredibly popular version of pinball – also a source of enormous economic turnover.

A veritable wealth of information about the seamier side of entertainment in Japanese cities is to be found in Ian Buruma's (1985) book, *A Japanese Mirror*, and in Nick Bornoff's (1991) book, *The Pink Samurai*. There would seem to be much less stigma attached to the pursuit of erotic entertainment in Japan, and 'respectable' company employees quite happily engage in all kinds of activities which their Western contemporaries (or, at least, their wives) might find distasteful. Japanese wives are supposed to turn a blind eye to these extra-marital activities, and many become accustomed to seeing their husbands regularly arrive home late and drunk. Men with the resources have even been accustomed to maintaining a mistress or two, as well as their family homes, although this practice is becoming less acceptable in recent years, at least among politicians.

An abundance of violent and erotic books and films, albeit legally restricted, permit men to live vicariously even beyond the lives in which they are allowed to indulge, and Buruma argues that this and the sometimes excessive violence of films, comics and television programmes makes it possible for people to live in quiet and apparently uneventful harmony in the real world. Essentially, his thesis is that Japanese men (and women) are able to maintain the *tatemae* of harmonious existence with their friends, relatives and colleagues, partly because of the many possibilities for vicarious and fantasy violence and eroticism: 'What one sees on the screen, on stage or in the comic books, is usually precisely the reverse of normal behaviour' (1985:225).

In fact, many of the films made by younger directors, along with the works of a new generation of writers, have sought to reject the lifestyle that this thesis implies. They tend to portray it as characterised by an overwhelming emptiness, and seek an alternative identity through a long and sometimes tedious process of self-examination and consideration of 'other' possibilities. A good analysis of this process in Japanese cinema, with excellent examples and discussions of films and their directors, is to be found in an article by Aaron Gerow (2002), who also illustrates the contemporary interest in diversity within Japanese society itself. He lists many recent films about the Korean community, for example, as well as films shot in Okinawa (see also Molasky 1999 for Okinawan literature and Roberson 2001 for music). Murakami's *Norwegian Wood* (2000) is an example of a novel that portrays the emptiness of a nightlife that is even seen as rather conservative.

From the point of view of the women who work in the 'water trade', they are often those who have failed in the pursuit of accepted family life. They may be divorced or separated from previous husbands, or they may never have married. They often have children whom they must bring up alone, and the work they do in the evenings will bring in a good income. Working as a hostess in a bar or nightclub, without any commitment to providing further sexual services, pays quite well, and if a woman can raise the capital to set up her own bar, she may then establish the security of a regular clientele. One woman of my acquaintance gave up her job as a bank clerk to run a bar when her husband, who had also been in the bank, fell too ill to work. This way she was better able to make ends meet. Other women are the regular mistresses of men who help them financially, and they maintain long-term relations in the way described above.

At the aristocratic end of the scale, there are women who devote their lives to this world of entertainment, and they may have started training even before they reached puberty. These are the *geisha*, who have become well known in the wider world through the best-selling novel by Arthur Golden (1998). An anthropological account of the lives of some of the most accomplished Kyoto *geisha* is to be found in a book by Liza Crihfield Dalby (1983), who carried out research by training as a *geisha* herself for a period. She describes with great clarity and insight the lives of these artists, the relations between them and the professional way in which they carry out their work. A more recent study was made by Leslie Downer (2000), who also became quite close to several practising *geisha*, and Gaye Rowley's translation of the autobiography of a *geisha* (Masuda 2003), reveals some of the less glamorous background to this life.

Each *geisha* is highly accomplished in particular skills such as playing the *koto*, dancing or singing, but they all train for years in the more general arts of caring for their guests (or, strictly speaking, clients). Nothing is left to chance, and they learn how to walk gracefully, how to sit, stand up, pass through a door, how to listen, how to talk, how to laugh and even how to cry when the occasion demands. They also learn how to serve drinks and all manner of snacks and food, although there are maids in the best establishments who prepare the refreshments and carry them to the guest room. Nowadays, there are very few real *geisha* left in Japan, and they are extremely expensive to hire. Thus the women who are involved tend to mix with an elite of Japanese men, and their own status in society reflects to some extent these associations.

Within particular teahouses, to which *geisha* become attached when they decide to take up such a career, the women organise themselves hierarchically in relations again based on the family model of mother/daughter or younger and older sisters. Each teahouse has a 'mother' who takes ultimate responsibility for her charges, and each individual *geisha* is linked to a particular senior or 'elder sister', who helps with her training. Eventually she, too, will have a junior beneath her to whom she is expected to pass on her skills. These relationships are again long term, and they illustrate the inverted V model quite well. Since less highly trained entertainers, such as hostesses, have modelled themselves to some extent on the *geisha* image, this could also help to explain the wider use of the term *mama-san*, although there is undoubtedly something in the psychological explanations as well. Buruma (1985) traces the power of the motherly image back to the early Japanese mythology of Amaterasu Omikami and her relations.

Although the entertainment industry may be seen as a source of employment for women, who may well have chosen to be there and be earning well, it also has a less respectable past reputation. In times of economic hardship, it has been a well-known practice for a struggling family to 'sell' a daughter to a brothel, or *geisha* house, in order to feed the rest of the family. An outright payment would be made which would represent several years of training and service for their daughter who would live in the house, but be literally expected to pay off her own debt to the brothel through her work. The film *Street of Shame* is a depiction of just such a brothel during the period of political discussions about legislation to terminate these practices, and it portrays the variety of ways in which women involved came to terms (or failed to come to terms) with their situation.

Nightlife for young people in Japan these days is a far cry from these ancient worlds, however, and the work of anthropologist Ian Condry (2000, 2001) provides an excellent insight into establishments that open only when the businessmen are rolling home, and close as they set off for work.

Japanese hip-hop music provides the focus for his research, and his argument reiterates the idea that copying an outside art form, in this case the rap music of the black American ghettos, by no means precludes a subsequent creativity in music, dance and the culture that goes with them. This is masked somewhat by the clothes and even dreadlocks chosen by participants, but young people in turn-of-the-century Japan sport a huge variety of hair-styles and colour, and their apparel also expresses an apparently borderless range of inspiration and influence. Stevens and Hosokawa (2001) is another anthropological study that examines contemporary music in Japan, this time as represented on television, and Atkins (2002) is a good source on jazz in Japan.

TRIPS AND TOURISM

Another very popular use of leisure time in Japan is the taking of trips of one sort or another. The country is peppered with attractions which range from the natural beauty of the landscape, often culturally elaborated with religious edifices or depicted in enclosed and miniature form in gardens, through artificially maintained traditional villages and wildlife sanctuaries, to the ultimate expressions of technological achievement such as those displayed at Disneyland and Universal Studios Japan. There is also an extensive and efficient transport network. Planes, trains and ferry boats are usually more reliable over long distances than vehicles that use the over-burdened roads, but all forms of transport are well patronised, and full to capacity over national holidays. Japanese tourists are also a common sight abroad, and this propensity for travel, which now incorporates most countries of the world, has made a strong contribution to the new global worldview briefly discussed in Chapter 1.

Activities are also varied. For the young and fit, skiing, surfing and diving are popular, and they also enjoy visits to the abundant hot springs, still a favourite choice for their grandparents. We have already seen that aspiring managers may choose to spend time playing golf together, others may choose a more unstructured walk in open country. For these, sightseeing may be enough incentive to make a trip, others may travel to the countryside to engage in hunting or fishing, as mentioned in Chapter 4. Pilgrimage to specific shrines or temples continue an ancient reason for travel, and sometimes a whole itinerary is fixed by the preferred order of visit. We have already discussed visits to quaint country towns, preserved ancient villages and other sites of a lost Japan, and several anthropologists have observed this theme of nostalgia. Nelson Graburn (1995) is one source on the subject.

In my study of Japanese theme parks that depict foreign countries as well as old Japanese villages and historical sites, I found that a strong motivation was the pursuit of something new, something unusual to delight and amuse. Those who have the wherewithal may travel abroad, but others can have a pretty good day out by visiting a re-creation of a certain cultural theme with far less time and hassle. Some parks try to give a taste of whole countries like Germany, Spain and Holland, others focus on a single writer or a specific story for their theme. In Hokkaido, there are parks that focus on Hans Christian Anderson and the Brothers Grimm, another tried to recreate the surroundings experienced by Anne of Green Gables. In Tōhoku, a Swiss Park chose Heidi for their theme, and in the south of Chiba prefecture, a

Figure 10.2 A model of the young William Shakespeare, his son Hamnet on his knee, sits at the window of the reconstruction of his birthplace in a small town in Japan – said to be dreaming of his future life as he gazes down the road to London.

park at Maruyama has even built a reconstruction of the birthplace of William Shakespeare as a tourist attraction.

These parks usually also offer appropriate shows, such as theatre, dance and cultural festivals, as well as local food and drink to try and an abundance of souvenir shops. Some have rides, building on the local theme, and clearly a strong influence in their creation was the popularity of Tokyo Disneyland, which offers a mini holiday in America as well as all the play. An ethnographic study of this world-class theme park by Aviad Raz (1999) also argues against the idea that this park infiltrated a huge new influx of American culture into Japan. Instead he shows how it has been modified specifically to appeal to its Japanese customers and the way that it draws on the characteristics of previous Japanese pleasure parks in the reconstruction of some of its attractions. Likewise, Universal Studios Japan, features films that were already popular amongst Japanese potential visitors, and depicts a kind of 1950s America that recreates the setting of some of the classic favourites. Ohnuki-Tierney's (1997) study on the Japanese version of McDonald's makes a similar point.

Trips abroad are also very often made around specific objectives such as tracking down the birthplace of famous writers, or locating the sites seen in some favourite films or novels. The keepers of the tiny cottage where Beatrix Potter was born in the Lake District in England have had to ask Japanese tourists to stay away, so numerous did they become, and in the Yorkshire Moors around the home of the Bröntes signposts have been erected in Japanese. Golf in Scotland has become so popular with Japanese visitors that some of the older hotels have been bought up by Japanese tourist companies to accommodate them in the style they expect. Travellers with more time on their hands may sign up for courses in foreign skills, and the anthropologist Merry White carried out fieldwork in Italy with Japanese chefs, housewives and others who wanted to acquire 'authentic' Italian culinary skills. For young people, India and Nepal are popular destinations, where trekking in the hills may be combined with learning something of other Asian peoples.

The length of trips is very variable, and while groups such as these might manage several weeks abroad together, the majority of Japanese people seem happy to take very short trips away from their regular routines. Two or three nights away is popular, and these are usually described as 'three days and two nights', or 'four days and three nights', with tour operators packing as much as possible into the available time. Real cultural diversity may again be sought for these trips, and Okinawa is a popular location, where local music may be a focus of the visit, alongside the sunshine and sea sports. Other locations within Asia have also become popular in recent years, and Bali is (or was) a favoured destination, though visits are made to a multitude of other destinations for their local cultural features as well as the chance to get away.

Day trips are also common and even shorter outings to view some local natural feature are well-known pastimes. One of the most ancient and famous of these is cherry-blossom viewing in the early spring, and Emiko Ohnuki-Tierney (1998) has analysed some of the meaning and symbolism of such an outing, which invariably also involves the consumption of alcohol – traditionally rice wine – with a group of friends. People go out to view plum blossom, fiery summer blooms and autumn leaves as well, but nothing is quite as Japanese as that delicate, ephemeral cherry blossom!

An even shorter trip away might be to visit one of the ubiquitous 'love hotels' found in Japan, and here the cost of the stay can be limited to a matter of hours. Fantasy and cultural diversity again form popular themes, and the buildings sometimes stand out in the landscape for their extraordinary features. Fairytale castles provide one model, a variety of exotic architecture another, and I have even seen whole buildings devoted to the depiction of a huge wild animal. Inside, there are photographs of the décor of the various rooms on offer at the time, and these may provide a coordinated theme of a particular country, for example, with murals and even television film of the scenery, accompanied by mood-making local music. Because of the limited size of some family homes, it is said that these facilities may even be used by married couples seeking privacy, but the clientele are not vetted before they are sold a room.

Companions for trips are in general rather varied. Travel with peers is popular, and since the annual class outings start at kindergarten in Japan, most people grow up with the experience. School classes visit sites of historical importance, as well as locations known for fun and play, and former classmates may travel together later in life. Age-mate groups often travel together from my area of research in Kyushu, and this probably dates back at least to the nationally common custom of groups saving to send one or two of their members to the shrine of Amaterasu at Ise. Nowadays hot springs seem to be more popular, and even some foreign trips, but most of the villagers have also been to Ise. Company employees, who are said rarely to take all the holidays to which they are entitled, do spend time away together, as we have seen, perhaps at the company's own accommodation, or visiting other parts of Asia known for their night life.

The family holiday is becoming more popular, particularly to the seaside, but in general such trips tend to be much shorter than the 'vacations' which are common in other parts of the world. Nor will it usually involve more than the nuclear parent–children group. Two nights away is perhaps typical, and the father of the family will be itchy to get back to work after what he may well describe as 'family duty'. Families also go out on day trips from time to time, Sundays and national holidays being particularly popular, and theme parks are good destinations for these. They also travel together to visit the parents' own family homes at New Year or the *Bon* summer festival. Otherwise individual members of the family tend to travel with their own peers or contemporaries. The lone traveller used to be rather rare, except perhaps for young people travelling abroad, but even these seem to have become more common in the past few years.

Members of the family are not forgotten, however, and one of the main purposes of travel seems to be the purchase of a large number of presents to take back to those who remain behind. For a major trip, it has been customary for friends and neighbours to organise a send-off with a gift of money, and these well wishers are also remembered when the presents are purchased. It is also important to bring back souvenirs of the trip, and most tourist resorts have developed their own specialities to cater to these two needs. These *miyage* may be bought in airports and stations, and major cities such as Tokyo sport a selection from different regions for those who left their purchases too late! In this practice, the traveller may still be seen as going away in part as a representative of his or her *uchi* group.

Another related *sine qua non* of the venture is to record all the highlights of the trip in photographic record (see Figure 10.3). For this purpose, Japanese

Figure 10.3 The Imperial Palace, which occupies a large area of land in the centre of Tokyo, forms a popular backdrop for photographs of groups visiting the city.

tourists are always willing to help out total strangers by taking photographs for them, because the required picture involves the whole travel group posing together in front of each major site or famous place visited. There is apparently no need to record the informal moments, and albums are really only interesting if one knows the people, partly because the site itself is often largely obscured by the group lined up in front of it. The chief object of the exercise seems to be to provide 'proof' that one has been to the places involved, and generally to legitimise the event. Many famous sites also have stamps that one can collect as further 'proof' of one's visits.

CONCLUSION

This chapter has introduced a vast range of activities under the broad headings of arts, entertainment and leisure, and there are many we have neglected altogether. We have, however, again identified some of the principles outlined in previous chapters: the familiar distinction between *uchi* and *soto*, the principles of hierarchical relations that characterise the *ie*, among other things, and the importance of ritual. Japan uses arts and customary forms of entertainment to impress the outside world, and it is in these same arts and accomplishments that individual Japanese often find satisfaction and spiritual strength. It is through different worlds of art and popular culture, too, that ideas are introduced from outside, reinvented and dispatched again, in some cases to become global household names. And it is undoubtedly through exchanges such as these that Japan takes a deserved place among contributors to the new cyberworld of computer games and digital gadgets. In the next chapter we turn to an earlier attempt on Japan's part to join a wider community.

REFERENCES AND FURTHER READING

Allison, Anne, *Nightwork: Sexuality, Pleasure, and Corporate Masculinity in a Tokyo Hostess Club* (University of Chicago Press, Chicago and London, 1994)

Anderson, Jennifer L., *Japanese Tea Ritual* (State University of New York Press, Albany, 1991)

Atkins, A. Taylor, *Blue Nippon: Authenticating Jazz in Japan* (Duke University Press, Durham NC and London, 2002)

Barrett, Gregory, *Archetypes in Japanese Film* (Associated University Presses, London and Toronto, 1989)

Ben-Ari, Eyal, 'Posing, Posturing and Photographic Presences: A Rite of Passage in a Japanese Commuter Village', *Man* (n.s.), 26 (1991), pp. 87–104

Ben-Ari, Eyal, 'Golf, Organization and "Body Projects": Japanese Business Executives in Singapore', in Sepp Linhart and Sabine Frühstück, *The Culture of Japan as Seen through its Leisure* (State University of New York Press, New York, 1998), pp. 139–61

Bornoff, Nick, *The Pink Samurai: The Pursuit and Politics of Sex in Japan* (Grafton, 1991)

Brandon, James R., *Nō and Kyōgen in the Contemporary World* (University of Hawaii Press, Honolulu, 1997)

Brown, Steven, *Theatricalities of Power: The Cultural Politics of Noh* (Stanford University Press, Stanford, CA, 2001)

Buruma, Ian, *A Japanese Mirror* (Penguin Books, Harmondsworth, 1985)

Coaldrake, A. Kimi, *Women's Gidayū and the Japanese Theatre Tradition* (Routledge, London, 1997)

Coaldrake, William H., *The Way of the Carpenter* (Weatherhill, New York and Tokyo, 1990)

Condry, Ian, 'The Social Production of Difference: Imitation and Authenticity in Japanese Rap Music', in Uta Poiger and Heide Fehrenbach (eds), *Transactions, Transgressions, Transformations: American Culture in Western Europe and Japan* (Berghahn Books, Oxford and New York, 2000), pp. 166–84

——'Japanese Hip-Hop and the Globalization of Popular Culture', in George Gmelch and Walter Zenner (eds), *Urban Life: Readings in the Anthropology of the City* (Waveland Press, Prospect Heights, IL, 2001), pp. 357–87

Cox, Rupert, *The Zen Arts: An Anthropological Study of the Culture of Aesthetic Form in Japan* (RoutledgeCurzon, London, 2002)

Dalby, Liza Crihfield, *Geisha* (University of California Press, Berkeley, 1983, with a new preface, 1998)

Dalla Chiesa, Simone, 'When the Goal is Not a Goal: Japanese School Football Players Working Hard at their Game', in Joy Hendry and Massimo Raveri (eds), *Japan at Play: The Ludic and the Logic of Power* (Routledge, London, 2002), pp. 186–98

Downer, Leslie, *Geisha: The Secret History of a Vanishing World* (Headline, London, 2000)

Gerow, Aaron, 'Recognising "Others" in a New Japanese Cinema', *The Japan Foundation Newsletter*, XXIX, 2 (2002), pp. 1–6

Graburn, Nelson, 'The Past and Present in Japan: Nostalgia and Neo-Traditionalism in Contemporary Japanese Domestic Tourism', in Richard Butler and Douglas Pearce (eds), *Change in Tourism: People, Places, Processes* (Routledge, London, 1995)

Hall, John Whitney and Richard K. Beardsley, *Twelve Doors to Japan* (McGraw Hill, New York, 1965), Chapters 5 and 6

Hayakawa Masao, *The Garden Art of Japan* (Weatherhill, New York and Heibonsha, Tokyo, 1973)

Hendry, Joy, *The Orient Strikes Back: A Global View of Cultural Display* (Berg, Oxford, 2000)

Hendry, Joy and Massimo Raveri (eds), *Japan at Play: The Ludic and the Logic of Power* (Routledge, London, 2002)

Hori, G. Victor Sogen, 'Teaching and Learning in the Rinzai Zen Monastery', *Journal of Japanese Studies*, 20, 1 (1994), pp. 5–35

Horne, John and Wolfram Manzenreiter (eds), *Japan, Korea and the 2002 World Cup* (Routledge, London, 2002)

Hughes, David, 'Japanese "New Folk Songs" Old and New', *Asian Music*, 22, 1 (1991)

Katō, Shūichi, *Form, Style, Tradition: Reflections on Japanese Art and Society* (Kodansha International, Tokyo, 1981)

Kelly, William, 'Blood and Guts in Japanese Professional Baseball', in Sepp Linhart and Sabine Frühstück, *The Culture of Japan as Seen through its Leisure* (State University of New York Press, New York, 1998), pp. 95–111

Kelly, William H., 'Training for Leisure: *Karaoke* and the Seriousness of Play in Japan', in Joy Hendry and Massimo Raveri (eds), *Japan at Play: The Ludic and the Logic of Power* (Routledge, London, 2002), pp. 152–68

Kinsella, Sharon, *Adult Manga: Culture and Power in Contemporary Japanese Society* (Curzon, Richmond, Surrey, 2000)

Kondo, Dorinne, 'The Way of Tea: A Symbolic Analysis', *Man*, 20, 2 (1985), pp. 287–306

Linhart, Sepp, 'Sakariba: Zone of "Evaporation" between Work and Home', in Joy Hendry (ed.), *Interpreting Japanese Society: Anthropological Approaches* (Routledge, London, 1998), pp. 231–42

Linhart, Sepp and Sabine Frühstück, *The Culture of Japan as Seen through its Leisure*, (State University of New York Press, New York, 1998)

Lunsing, Wim, '*Kono Sekai* (The Japanese Gay Scene): Communities or Just Playing Around?' in Joy Hendry and Massimo Raveri (eds), *Japan at Play: The Ludic and the Logic of Power* (Routledge, London, 2002), pp. 57–71

McLelland, Mark J., *Male Homosexuality in Modern Japan: Cultural Myths and Social Realities* (Curzon Press, Richmond, Surrey, 2000)

Manzenreiter, Wolfram, 'Time, Space and Money: Cultural Dimensions of the "Pachinko" Games', in Sepp Linhart and Sabine Frühstück, *The Culture of Japan as Seen through its Leisure* (State University of New York Press, New York, 1998), pp. 359–81

Martinez, D.P., *The Worlds of Japanese Popular Culture: Gender, Shifting Boundaries and Global Cultures* (Cambridge University Press, Cambridge, 1998)

Matthew, Robert, *Japanese Science Fiction: A View of a Changing Society* (Routledge, London, 1989)

Moeran, Brian, *Folk Art Potters of Japan: Beyond an Anthropology of Aesthetics* (Curzon, Richmond, Surrey, 1997)

Molasky, Michael, *The American Occupation of Japan and Okinawa: Literature and Memory* (Routledge, London, 1999)

Munroe, Alexandra (ed.), *Scream against Sky* (Harry N. Abrams, New York, 1994)

Nagashima, Nobuhiro, 'Gambling and Changing Japanese Attitudes Toward It', in Sepp Linhart and Sabine Frühstück, *The Culture of Japan as Seen through its Leisure* (State University of New York Press, New York, 1998), pp. 345–58

O'Neill, P.G., 'Organization and Authority in the Traditional Arts', *Modern Asian Studies*, 18, 4 (1984), pp. 631–45

Ohnuki-Tierney, Emiko, 'McDonald's in Japan: Changing Manners and Etiquette', in James L. Watson (ed.), *Golden Arches East: McDonald's in East Asia* (Stanford University Press, Stanford, CA, 1997)

—— 'Cherry Blossoms and the Viewing: A Window onto Japanese Culture', in Sepp Linhart and Sabine Frühstück, *The Culture of Japan as Seen through its Leisure* (State University of New York Press, New York, 1998), pp. 213–36

Powell, Brian, *Japan's Modern Theatre: A Century of Change and Continuity* (Routledge-Curzon, London, 2002)

Powell, Irena, *Writers and Society in Modern Japan* (Macmillan, London, 1983)

Raz, Aviad, *Riding The Black Ship: Japan and Tokyo Disneyland* (Harvard University Press, Cambridge, MA and London, 1999)

Raz, Jacob, *Audience and Actors: A Study of their Interaction in the Japanese Traditional Theatre* (E.J. Brill, Leiden, 1983)

Reader, Ian, 'Dead to the World: Pilgrims in Shikoku', in Ian Reader and Tony Walter (eds), *Pilgrimage in Popular Culture* (Macmillan, London, 1993)

Roberson, James, 'Uchinaa Pop: Place and Identity in Contemporary Okinawan Popular Music', *Critical Asian Studies*, 33, 2 (2001), pp. 211–42

Robertson, Jennifer, *Takarazuka: Sexual Politics and Popular Culture in Modern Japan* (University of California Press, Berkeley, Los Angeles and London, 1998)

Rodriguez del Alisal, Maria-Dolores, 'Ludic Elements in Japanese Attitudes to *Tsukuru*', in Joy Hendry and Massimo Raveri (eds), *Japan at Play: The Ludic and the Logic of Power* (Routledge, London, 2002), pp. 84–98

Singleton, John (ed.), *Learning in Likely Places: Varieties of Apprenticeship in Japan* (Cambridge University Press, Cambridge, 1998)

Smith, Robert J., 'Transmitting Tradition by the Rules: An Anthropological Interpretation of the *Iemoto* System', in John Singleton (ed.), *Learning in Likely Places: Varieties of Apprenticeship in Japan* (Cambridge University Press, Cambridge, 1998), pp. 23–34

Stevens, Carolyn and Shūhei Hosokawa, 'So Close and Yet So Far: Humanizing Celebrity in Japanese Music Variety Show, 1960s–1990s', in Brian Moeran (ed.), *Asian Media Productions* (Curzon, Richmond, Surrey, 2001)

Valentine, James, 'Models of Performance: Space, Time and Social Organisation in Japanese Dance', in Joy Hendry (ed.), *Interpreting Japanese Society: Anthropological Approaches* (Routledge, London, 1998), pp. 259–81

NOVELS AND LIGHTER READING

Golden, Arthur, *Memoirs of a Geisha* (Vintage, London, 1998)

Greenfeld, Karl Taro, *Speed Tribes: Days and Nights With Japan's Next Generation* (HarperCollins, London, 1995)

Ishiguro Kazuo, *An Artist of the Floating World* (Faber & Faber, London, 1985)

Kawabata, Yasunari, *Beauty and Sadness* (Penguin, Harmondsworth, 1979)

Morley, John David, *Pictures from the Water Trade* (Andre Deutsch, London, 1985; Flamingo, London, 1985)

Murakami, Hiroki, trans. Jay Rubin, *Norwegian Wood* (The Harvill Press, London, 2000)

Masuda Sayo, trans. G.G. Rowley, *Autobiography of a Geisha* (Columbia University Press, New York, 2003)

FILMS

Miyamoto Musashi series (Tomu Uchida)

Rikyū (1990 Hiroshi Teshigawara)

Shall We Dance? (1996 Masayuki Suō)

Street of Shame (*Akasen Chitai*) (1956 Kenji Mizoguchi)

Tampopo (1985 Jūzō Itami)

11 Government and the craft of politics

INTRODUCTION

This chapter and the next bring us finally into an area that will seem, superficially at least, very familiar to a Western reader, since Japan's political and legal systems have in the past century been twice modelled on Western prototypes. As outlined in Chapter 1, the Meiji period witnessed the establishment of a bicameral parliamentary system, influenced by Germany, France and England, and, during the Allied Occupation, this system underwent a thorough, American-style 'democratisation' process. The language of politics in Japan is thus easily rendered into English – indeed, the 1947 Constitution was first drafted in English – and Japan plays a recognisable role in international political arenas.

Under the surface, however, Japan still has its own way of doing things, just as any nation does, and it is one of the aims of an anthropological approach to penetrate the deeper levels of operation behind the familiar facade. Unfortunately this is an area which has been rather little studied by anthropologists in Japan, except at the most local level of the community, so we must rely for the wider system on the materials provided by political scientists, who are, of course, by no means unaware of the problem. The work of Arthur Stockwin (1999) and Ian Neary (2002a) has been particularly helpful, as always, and I am indebted to the latter for the idea of using the term 'craft' to characterise the activities of Japanese politicians, though an extension to the less positive 'crafty' would be entirely my own.

We also have available by now a good deal of contextual material for approaching our final two topics. The historical precedents for the present system of government were outlined in Chapter 1, and we have acquired a good deal of information about other areas of Japanese society that offers a framework for the relationships between politicians. This includes ideas of continuity and loyalty presented in Chapters 2 and 10, aspects of early training such as an emphasis on the importance of reciprocity discussed in

Chapter 3, the importance of community seen in Chapter 4, and notions of relative hierarchy explained in some detail in Chapter 6. Some examples of the outcome of governmental deliberations have been discussed as well, in the new policies regarding day care for children and old people, home help facilities and other new initiatives for the encouragement of women into the workplace.

This chapter will open with an outline of the system of government in Japan, describing its institutional components, the principles by which they operate and some recent reforms that have been made. It will then move on to investigate the roles played by its human participants, the way in which they ally themselves with each other for political purposes and the way in which they achieve support. It will also look at the role of the voting public, the extent to which they participate in political activities, the way they make decisions about political matters and the opportunities they have for moving into political arenas. Finally, I will turn to consider some popular political movements including a much-publicised move to develop a stronger 'civil society' in Japan. Judicial matters will be left for the following chapter, which will focus on social control at a more microscopic level.

GOVERNMENT INSTITUTIONS

Despite the role of the imperial line in providing the Japanese people with an identity and a unity, the Emperor himself has no political power. The Constitution declares him a symbol of the state, with duties confined to ceremonial and diplomatic affairs. Like the Queen of England, he opens parliament, attests the appointment of ministers and ambassadors, awards honours and receives foreign royalty and ambassadors. He thus pursues a role not unlike that of most of his predecessors, retaining the dignity of distance from the everyday political affairs of the nation. Members of his immediate family play similar roles. At present, the heir is supposed only to be a male, but the birth of a daughter to the Crown Prince and Princess, after eight years of marriage, has sparked a debate about changing this anyway rather recent rule.

The active government has three branches: legislative, administrative and judiciary. Legislative power is in the hands of the Diet, a parliament composed of a House of Representatives and a House of Councillors, both comprising elected members since the Occupation, when the latter replaced the European-style House of Peers. Administrative power falls to the Cabinet, a body of ministers, headed by the Prime Minister, responsible to the Diet, but supported by a very strong bureaucracy of civil servants. Judicial power is invested in the court system, headed by the Supreme Court. Judges are appointed by the Cabinet, with the exception of the Chief Justice, whose appointment is officially conferred by the Emperor, and the courts have the power to rule on the constitutionality of laws and orders.

The House of Representatives currently has 480 members who serve for a maximum term of four years. Three hundred are elected from single-seat constituencies, with the remaining 180 determined through a system of proportional representation that involves voting for lists prepared by political parties in regional blocks. There are plenary sessions, which are presided over by a speaker to maintain order, and there are also smaller committees. The House of Councillors, the upper house, has 242 members, 146 elected from the prefectures in numbers proportional to their populations, and 96 from a national constituency. They serve for a period of six years, but elections are held every three years for half the seats. Together the houses make laws, raise and spend public money, and designate the Prime Minister. The House of Representatives is more powerful in that it can overrule the House of Councillors under certain circumstances, although bills should usually be approved by both Houses before they become law.

The Prime Minister is chosen from the Diet members by Diet resolution. He is usually the leader of the party with a majority in the House of Representatives, but a leader of a minority party might be chosen to hold together a coalition government as happened in the mid-1990s. The Prime Minister chooses the Cabinet, although it too is ultimately responsible to the overall Diet. Its work includes the administration of the law, the management of internal and external affairs, and the preparation and submission of the budget. In practice, full advantage is taken of the powerful supporting bureaucracy, and many Cabinet decisions may in fact be arrived at prior to meetings, especially in the Conference of Administrative Vice-Ministers, that is the heads of government ministries. However, the number of ministries was slimmed down in January 2001 from 23 to 13, and one of the aims was to redress this balance of power towards elected politicians, particularly the Prime Minister.

Serious dissent within the Cabinet is rare, as decisions are supposed to be made by consensus, and dissent therefore usually leads to resignation or dismissal. However, there is quite a high turnover of ministers, including the Prime Minister, whose average period of office in the post-war period has been only just over two years. This flexibility is an integral part of a system that requires considerable attention to the honouring of reciprocal arrangements, one of the 'crafts' of Japanese politics, enabling the Prime Minister to avail himself of the resources within his party and to reward supporters who helped him to achieve his own position. It has also been an important way of maintaining representation from the different factions that make up the parties in government at any one time, although Jun'ichiro

Figure 11.1 The 'Diet' or Japanese parliament can be seen here through one of the gates of the Imperial Palace. In many ways the originally German system of government operates with heavy Japanese modifications in practice, although the Emperor has no power.

Koizumi, the Prime Minister in power as this edition goes to press, claims to be replacing factional representation with decisions made on merit. As in other walks of life, these factions are ultimately the way in which human relations are ordered, and the balance within and between them forms much of the stuff of politics, so it will be interesting to see how Koizumi's words go beyond the *tatemae* of political rhetoric.

The bureaucratic staff of the ministries maintains a solid, stable base for the day-to-day administration of business, and the personnel represent the elite of the nation's potential, since they are usually recruited from the graduates of the best universities. This is a pattern that was established in

1887 with the introduction of an examination to select the best candidates. In the early modern period, before political parties were established, there was no clear distinction between the higher-ranking bureaucrats and the political leaders who were in charge of decision-making, and even after the parties emerged, many of their leaders were recruited from the bureaucracy. Until the end of the Second World War, too, imperial prerogatives were exercised by the bureaucracy, which became particularly powerful again after party government was abandoned in 1932 and power was shared with the increasingly dominant military regime.

After the war, the Americans removed the armed forces and encouraged the re-establishment of competing political parties, which had been merged into a single pro-government party in 1940. The bureaucracy has nevertheless remained powerful, both in policy formation and in the drafting of legislation. It will be interesting to see how successful the reforms of January 2001 turn out to be since the organisation of the sections of the new ministries looks little different in practice from the old line-up (Neary 2002a:125 has a good diagram). Some have argued that the bureaucracy in Japan forms the central axis of the political system, and that its power actually increased in post-war years. It also still supplies a substantial number of candidates for political office among career bureaucrats who have served their years in the Civil Service as the nature of the hierarchical system that operates here, as elsewhere, finds a majority 'retiring' before they reach 55.

At the local level, there are elected assemblies for the prefectures, cities, towns and 'villages', including Tokyo wards. The mayors and prefectural governors are elected separately, and these tend to have much longer terms of office, often remaining in power for several consecutive four-year periods. The units they head are responsible for a variety of local affairs, including some taxation, although financially they have been very dependent on subsidies and other aid from central government. A move to devolve more power to local government has been part of a recent raft of reforms, however. Ultimately, at the local level of the community, there is still often a fair degree of autonomy, as was described in Chapter 4. This feature of community life has probably been rather persistent throughout several changes at higher levels, and it is no doubt related to the strong *uchi/soto* distinction in Japanese society.

ELECTORAL SYSTEM

Elections were introduced into Japan in 1889, but the franchise was at first limited to a small percentage of men, depending on qualifications of residence and tax assessment. In 1925, universal male suffrage was introduced for adults of 25 and over, but women were only given a vote in 1945, when the voting age was reduced to 20. Until 1945, too, it was only members of the House of Representatives who were elected, and the power of these was quite limited. Now, control of a majority of the seats in this house gives a party virtual control over the legislative and administrative branches of government, since the leader of the party in power usually becomes Prime Minister.

Elections for the House of Representatives are thus the most significant nationally, and they are also the ones that have over the years engendered the most controversy. Until a measure of political reform in 1994, each constituency returned between three and five members, depending on its size. Everyone had one non-transferable vote, and the designated number of candidates who won the most votes were elected. One of the results of this system was that in districts with a dense population more votes were required for the election of one candidate than in districts with a sparse population. An extreme example of this disparity was to compare Chiba district 4, which in the 1983 election required an average of 499,763 votes to gain a seat, with Hyogo district 5, which required only 110,051. One vote in Hyogo 5 was thus equivalent to more than four votes in Chiba 4. In fact, the election was declared unconstitutional by the Supreme Court because of this disparity, as several previous elections had been.

Prior to the 1986 election, eight new seats were created in the most populous districts, and seven removed from the least dense, but the coalition government elected in 1993 put through a more radical new system. This involved electing 300 of the members of the House of Representatives from single-seat constituencies and 200 from a national system with eleven districts, each with a slate of members proportional to the population. In 2000, the number of seats chosen by proportional representation was reduced to 180. Each voter is entitled to choose both an individual and a party, and politicians may thus have two chances to gain a seat. Even this system was something of a compromise, necessary to maintain the balance of power between the coalition parties, which of course have views related to their own interests, and it may still be modified further.

Elections for the House of Councillors are less controversial but there have been reforms here too. Most prefectures are large and therefore include both urban and rural areas, and the number of representatives is proportional to the population, but there has still been a severe discrepancy in the value of a vote between different prefectures. The national constituency is evidently more representative. In the 1983 election, a system of proportional representation was introduced where the voters were asked to select a candidate for the prefecture and a party for the national constituency. However, the latter was reformed again in 2001, so that voters may now choose either a party or a candidate in the national constituency. At the same time, the overall number of seats was reduced by 10, 6 in the prefectures and 4 on the national slate. Probably because the candidates are less likely to be locally known figures than for the House of Representatives, elections generate rather less excitement, but the House of Councillors also ultimately has less power.

Local elections, on the other hand, are capable of inspiring more enthusiasm. Candidates are likely to be influential local figures, and the abundance of personal connections that they build up usually ensures a reasonable level of support. In rural areas, in particular, there is often most interest in local elections since these relate more apparently to the real world of everyday life experienced by the voters. It also reflects a general emphasis in Japanese society on face-to-face interaction. The figures for electoral participation have also generally borne out this emphasis on local interest, especially in rural areas.

Campaigning is rather severely restricted, however. Activities may not begin until one month before the election, and there is an upper limit on the amount of money to be spent, the number of personnel who may be involved, the number of speeches which may be made, and the advertising and posters which may be put up. House calls and leaflets are prohibited. Instead the candidates and their supporters drive around the constituency in heavily decorated vehicles, topped with loud speakers, literally allowing their pleas for votes to echo around the district. From time to time, they stop and make speeches, sometimes setting up quite a display to attract attention before they start. These speeches tend to be very formal and uninformative, however, and it doesn't really seem to matter if they can't be heard. In rural areas, they stop beside fields and on hillsides, where their voices are carried off on the wind, but they ensure that the names on their cars are written large enough for the farmers to read.

Ultimately, the campaign probably plays only a minor part in attracting votes, although it may ensure that people have the appropriate names firmly in their heads when they go to the polls and they have to write the name of the candidate on the ballot paper. Politicians use different methods to ensure their support, and the voters use other criteria to make decisions about whom to support, but these factors will be considered in later sections. First, it is necessary to explain the party system in Japan.

THE PARTIES AND SOME RECENT REALIGNMENT

Political parties have existed in Japan since 1874, although their names and the aims they represent have undergone many changes since that time, and there have been a total approaching 200. They provide an excellent example of an amalgamation of imported and Japanese principles of formation. The parties themselves may be described for the ideologies they espouse, and their activities may be described in terms of their pursuit or modification of those aims. Likewise, the behaviour of the politicians and other members of the parties may be interpreted in terms of their own personal development of ideals and principles. At the same time, political parties may also be seen as rather loose amalgamations of factions, in practice hierarchical groups formed along the lines described in Chapter 6, and the fission and fusion that occurs within and between them is one of the reasons why there have been so many.

To start with the factions, politicians and their supporters may be described as being formed into groups based on links of personal allegiance. An aspiring politician thus finds one of the best courses of action is to seek alignment with an established politician and thereby become part of the wider group to which he (or she) belongs. The senior politician will then help the younger one indefinitely in exchange for support and unfailing loyalty. A series of dyadic relations of this sort ensures a solid base of support for any particular politician, who will in turn have similar relations with even more established politicians higher up the pyramid. These, in turn, can draw on an increasingly broad support group the higher up they go.

As Nakane (1973, see Chapter 6) pointed out, however, problems arise when a person at the peak of the pyramid resigns. Unless there is a clear method of choosing a successor, this leads to competition between the most immediate inferiors. It is at this stage that the group may split into factions headed by different members of the secondary level, and this is indeed what happens with political groups. On the other hand, political strength requires greater numbers, so groups with different leaders will align themselves into a coalition in pursuit of this strength. Political parties in Japan are thus often made up of such coalitions, and while some such alliances and splits are contained within a party, others will be serious or ideological enough to engender new parties. A spate of these emerged in the climate of political unrest that led up to the election in 1993, and indeed, has continued to characterise much of the 1990s and the turn of the millennium.

Until that time, there had been a clear split between the right and left in Japanese politics, and the right had maintained power since 1948, although the overall majority had risen and fallen over the years. The largest right-wing party, the Liberal Democratic Party (LDP), represents an alliance forged in 1955 between the previous Liberal and Democratic (or Progressive) Parties, largely in response to a similar alliance in their major left-wing opposition, the Japan Socialist Party (JSP). At that time, the only other left-wing party was the Japan Communist Party (JCP), but since then there have been various quite major new realignments. Another influential party is the *Kōmeitō*, or 'Clean Government Party', a middle-of-the-road group spawned by the 'new' religious movement Sōka Gakkai, and it has continued to play an important role in coalitions of the major power groups during the restructuring of the last decade of the twentieth century.

The Liberal Democratic Party, which actually only briefly lost its hegemony in 1993, is a 'catch-all' party, deriving its support from business, agriculturalists, professionals and some religious groups. Its parliamentary members are drawn from local politicians, business people, former secretaries and the family of Diet members, and another substantial proportion of them, including women, are those bureaucrats who move into politics after a career in one of the ministries. There are also smaller numbers of professional people, journalists and lawyers. Most of them have university degrees, many graduating from the prestigious Tokyo University. Their average age had been high, however, and in the years preceding the defeat there was a growing division between the die-hard members of the old school and younger politicians who were advocating reform. Except for elections, most of the party's business was run by professional politicians, who chose a president every two years. He became Prime Minister, but as one of his chief roles was maintaining the support of leaders of factions other than his own, he made as many decisions as possible in committees, and party policies tended to be rather vague and flexible, usually the result of compromise.

In the early 1990s, a series of scandals involving prime ministers, and a failed attempt at electoral reform, brought matters to a head, and three new parties were spawned from this larger, somewhat amorphous amalgamation of groups in the space of just over a year. These defections were enough to bring down the LDP, as had been calculated, and in the election that followed a coalition was formed with other opposition parties. Winds of change were in the air, and much reform was sought including anti-corruption legislation, electoral reorganisation, financial and industrial deregulation, and more power to local government. The new arrangement was popular, but the cabinet of representatives included several with little experience of office, and this gave bureaucrats an edge that probably slowed up the process of reform and allowed the LDP to retrench.

An interesting part of the alliance came from the Japan Socialist Party (JSP), for long a major party of opposition, but at that time with dwindling support. Like the LDP, it had to contain as many hues as it had factions over the years, and it also experienced trouble maintaining unity and strong leadership. Its major financial support came from the General Council of Labour Unions (*Sōhyō*), and many parliamentary members were former union leaders, but as we have already seen union activity is declining. Other members rose through local government, and again, a substantial proportion were university educated. The party had long passed its heyday of strength, but its election in 1986 of Takako Doi, the first female party leader in Japan, had a great revitalising effect, and in 1989 she led her party to success in the Upper House elections and the following year gained 50 new seats in the Lower House.

Ironically in the 1993 election that brought down the LDP, the JSP lost half its seats, but by agreeing to support the mixed new coalition, it gained 5 seats in the Cabinet and came into executive power for the first time since 1948. More was to come, though it proved to be a swan-song. The next few months witnessed bickering and realignment among the coalition parties as they tried to institute the reform, and a serious threat to create yet another new 'Renovation' party that would exclude the JSP. This caused them to move their alliance over to their former rivals, the diminished LDP, which brought the big party leaders back into the Cabinet only 11 months after they had lost power, but with Tomiichi Murayama, then the leader of the JSP, as Prime Minister. This apparent sacrifice of ideology for the sake of power proved too much for the supporters of the JSP, however, and after an albeit unfortunate 18 months that included the Kobe earthquake and the Aum sarin gas attack, Murayama lost both his own power and that of his party.

Actually, their main left-wing rivals, the Democratic Socialist Party (DSP), founded by a substantial wing of the JSP in 1960, had sometimes allied itself with the LDP on particular issues, especially at the level of local government, and the latest main opposition party is now much more centrist. It would be confusing here to go into all the different parties that were created, aligned and realigned in the last few years of the twentieth century, but as the new century gets underway, Japan has an uncannily familiar scenario. Again there is a Liberal Democratic Party that holds a majority in the House of Representatives, though it still has to negotiate power in the House of Councillors. The main opposition party is now called the Democratic Party of Japan (DPJ) and it comprises former members of the JSP as well as the DSP, one of the new groups mentioned above, and others seeking change such as greater transparency in government.

Much of the promised reform has taken place, however, and the success of Takako Doi has been followed by the entrance of several other women into prominent positions in various political parties. The LDP began to appoint women to the Cabinet as well, and Koizumi, the Prime Minister as this book goes to press, went into power with no fewer than five, also promising much reform. He was for a while very popular, though his less than harmonious relationship with his first female foreign minister, also popular Makiko Tanaka, began to test his support. Koizumi has done very well for his party considering how disillusioned the Japanese electorate currently is with the failure of its government to resolve the economic situation. Many are also disappointed with Japan's agreement to change its legislation and allow military support for America's aggressive incursions in the Middle East and Central Asia.

POLITICIANS AND THEIR PATHS TO SUCCESS

It was noted above that the election campaign itself probably plays only a minor part in attracting votes, and this section returns to the question of how politicians achieve support when they stand for election. There are, of course, several roads to success, and we cannot hope to cover all the various possibilities, but we can look at some of the likely paths. In a country which values long-term personal allegiance, it is perhaps only to be expected that the accumulation of support is unlikely to be achieved overnight.

In rural and provincial areas, in particular, people who become politicians tend to be well-known figures in the area. They often start their political careers in the local assembly, but before they enter politics at all, they have usually built up a reputation as persons of some considerable status in the community. This status is achieved in various ways. In the past, an important component was good local family connections, and a newcomer to the district would have little chance of political success. Nowadays, education can to some extent compensate for a lack of 'breeding', and a recent governor of Nagano – the prefecture that hosted the Winter Olympics in 1998 – Yasuo Tanaka, came as an outsider to politics, but had won an award for a nationally acclaimed novel while a student at a prestigious university. He had also been an active volunteer in the aftermath of the Kobe earthquake, but an aspiring politician needs also to show some concern for community matters.

Typically, a businessman or woman will begin by allocating funds to various needy local causes, and will start also to sit on the committees of local organisations. These may be economically important, such as the local Chamber of Commerce, or they may be less directly related to business, such as the PTA or shrine wardens' organisations. Important projects in the area would be targets for their attention, and a few splendid achievements would certainly ensure long-term note. A farmer/politician in the area of

Kyushu where I worked had initiated a huge project to excavate a vast area of hillside and convert it into tea fields, parcels of which were purchased on easy terms by many of the local farmers. Their enhanced standard of living, as the tea crops began to bring in a profit, ensured their political support for this innovator for many years to come.

In the same way, members of all the groups and organisations supported by this local leader would know and trust him. Moreover, in a Japanese context, they would feel obligated to him for his service to their interests. In return for his benevolence, they would expect to express their loyalty, and in the absence of any stronger loyalties, they would be likely to vote for him were he to stand for election. In many parts of Japan, this personal allegiance is still much stronger than party issues, and large support groups have been known to maintain their loyalty despite a change of party by their leader. The politician, for his (or her) part, gives time and resources to as many support groups as he (or she) can afford. He (or she) attracts loyalty by dispensing benevolence and material benefits, and by belonging to as many *uchi* groups as he (or she) can.

At the level of local elections, candidates do not stand for particular constituencies, but as part of a multi-member slate to serve the city, town or village at large. They are usually supported by the area in which they live, however, even if only for pragmatic reasons of self-interest, and neighbours would probably only vote elsewhere if they had a relative running who lived in a different district. When a politician comes to stand for the Diet, however, it is necessary to draw on a larger circle of connections, and experience in local politics may stand him (or her) in good stead. With time, and political advancement, an individual politician will probably have less and less time for direct participation in local events, and it is here that he (or she) can make use of younger aspiring politicians to help out. A wise national politician retains a solid base of support of this kind while pursuing a career at national level.

In urban areas, where the sheer density and variety of population makes it difficult to build up personal allegiances of the kind found in rural and provincial areas, the 'supporters' club' or 'personal support group' (*kōenkai*) has become an institution, although they are found in rural areas too. Its aims are to foster and nurture support for a particular politician, to run the election campaigns and to deal with the press, the police and the general public. It will also organise 'surgeries' when the politician is in the locality. For a successful Diet member, this organisation may have busy branches throughout the constituency, each with local subordinate politicians as officials. In some cases, these activities have been so successfully organised that the system has been called a 'political machine'.

By now, our individual politician has moved well into the area of the inverted V model, described in Chapter 6. He has not arrived there without incurring a number of debts and obligations, however, and he will have continuing commitments to his seniors and juniors throughout his political life. This is an important principle to understand about Japanese politics, because there is a great deal of reciprocal exchange involved, and this has sometimes been described in critical terms by Western observers. Politicians are also usually personally associated with a variety of interest groups on whose votes they can count, but in return they must respond to their requests, when necessary. Indeed, success in the polls depends on the maintenance of such support, as may the financial backing of an election campaign. It is when arrangements such as these stray across the ever-shifting boundaries of behaviour regarded as unacceptable in a 'civilised' society that accusations of corruption become another effective tool in the political craftsman's bag.

Political leadership in Japan thus depends less on oratorical skills and a charismatic personality than on maintaining strong links of personal allegiance and a reputation for loyalty and sincerity. It depends on length of service, connections with sources of funds and an ability to deal diplomatically and effectively with any number of different demands and requests. As one rises higher in the ranks, it also depends on possessing the skill to maintain harmony among one's subordinates, who may be pressing for their own success. A politician must try to share his largesse with equanimity, and the role of the Prime Minister is, of course, paramount in this respect.

The conflicts between the traditional Japanese side of the game, and the imported rules by which it is ostensibly played, were harshly illustrated in the Lockheed scandal. Prime Minister Kakuei Tanaka was imprisoned for falling foul of the law in an international deal, but he never lost his support groups, even when he was paralysed by a stroke. His daughter, Makiko, is the same politician who became foreign minister and fell out with Koizumi. Since that time, there have been many more financial scandals, some with sexual innuendoes, and these have increasingly been shocking to Japanese voters as well as to foreign commentators. Indeed, it was in the wake of one of these that the spate of new parties was formed in 1992.

The reader will have noticed that the male pronoun has been mostly used throughout this section, though sometimes with the female one in brackets. This was intentional, for women have only recently begun to enter the usual male paths through politics in Japan. There are some female political leaders, and their numbers are increasing. Indeed Koizumi appointed five women to his first cabinet, as we have seen, and he has now had two female foreign ministers. They are rarely able to build up the kind of support network that a man can, however, and they tend to come into the system in different ways. They may, for example, simply inherit the support group of a deceased or incapacitated husband, father or brother. This is not out of keeping with the old *ie* principles of replacement by other members of the house, and women have sometimes been very successful in this way.

Women have for long been active members of *kōenkai*, particularly if their husbands or fathers are involved. They have usually played supporting roles, however, and may see their own ambitions as reflections of those of the men they support. Women who are politically active in their own right have until recently had more success in left-wing parties, as the election of a woman as leader of the JSP has shown, although the JCP is perhaps even more open to advancement for women. Susan Pharr's (1981) now rather dated book was a good discussion of political women in a variety of arenas, from student members of the Red Army to wives who devote their lives to their husbands' political careers. Leblanc (1999) is more up to date. A few politicians, both men and women, first achieve fame and success in a completely different field, such as television or novel writing, as we saw above, and then use their names to attract votes. This type of arrangement is more common in urban areas, where there is less likelihood of a locally known person accumulating votes.

POPULAR PARTICIPATION IN POLITICS

A corollary of the system of allegiances described above is that the voting behaviour of individuals is often determined not by personal choice, but by membership in some *uchi* group which demands loyalty. In the farming area where I worked, for example, local elections commanded support on kin or residential lines, and for national elections, decisions tended to be made according to occupational allegiances. Farmers have on the whole felt that the LDP represented their interests, and if a local candidate showed some personal interest in one of the agricultural or horticultural specialist groups, then that faction is probably chosen. However, proximity of residence, or some other long-term relationship might be a closer link. In any case, the community otherwise takes little interest in the affairs of national politics.

These principles operate in similar ways for people in many different walks of life, and anthropologists have often referred only briefly to national politics in a community study on the grounds that little interest is shown. One's vote tends to be determined by one's position in society: one's occupational group, one's place of residence and one's personal and group allegiances. For those who become more actively involved in party politics, their hands are even more tied. They become part of the base of support and the complicated series of exchanges, so not only their own vote but as many others as they can command become tied to the system they have joined.

This is not the end of political participation, however, and this chapter would be incomplete without a consideration of informal local political activity. For in many areas of Japanese life, people who perceive a need will band together with others who share their perception and take direct action of their own. This may or may not ultimately involve the lobbying of professional politicians. Sometimes people are able to solve their own problems at a local level, and this is in keeping with the general autonomy associated with the smallest political units. Alternatively, the people concerned will become one of the interest groups on whom a politician, who might help them achieve their goals, would be able to count for future support, and they have allocated their vote in an effective way. There are also an increasing number of non-governmental and non-profit organisations in Japan which form part of the recent movement to strengthen 'civil society' that has been mentioned in previous chapters.

Some of the most effective political movements have been those of the minority groups already discussed in Chapter 6, where we saw, for example, that the 'special measures' achieved by the Buraku Liberation League have been so successful that they have been dropped to avoid further discrimination. The Korean community has been another group active in seeking treatment equal to that of ordinary Japanese citizens. They have managed to get rid of a discriminatory law that obliged them to register their fingerprints, like foreigners temporarily resident in Japan, even though they had been born and brought up there, but there are still many cases of discrimination in the workplace and the movement continues. We saw in Chapter 6 too that the demands of Ainu activists have achieved some success in bringing about changes in the law, and in securing fair representation, but they continue to seek designation as 'indigenous people' recognisable in an international context.

Another well-publicised example of popular political activity is to be found in environmental protest groups, especially those who have reacted to threats to their residential areas by the waste of large enterprises and the building of golf courses. The movements against harmful industrial waste epitomised by that causing the so-called Minamata disease were often long and hard fought, sometimes quite spectacular, and many eventually successful. They attracted the attention of several political scientists, and an early study by Margaret McKean (1981) was a good documentation of the phenomenon. A collection of essays published in the same year by Steiner, Krauss and Flanagan (1981) looked at the wider subject of *Political Opposition and Local Politics in Japan*. Broadbent (1998) is a more recent source. An interesting study by Peng-Er Lam (1999), entitled *Green Politics in Japan*, examines the extent of the support of the big parties to environmental movements, and charts the development of the Network Movement (NET), a potential green party, so far only successful at a local level.

Much of the focus of Lam's book is on a movement regarded as parent to NET, a consumer cooperative known as the *Seikatsu Club*, or 'livelihood club', one of the groups mentioned in Chapter 2 that seek to bring safe, cheap food directly from producers into Japanese homes. These groups are largely run by full-time housewives, as they have required attendance at a delivery point for sorting and receipt, but some feminist complaints have made the system more user-friendly to women out at work all day. They have encouraged the development of the production of organically grown foods, as well as cutting out the profits of the 'middlemen'. The *Seikatsu Club* was also the group mentioned in Chapter 2 that was awarded a Swedish prize for creating an alternative economy, and somewhat in the same vein, it has developed an alternative political movement as well. At this level of local political activity women are strong and effective participants, but they may still be represented by a man in formal encounters, and Lam calls for them to take on the roles of leadership as well.

From an anthropological point of view this kind of action represents another example of the force of face-to-face interaction in Japanese society. Most of these groups make progress because they are working with local *uchi* groups to achieve local aims despite the overarching movement that the consumer cooperatives have become. In a traditional community, it was usually more effective for neighbours to cooperate to achieve some goal which they shared than to appeal individually to the impersonal institutions of which they formed only a minor part. The continuing existence of fire-fighting corps, road-mending squads and women's consumer groups attests to the way this preference for a degree of local autonomy persists. Even in new neighbourhoods, self-help groups are soon formed, and these draw on the social patterns that developed in older communities.

A good case study of such activity is to be found in the book by Eyal Ben-Ari (1991) already referred to in Chapter 4. He analyses in some considerable detail the way members of a new community near Kyoto came together to solve the problems they were suffering due to a lack of services. He discusses the various options open to the residents, the way they themselves considered all the possibilities and the means by which they eventually achieved their aims. The self-help group that they set up is a prototype also found elsewhere, and once established it can be activated for other purposes in the future. In effect, the new neighbours have drawn on one of the strengths of the old, relatively autonomous community, but they also make good use of their residents' links with the sophistications of the outside world.

At this level of politics in the smallest local unit, there are a number of anthropological sources that have documented political behaviour over the post-war years. This is the face-to-face level with which anthropology is particularly familiar, and several authors have analysed the paths to power and influence within the community. The study by Beardsley, Hall and Ward (1959) was an early example of one community and that by Fukutake (1972) is a more general survey of rural Japan. Moeran (1998) has discussed the role of drinking in political behaviour in a rural community in Kyushu, and the importance of remembering, though not mentioning, matters that were discussed under the influence of several cups. The work of Ted Bestor (1989) in a Tokyo neighbourhood, already discussed in Chapter 4, fills a gap with regard to political behaviour in a local urban situation.

Ultimately, political action would still seem to be most effective at this local level, and the increasing number of volunteers willing to work for causes important to their communities (reported from Nakano's (2000) work in Chapter 4) has helped to create the new emphasis on the power of civil society. Reactions to government failure after the Kobe earthquake, plus a willingness for volunteers to step out of their own patch for a serious enough disaster, helped to consolidate support for a new Special Nonprofit Organisation Law (NPO Law), eventually passed in 1998. This allows considerable deregulation for NPOs and non-government organisations (NGOs) and a new boost in the decentralisation of power away from the bureaucracy that Robert Pekkanen (2000) has identified as an important shift in state–civil relations. It could also be seen as a timely recognition that the real craft of exercising power in Japan still lies at a very grass-roots level.

CONCLUSION

This chapter has set out to show how an originally imported system of politics works in a historically quite different host culture. The institutions are recognisable, but the behaviour within them is not so clear. Indeed, some integral parts of the Japanese version of the system have been shown to be quite corrupt by the standards of the societies from which the framework was adopted, and this fact has increasingly been disturbing the voting public. Reform is in the air, and more is promised, but some of it seems incompatible with much of the basis of social relations in the wider society and it will be interesting to see how far it comes off. The success of the government in power as this edition goes to press rides to some extent on its ability to bring Japan out of the economic doldrums, but in the meantime, it is dealing quite effectively with other grass-roots demands and has incorporated new political movements.

REFERENCES AND FURTHER READING

Beardsley, Richard K., John W. Hall and Robert E. Ward, *Village Japan* (University of Chicago Press, Chicago, 1959), chapters 12 and 13

Ben-Ari, Eyal, *Changing Japanese Suburbia: A Study of Two Present-Day Localities* (Kegan Paul International, Tokyo, 1991)

Bestor, Theodore, *Neighbourhood Tokyo* (Stanford University Press, Stanford, CA, 1989), especially Chapter 3

Broadbent, Jeffrey, *Environmental Politics in Japan: Networks of Power and Protest* (Cambridge University Press, Cambridge, 1998)

Curtis, Gerald L. *The Japanese Way of Politics* (Columbia University Press, New York, 1988)

Flanagan, Scott C., S. Kohei, I. Miyake, B.M. Richardson and J. Watanabe, *The Japanese Voter* (Yale University Press, New Haven and London, 1991)

Fukutake, Tadashi, *Japanese Rural Society* (trans. R.P. Dore, Cornell University Press, Ithaca, 1972)

Healey, Graham, 'Politics and Politicians', in Howard Smith (ed.), *Inside Japan* (British Broadcasting Association, London, 1981), pp. 155–86

Iritani, Toshio, 'The Emergence of the Hosokawa Coalition: A Significant Break in the Continuity of Japanese Politics?', *Japan Forum*, 6, 1 (1994), pp. 1–7

Johnson, Stephen, 'Continuity and Change in Japanese Electoral Patterns: The 1993 General Election in Yamanashi', *Japan Forum*, 6, 1 (1994), pp. 8–20

Lam, Peng-Er, *Green Politics in Japan* (Routledge, London, 1999)

Leblanc, Robin, *Bicycle Citizens* (University of California Press, Berkeley, 1999)

McKean, Margaret, *Environmental Politics and Citizen Politics in Japan* (California University Press, Berkeley, 1981)

Moeran, Brian, 'One Over the Seven: Sake Drinking in a Japanese Potting Community', in Joy Hendry (ed.), *Interpreting Japanese Society: Anthropological Approaches* (Routledge, London, 1998), pp. 243–58

Neary, Ian, *The State and Politics in Japan* (Polity Press, Cambridge, 2002a)

Okimoto, Daniel I., and T.P. Rohlen, *Inside the Japanese System* (Stanford University Press, Stanford, 1988)

Pekkanen, Robert, 'Japan's New Politics: The Case of the NPO Law', *Journal of Japanese Studies*, 26, 1 (2000), pp. 111–49

Pempel, T., *Policy and Politics in Japan, Creative Conservatism* (Temple University Press, Philadelphia, 1982)

Pharr, Susan J., *Political Women in Japan: The Search for a Place in Political Life* (University of California Press, Berkeley, 1981)

Steiner, K., E.S. Krauss and S.C. Flanagan, *Political Opposition and Local Politics in Japan* (Princeton University Press, Princeton, NJ, 1981)

Stockwin, J.A.A., *Dynamic and Immobilist Politics in Japan* (University of Hawaii Press, Honolulu, 1988)

—— *Governing Japan* (Blackwell Publishers, Oxford, third edition, 1999)

van Wolferen, Karel, *The Enigma of Japanese Power* (Macmillan, London, 1989)

RELATED NOVELS

Eisler, Barry, *Rain Fall* (Penguin Putnam, New York, 2002)
Mishima, Yukio, *After the Banquet* (Charles E. Tuttle, Tokyo, 1967)

FILMS

Annular Eclipse (*Kinkanshoku*) (1975 Satsuo Yamamoto)
As Iwate Goes: Is Politics Local? (Asian Educational Media Services, 1998)
The Bad Sleep Well (*Warui Yatsu hodo Yoku Nemuru*) (1960 Akira Kurosawa)
Japan Foundering (*Nihon Chinbotsu*) (1973 Shiro Moritani)
A Taxing Woman (*Marusa no Onna*) (1987 Jūzō Itami)

12 The legal system and social control

INTRODUCTION

Social control is anthropological terminology for the mechanisms a society uses to maintain order in social life. There are usually mechanisms both to encourage behaviour that is approved by the society and to discourage that which is unacceptable, so that as they are brought into play they reinforce the values that underlie them. These mechanisms range from the spontaneous reactions of friends and neighbours, such as admiration, gossip or ostracism, to the highly organised system of honours and punishments which are distributed by agencies of the state in which the society is found. In a small-scale society, or close-knit group, the former are usually more effective in practice than the latter, whose part is greater the more complex and anonymous a society becomes.

In any particular society, the value system or systems on which mechanisms of social control are based, is inextricably tied up with other important aspects of the cosmology or worldview of that society, so that an understanding of social control must be placed in the context of such information. Thus, for example, Evans-Pritchard (1937) argued that beliefs about witchcraft play an important part in the social control of the Azande people of the Sudan, and elsewhere notions of ancestral or spiritual retribution have been shown to play a comparable role. Similarly, systems of law need a set of principles on which to be based, and these principles may or may not coincide with those underlying the more informal mechanisms.

In a complex society like Japan, there are understandably a large number of factors that play a part, and indeed, several of them have already been discussed in other contexts. These will be referred to during the course of the chapter. Much of the formal legal system will be superficially recognisable to a Western reader, as the political system was, largely because it was imported from Europe, but there is again a considerable discrepancy between the principles which were imported with it, and modified by the

Allied Occupation, and the principles which underlie indigenous, less formal methods of social control. This chapter will briefly describe the official legal system, and its enforcement, but it will also devote space to discussing the way it is used, or not used, and indeed some of the other ways in which order is achieved in Japanese society.

One important general aspect of social control should be mentioned here, because it raises an issue that has been of some interest amongst commentators on Japan. This is the area known as dispute resolution. In Simon Roberts' (1979) excellent introduction to legal anthropology, *Order and Dispute*, he emphasises the importance of moving away from our ethnocentric ideas about law and its enforcement, and he starts instead with two 'simple assumptions' about society. First, 'that a degree of order and regularity *must* be maintained in any human group if the basic processes of life are to be sustained', and, second, 'that quarrels will inevitably arise, and that these may disrupt that order if they are not resolved or at least contained'. He thus sets out to examine the ways in which people maintain order and deal with disputes (1979:13–14).

Roberts is particularly concerned with small-scale societies, but these assumptions would seem to be valid anywhere, at least at the face-to-face level. Indeed, anthropologists usually assume that quarrels are inevitable, and one aspect of social control is therefore concerned with the mechanisms that are available to deal with dispute. In the case of Japan, so much has been made of the strong value attached to harmony, as if this in itself would do away with disputes, that some commentators have reacted by placing an equally strong emphasis on conflict in Japanese society. The positive value attached to harmony is evidently an aspect of social control which must not be ignored, but it by no means ensures that there will be no conflict, as the fruits of this reaction make clear (see, for example, Eisenstadt and Ben-Ari 1990; Krauss *et al.* 1984). We will return to this problem after presenting some aspects of social control, starting with the most formal and conspicuous means of dispute resolution, the courts.

LAWS AND COURTS

Japan has had a set of written laws since at least the early eighth century, when the influx of influence from China included the basis of the Taihō code, which was promulgated in 702, and the subsequent Yōrō code of 718. These formed the foundations of a formal legal system, although there were of course modifications to their content and administration over the centuries that followed, particularly in the degree to which they were made locally variable. For example, radical revisions took place in the early Tokugawa period, when a system, which has been described as centralised feudal law, was instigated by the shogunate. There were separate codes at that time for imperial court nobles, for *daimyō* (local lords), for samurai and for commoners. Administration of the law was largely carried out by local magistrates, although serious disputes could be brought to the central offices of the shogunate.

This system was entirely inadequate for the international country Japan was becoming at the start of the Meiji period, however. Under pressure from foreign countries, which insisted on rights of extra-territoriality in view of the weaknesses of the Japanese legal system, scholars began to debate the possibilities of various European legal codes for the needs of the Japanese case. The Meiji codes were at first heavily influenced by the French system, even being drawn up under the guidance of an adviser from the French government, but there were later influences from Germany and England. Major revisions were, of course, introduced during the Allied Occupation after the Second World War, when the influences were largely from the United States. That these influences are foreign is starkly clear in the three main principles of the 1947 Constitution which, as we noted in Chapter 1, aimed to introduce the ideals of democracy. They are: sovereignty of the people, pacifism and a respect for basic human rights, which include equality, liberty and life.

These principles are almost completely at odds with previous Japanese values, as a glance back at Chapter 1 will make clear, although this does not mean that the aims they represent are entirely inconsistent with the aims achieved in other ways in Japanese social relations. Japanese lawyer Takeyoshi Kawashima (1967) has argued, for example, that the lack of a notion of 'right' in Japan, where an individual is involved instead in a variety of 'obligations', 'does not mean, that a sense of respect for the honor, life and feelings of other persons did not exist' (1967:264–5), as we saw in Chapter 3. After considerable resistance and some collective dragging of feet, however, Japan has finally signed and implemented most elements of the UN's Universal Declaration on Human Rights. Ian Neary (2002b) is a good comprehensive source on the development and use of ideas of 'human rights' in Japan, placed in a broader Asian context by considering it together with Korea and Taiwan, who shared some of Japan's prior conflicting influences. Feldman (2000) discusses the meaning of 'rights' in a Japanese context, specifically in the context of AIDS sufferers and health policy.

Evidence would seem to suggest, however, that the present legal system still represents another example of an imported edifice, with rather different workings in the everyday life of activities on the ground. We will consider both, but in the meantime it is interesting to note that the Ministry of Justice in Tokyo kept for many years a European-style brick exterior, while the

Figure 12.1 The former Ministry of Justice in Tokyo has a brick front reflecting the European influence in the creation of the Japanese legal system. Like the legal system, however, the actual building in use is constructed in a completely different way.

inside was gradually completely refurbished. Early in the 1990s an entirely new construction was built, but the old brick building remains standing in front of it, now containing a museum illustrating the 'Modernisation of Japan'.

As mentioned in Chapter 11, the 1947 Constitution also stipulates the separation of legislative, administrative and judicial powers, and the last, the subject of this section, was for the first time guaranteed independence from the others. As in the United States, it is headed by a Supreme Court, which has the ultimate power to decide on the constitutionality of any laws, orders or official acts, and to issue rules of practice and procedure. Under this there are 8 high courts, 50 district courts, 570 summary courts and 50 family courts. Family courts operate at the same regional levels as the district courts, but cover problems of domestic relations, juvenile delinquency and the criminal cases of adults who have contributed to minors' cases. Other cases start in the summary courts, unless they involve large sums of money, when they go directly to the district courts. The higher courts are largely for cases of appeal from below.

Justice is in the hands of judges, a jury system having been tried and rejected in the period preceding the Second World War, though there is a move to revive it to give people more representation (see Shinomiya 2002). Courts are presently allowed considerable discretion in administering punishments set out in the Penal Code, and also in suspending the execution of punishments where the circumstances seem to warrant this. Kawashima also suggested that a Japanese view of the relationship between legal rules and the social world is rather different from the state of tension that is taken for granted in Western society (1967:267). Nevertheless, the influences of the European and American adversarial systems adopted in Japan cannot be completely ignored, and a good examination of them is available in a collection of papers edited by Feeley and Miyazawa (2002).

One of the major features of this official Japanese system is the emphasis that is placed on compromise and conciliation. As a general rule, a judge seeks solutions to cases that satisfy both sides, and there is a reluctance to apply universal principles in which declarations are made about absolute right and wrong. Instead, the particular circumstances of each case are taken into consideration as far as possible, and a willingness to confess and apologise on the part of the accused will usually result in a fair measure of leniency. According to Japanese judges, the primary purpose of trials is to correct behaviour, not to punish it, and if an apology seems to be sincere, the aim is deemed to have been achieved. A recent source on this subject is Johnson and Johnson (2000), *Linking Community and Corrections in Japan*, which as the title suggests finds a strong preference for parole and probation within a community situation.

The Japanese system in practice is noted for its success in achieving a high rate of conviction, but a low prison population. In 1982, John Haley found the rate of conviction in cases that go to trial to be 99.9 per cent, but less than 3 per cent had a prison sentence imposed, and in 87 per cent of those cases, the terms were less than three years. Furthermore, two-thirds of the gaol sentences were regularly suspended, so that less than 2 per cent of all those convicted of a crime were ever imprisoned. Figures for 2002 showed a similar conviction rate, but 7.7 per cent had a prison sentence imposed, and this figure seems to have been gradually increasing (*FFJ* 2002:167). Nevertheless, it still seems to be in the interest of the defendant to be repentant, as Haley suggested, and an indication of sincerity may be to arrange to pay compensation to the victim of the crime before the case comes to trial. If the victim, in turn, writes a letter absolving the accused of further blame that would be even better. A situation of at least superficial harmony has been restored, and the crime is seen to have been appeased.

Examples of unrepentance sometimes receive extraordinary media attention. Three notorious cases have been recounted in some detail in a book by Norma Field (1991), *In the Realm of the Dying Emperor*, where she describes the actions of individuals who took a stand against the establishment during the year in which Emperor Hirohito died. One of these was an otherwise law-abiding supermarket owner in Okinawa who burned a Japanese flag, another a Christian woman who objected to the Shintō enshrinement (and deification) of her deceased husband and the third no lesser figure than the Mayor of Nagasaki who publically criticised the dying Emperor. The hue and cry that surrounded each of these cases, and the ostracism the protagonists experienced, well illustrates the general disapproval of people who adopt an unrepentant posture, and the result illustrates perfectly the way a system such as this closes in on people who refuse to toe the line. However, the book also recounts the gestures of support these people received, for example quoting in full some of the letters written to the Mayor of Nagasaki, who was the same mayor mentioned in Chapter 6 as being descended from a family of 'hidden Christians'.

ALTERNATIVE RESPONSES TO DISPUTE

Conciliation was a prominent feature of Tokugawa law, and the modern legal system also provides an official conciliation procedure as a well-used alternative to litigation and court trial. The conciliator may be a judge, alone, or he may be part of a lay committee, and if the parties can agree to a solution there will be no need to have a trial. If they fail to agree, the trial will follow. The classic work by Dan Henderson (1965) traced the development of the modern procedure from traditional practices, and discussed how it had changed in response to changes in society. A more recent description of the system is to be found in Oda's (1992) comprehensive discussion of *Japanese Law*, where he explains the possibilities and the reasons behind using them. These include saving time and the huge cost of litigation, and the preference for reaching agreement without confrontation, especially in the case of parties engaged in a long-term relationship (1992:84).

Divorce cases provide a good example of some possible conciliation mechanisms, especially as the role of the mediator in marriage has already been discussed in Chapter 8. In Japan, it is simply necessary to register divorce in the same way that one registers marriage, with both parties signing the document, and in fact the vast majority of divorce cases are settled informally. It is likely that a third party will have been asked by the family to help settle practical matters, and this may be the same go-between who brought the couple together in the first place, or it may be another person respected by both sides of the family. In case this informal system breaks down, a conciliation committee attached to every family court tries to resolve all cases before they may be presented to the court itself, and again, they usually achieve agreement. Some of the issues that brought the rare few divorce cases into even the Supreme Court are outlined in Oda (1992:236–7).

It was already mentioned briefly in Chapter 4 that mediation in the case of disputes is one of the roles of the head of a village or community. Indeed, it has generally been thought preferable to solve problems within the confines of an *uchi* group such as this, since resorting to the outside world is seen to bring shame on the whole community. Thus, boundary disputes, for example, are thought best settled at this local level where possible, and the villagers in the community where I worked were able to give me examples of cases that had been resolved in this way over the years. Kawashima (1963) cited the example of a farmer whose whole house was subject to the local sanction of ostracism by the community because his father had sued another farmer about the boundaries of their land (1963:45).

Another well-publicised case in 1983 involved a family whose 3-year-old son drowned in an irrigation pond while he was in the care of a neighbour. The bereaved family filed a suit involving sums totalling 28 million yen for negligence, not only against their neighbours, but also against a contractor who had deepened the pond without putting a fence round it, and against the city, the prefecture and the state. The district court ordered the neighbours to pay 5 million yen, but exonerated the other defendants. The case was given much publicity on radio and television, as well as in the newspapers. Within a few days, the family who had lost their son received between 500 and 600 anonymous phone calls and some 50 letters and postcards condemning them in abusive language for taking legal action against their neighbours, particularly because they had won their case. Moreover, the father of the family lost his job, and the other children in the family were subjected to derision at school.

Meanwhile, the neighbours appealed. This action provoked a similar response from the general public, suggesting that appealing to the courts even in self-defence was regarded as inappropriate in the case of relations between neighbours. In fact, within a week of the first decision, the bereaved family succumbed to the social pressure and withdrew its case, but by this time they had done irreparable damage to their reputation, and they were forced to move out of the district. That the matter was a tragedy, no one could deny, but it was evidently not regarded as a solution to bring a dispute between neighbours into the public gaze in this way. It is likely that the whole community had anyway responded with gifts of sympathy to the bereaved family, and appealing to the impersonal machinery of the outside world would perhaps seem like a rejection of this community support.

There are other reasons, too, why individuals, companies and other parties involved in disputes will usually prefer to avoid the shame of a court case, whatever the outcome. The public apology that might be required entails an enormous loss of face, according to Haley (1982:275–6), who has pointed out the extensive practical consequences which may result since so much in Japanese life is dependent on one's personal reputation and connections. Thus, he explains, companies will prefer informally to pay enormous sums of compensation rather than make a public apology. Modern forms of *mura hachibu*, or village ostracism, for someone who loses their reputation in the community include the denial of loans, the boycotting of goods and a general reluctance to have any further business dealings with them. This would be tolerable if the transacting of business could easily be set up again, but long-term relations are so important that they are on the whole treasured with care and caution.

The force of ostracism as a sanction was illustrated in Chapter 3, when children were learning that they really had little option but to conform with the expected behaviour in kindergartens, and it appeared again in Chapter 4 as a negative sanction for stepping out of line within a village community. In both cases, the sanction is particularly effective because it is little used, the threat of such an outcome usually being a sufficient deterrent. In a similar way, people can usually rely on their business partners to conform to expectations in the interest of maintaining their business links in the community, and Japanese contracts are typically rather informal affairs emphasising the importance of 'goodwill' between the parties involved.

Ideally, then, disputes should be solved privately, if necessary with the intervention of a trusted third party to act as a mediator, a role that we have already discussed as important in Chapter 8. There, the emphasis was on the bringing together of two previous strangers for the purpose of marriage, but it was pointed out that the role is found elsewhere since it is a method of bringing people from 'the outside' (*soto*) into one's *uchi* group. Introductions are important because in general one tries to conduct one's life within a circle of *uchi* relations, and in any activity one can only benefit from a personal connection or perhaps a letter of guarantee. In times of dispute, in particular, then, it is preferred to keep the affair within bounded limits.

POSITIVE METHODS OF MAINTAINING ORDER

From the above discussion it will have become apparent that relations in Japanese society are where possible based on personal connections and face-to-face interaction. The preservation of this arrangement, which has often been lost elsewhere in modern times, is evidently one of the positive aspects of the maintenance of order in Japanese life, and, in the complex industrialised society which Japan has become, it is no mean feat. Some of the ways in which this is still achieved, despite the anomie that afflicts many other industrialised countries, have already been discussed in previous chapters, but this is a good opportunity for a summary.

In the first place, there is the development from an early age of the importance of the *uchi* group, the 'inside' of security, as opposed to the unknown dangers of the outside world. This is accompanied by the idea, learnt first in the home, but afterwards applied elsewhere, that one should put the needs of the *uchi* group before one's own. One's personal behaviour is also often representative of some wider group, whether it be the family, the school, the village or the company, and as a person goes about their life they are expected to remember how their own behaviour will reflect on the groups to which they belong. In Chapter 2, this principle was discussed as part of kindergarten training, where teachers make effective use of peer group pressure to see that the children behave in an orderly manner and develop a sense of responsibility to this wider entity of which they are part.

In the traditional community, too, similar principles operated effectively to ensure much controlled behaviour. One example is the 100 per cent tax payment that was usual when a community paid as a unit. In the past, neighbours would have had to make up the shortfall if an individual house defaulted. Today the ultimate responsibility rests with the individual or family concerned, but it may still be regarded as letting down the whole community if one house doesn't pay. For similar reasons, every house usually participates in cooperative activities to take care of village property, to keep the roads mended and the shrine weeded. The continuing reciprocal relations between houses also help to keep channels of communication open, and to minimise differences that may arise. As was pointed out in Chapter 4, membership in such a community involves a series of obligations and duties, but it also provides a considerable degree of security.

Living within a small-scale community such as this also renders informal sanctions such as gossip and ridicule quite effective. A family that behaves in a way that is radically different from the others invites neighbourly disapproval, and cooperation may be withdrawn altogether if they step seriously out of line. It used to be common for people who have had a possible marriage partner suggested for their son or daughter to travel to the community of the family concerned and ask amongst the neighbours and perhaps in the local shop what the family is like. This possibility may well have helped to maintain amicable relations between neighbours. One of the few intra-village (or endogamous) marriages in the village where I worked was said to be because both families had difficult mothers-in-law and no one from outside would have them once they learned about the problem!

The all-pervasive hierarchical principle is another effective example of how personal relations remain important. In many walks of life individuals can only proceed up a scale of advancement by remaining loyal to their superiors and cooperating within a structured situation. The maintenance of order is aided here because there are certain expectations between particular pairs of individuals who are bound up in long-term hierarchical relations. Usually the inferior is obliged to defer to the superior in cases of difference, but the superior is also expected to consult the inferior and take his feelings into consideration before making a decision.

This kind of relationship is based on old principles of *giri-ninjō*, which Noda (1976) describes as the Japanese system of rules that preceded the modern legal system. *Giri* may be loosely translated as 'duty' and it refers to the various expectations that exist between particular sets of relations. In Chapter 2, for example, the expectations between parents and children were described, and there are similar sets between a teacher and pupil, master and apprentice, indeed between any pair of hierarchical relations of this kind. An important characteristic of this type of duty, however, is that the person to whom it is owed has no right to demand that it be fulfilled. A failure to fulfil such a duty would incur great loss of face, and this is usually sufficient incentive, but it would involve equal loss of face were the potential recipient to point this out.

Such a relationship is supposed to be based on feelings of affection, and the value of the relationship itself is supposedly greater than any of the actual duties by which it is marked. This affection is the human element of the relationship, the *ninjō*, and if anyone appears to act out of self-interest, rather than with human feeling, they would be subject to informal sanctions of disapproval. Some modern Japanese would perhaps deny that *giri-ninjō* relations are important in Japan today, but the makings of relations of this kind are still in evidence in the upbringing of children when their mothers teach them to think of others before they act, to refrain from behaviour which they would not like to receive and to give in to a younger child who is not yet old enough to understand. The rationale for such teaching brings us back to the value placed on harmony in social relations.

The value attached to harmony is often used as an ideological principle in Japan, and is said to date back to the Seventeen-Article Constitution of Prince Shotoku (574–622), which esteemed concord above all things as the subject of the first article. The Japanese word for this concept is *wa*, which is also sometimes used to stand for Japan or Japaneseness, and it has a set of connotations rather different from those of the English word and somewhat manipulable according to political need (Itō 1998). Kawashima (1967:264) quotes from a book by Ono Seiichiro, in which harmony is described as consisting in 'not making distinctions; if a distinction between good and bad can be made, then there *wa* (harmony) does not exist'. This notion evidently underlies the behaviour of judges when they seek to conciliate rather than to apply universalistic principles of right and wrong. Recognising that there are two sides to a dispute, and seeking a compromise between the parties, helps resolve a conflict so that harmony may be restored.

THE POLICE SYSTEM

So far we have discussed rather diffuse methods of encouraging social order, and if Japan were a small-scale society, they might be sufficient. Even before industrialisation, however, Japan had enough problems in the control of her people to warrant an organised system of enforced order. In the Tokugawa period this was carried out by members of the warrior class, under the official guidance of local magistrates but, in effect, by means of the sword. The present policing system has been grafted on to the old one, but much of it has again been imported from the West. However, it has often been described as one of the most successful forces in the world. A good summary of the various stages of policing policy and practice in Japan since the war is to be found in an article by Christopher Aldous and Frank Leishman (1997).

The crime rate in Japan is extremely low, comparing favourably with most other industrialised countries in almost all categories of crime, and the arrest rate is correspondingly high. For example, in 2000, the rates per 100,000 population for homicide and theft, respectively, were 1.1 and 1,508 for Japan, as compared with 2.9 and 5,896 for England and Wales, and 5.7 and 3,742 for the United States. The arrest rates per 100 offences for the same crimes in the same year were 95.2 and 29.4 in Japan, 87.1 and 15.8 for England and Wales, and only 69.1 and 17.0 in the United States (*FFJ* 2002). Moreover, this success is achieved with a higher ratio of citizens to police than in most industrial nations.

Again, there are evidently diffuse forces of social control which are working with the police, and the title of an anthropological study of the Japanese police system gives away some of the secret. In *Police and Community in Japan* (Ames 1981), the author writes in the introduction, 'the police have not been moulded in a vacuum . . . they fit Japanese society like a glove fits the hand, and the societal hand has determined the form of the glove' (1981:1). Ames goes on to describe how the police adapt themselves to various areas of Japanese life, first to the cooperating regular communities, both rural and urban, then to non-conforming groups such as youthful protestors, disadvantaged minorities and out-and-out gangsters. He also discusses the way in which police officers are trained and maintained.

The local police offices found in rural areas of Japan epitomise the idea of community policing, and they are often mentioned as playing an important role in the prevention of crime. Typically, one police officer lives with his family in a house behind the office, and he is expected to integrate himself into the life of the community. His work includes regular visits to all the houses and factories within the district and he keeps a record of the entire population and their valuables. He also spends a regular daily period at his desk for consultation purposes, and his wife is paid a monthly allowance to answer the phone and look after visitors when her husband is out. The officer is usually accorded a fairly high measure of prestige in the community, and he will be invited to attend local events of any importance. He gets to know the district and its workings very thoroughly, and the local population comes to know and trust him.

Similar principles operate in the running of urban police boxes, but there is usually more work to be done, and several officers may be required to run one box. Again, regular visits are made to the families and enterprises in the area, and a record is kept of residents' details, such as those who work late and may be vulnerable or helpful in the observation of crime. The box is attended night and day for the reporting of crime or traffic accidents, and the local officer is often the first on the scene. There is also an important role in providing information and general help to the populace, and this may include the occasional loans of bus or train fares, the care of drunks and general advice to those who drop in for a chat. The police box takes on something of the air of a social centre at times.

In both urban and rural areas, the work of the police is usually supplemented by crime prevention and road safety groups, which are formed voluntarily by local residents from a particular *chōnaikai* (see Chapter 4 and the article by Nakano (2000) referred to there). Membership in such a group involves service at certain times of the year when there is a festival or a crime prevention programme. There are often also particularly cooperative residents who will keep the police box informed about any suspicious activities in the area, and a few selected houses are chosen to distribute information from time to time. The police, rather like teachers in the earlier stages of school and kindergarten life, take pains to remain on the same side as their charges, and they benefit from a good measure of cooperation in return.

The principle of neighbours watching over each other has a historical precedent in Japan, which has been a controversial issue at times. In the early policing days of the Tokugawa period, order was maintained at a local level by neighbourhood groups of about five houses, *goningumi* or five-man-groups, which were collectively responsible for order in the area where they lived. Thus, if one of the houses was up to no good, the others were expected to put pressure on the dissident to reform, or if that failed, they would report them to the higher authorities. The system was revived in wartime Japan for the purposes of government control, and it was criticised and abolished afterwards, but the principle of group responsibility for order at an informal level has by no means disappeared. It seems to work well as long as the arrangements are not abused by higher powers. It is of course the same principle again which is put to good use in schools.

This pattern is again only effective in face-to-face communities where neighbours know one another, and in many urban areas this is no longer the case. Nor is the positive image of police/community relations always successful in preventing crime. A useful study of police detective work, and the way in which they 'make crime', is to be found in Miyazawa (1992), a translation from Japanese of a rich and detailed study of the Japanese criminal justice system at work. It places the Japanese methods in their own social context, and provides some interesting comparisons with parallel situations in Europe and America.

ORGANISED CRIME

Japan also has a very active and highly organised underworld of gang activity, which is an interesting phenomenon at several levels. On one level, gang relations seem to epitomise the principles of social order, in that the hierarchical structure is firmly established and rigidly maintained so that relations are predictable and reliable. These relations are established at formal ceremonies, rather like marriages, when individual members become linked as father and son or brothers through the sharing of cups of sake. The partners thus formed can rely on one another for support and loyalty, and they take their places according to the further relations of the superior in the wider ranking of the gang. These long-term relations provide security and a place to belong for many of society's misfits and dropouts, and the *yakuza* gangs have been described as having a positive role to play in keeping even crime in order in Japan.

The gangs in themselves are not illegal. Each group maintains offices in the cities in which they operate, and they hold ceremonies such as funerals in full public gaze. As a rule, these *yakuza* gangs have legal 'front' occupations, and they live in peace with their neighbours, including the police. One of their connections is with the construction industry, and they are evident on the city streets as recruiters of day labourers, though they are not especially particular about the immigration status of the worker. On another level, they live quite outside the law, since many of the undercover enterprises they run are illegal. Their interests include gambling, prostitution, extortion, peddling, pornography and 'protection', and their territories run as far afield as Europe, South-east Asia, Hawaii and California.

They are also sometimes hired by legitimate enterprises for particular ends, for example by right-wing politicians to intimidate a left-wing group threatening trouble, or even by police to help with security during an important event. It would seem, then, that they do have a positive role to play in the maintenance of order, and since they absorb many of society's misfits, they also provide a haven for people who have no other niche in the organised social world which is Japan.

At this third level, then, gangsters make it possible for even the underside of Japan to be kept in control. Their relations with the police are generally rather cordial, even when they are involved in an investigation, and in the eyes of the general public they are sometimes seen as rather romantic, especially as they epitomise the old principles of *giri-ninjō*. Ames (1981:124) suggests that this is just the *tatemae* of the situation, however, and the *honne* is that these people are just criminals with a glamorous facade. Gill has examples of day labourers whose illusions have been shattered as well (2001:122–3). The police maintain good relations with them because this is the harmonious way to proceed. In reality, they would love to eradicate them, and they continually issue advice to the general public, through posters and the circulating neighbourhood notice-board, about helping to stamp out their activities.

On the whole the gangs have been too highly organised to be cracked, but problems do arise when factional strife develops, as they do in other areas where the principle described by Nakane obtains, and inter-gang warfare provides the police with legitimate reason for arresting members of the underworld. In 1991, new legislation was passed in the Diet in response to an escalation in the outbreaks of inter-group violence which was said to be making life intolerable for members of the public living or working near the offices and homes of these gangs. The aim of the law, which went into force in March 1992, was to curtail some of the more antisocial activities of these groups. It also outlines procedures for members of the general public who become victim to gang activities, and it aims too to help young people avoid being recruited.

From the point of view of the gangsters, the new law was said to be another example of a violation of human rights and therefore to go against the Japanese Constitution. They hired lawyers to analyse the small print, and quickly took various steps to retain their positions of leverage and their sources of income. An interesting article by Wolfgang Herbert (2000) examines some of the changes that have been made since that time, though he sees a decrease in overall membership as a cost-saving exercise in a time of recession rather than a success for the police. Some of their newer activities, such as the collection of debts and the occupation of land used as collateral, may also be directly related to the recession, as before 'the bubble' they were involved in harassing landowners to release land wanted for speculation. They are also reported to have extended the illegal trafficking of alien workers from a long-term practice of bringing women from South-east Asia to include the smuggling of Chinese men into Japan.

Jacob Raz (1992a,b) has carried out some excellent anthropological fieldwork amongst members of the Japanese underworld, and his publications are very revealing of their point of view. He focuses in particular on the itinerant branch of the *yakuza*, known as *tekiya*, whose members set up stalls at festivals and peddle food and wares, thereby creating a large part of the festival atmosphere. For this reason they see themselves as 'indispensable' to the 'Japaneseness' of this quintessentially Japanese event, located as it is at 'the heart of religious and community life' (1992a:105; 1992b:217–18). Raz also discusses the ways, through forms of self-presentation such as tattoos, style of dress and hair, in which members of the *yakuza* express their rejection of wider Japanese society, which many of them also perceive as having rejected them. Not a few are of Korean and *burakumin* origins. Nevertheless, Raz emphasises the way these groups, unlike the American mafia, operate wholly within a Japanese cultural context.

Another inside view of the *yakuza* world and its modern history is to be found in a fascinating book put together by a retired doctor, Saga Junichi (1989), based on a series of interviews with a dying friend and patient. *The Gambler's Tale* is a very personal account, but it well illustrates many of the ideas discussed above, such as the long-term loyalty amongst members of gangs and their hierarchical relations, as well as the resourcefulness of their members, especially in the desperate post-war years. It also depicts life in a couple of Japanese prisons.

CONCLUSION

The *tatemae–honne* distinction runs throughout the legal system and social control in Japan. The whole European-inspired arrangement of courts was set up to satisfy the world at large that Japan was capable of operating on the same terms as other 'civilised' countries. Indeed, the system is there to respond to the needs of those who call upon its facilities. For the most part, however, it continues to function along the lines of more customary practices that have quite different moral underpinnings. At the level of interpersonal relations the *tatemae* situation is, where possible, one of harmony, although, of course, there will be situations of conflict inside and outside the *uchi* groups to which people belong. The compromises that are reached sound splendid arrangements, but the *honne* may well be that one or more of the participants had little choice but to agree, just as partners in a 'consensus decision' may come away with something less than the satisfaction they will show on the surface. However, the ability to have a *tatemae* face for any situation is learned early in Japanese society, as was pointed out in Chapter 3, and this, too, is an important mechanism of social control. Indeed, it is perhaps one of the most effective of all.

To return, finally, to the problem mentioned at the beginning of the chapter of the opposing interpretations of Japanese society as either very harmonious or as full of conflict, we find that we do indeed draw on a similar distinction. Ishida Takeshi (1984) has proposed a very plausible way of reconciling these two views by using the notions of *omote* and *ura*, literally 'front' and 'back', but corresponding rather well to the notions of *tatemae* and *honne*, in juxtaposition with the notions of *uchi* and *soto*. He argues that the *omote* or surface relations between members of the same *uchi* group should be harmonious, and conflict which might well exist at the *ura* or underneath level is usually solved implicitly. At the *omote* level of *soto* relations, however, there should be no concessions and no compromise – hence the strong views of conflict. Even here, however, at the *ura* level, negotiation is possible if neither party loses face.

This chapter has tended to emphasise the harmonious side of the paradigm, but then it is concerned with social control, not social disorder. Surface relations between outsiders may well lead to open conflict anywhere in the world, and it reveals little about the Japanese mechanisms of social control to dwell on that superficial level. At a practical level, Japanese people would seem to prefer where possible to establish and expand their *uchi* relations with the security that follows, even if this means the loss of a degree of freedom. It is important to remember, however, that there are also people in Japan, as elsewhere, who feel that the system is too stifling, and once they reject the system, they have no option but to choose a path of direct conflict (or exile).

REFERENCES AND FURTHER READING

Aldous, C. and F. Leishman, 'Policing in Post-war Japan: Reform, Reversion and Reinvention', *International Journal of Sociology of Law*, 25, 3 (1997), pp. 135–54

Ames, Walter L., *Police and Community in Japan* (University of California Press, Berkeley, 1981)

Eisenstadt, S.N. and Eyal Ben-Ari (eds), *Japanese Models of Conflict Resolution* (Kegan Paul International, London and New York, 1990)

Evans-Pritchard, E.E., *Witchcraft, Oracles and Magic among the Azande* (Clarendon Press, Oxford, 1937)

Feeley, Malcolm M. and Setsuo Miyazawa, *The Japanese Adversary System in Context: Controversies and Comparisons* (Palgrave Macmillan, Basingstoke and New York, 2002)

Feldman, Eric A., *The Ritual of Rights in Japan: Law, Society and Health Policy* (Cambridge University Press, Cambridge, 2000)

FFJ – Facts and Figures of Japan (Foreign Press Centre, Japan, 2002)

Field, Norma, *In the Realm of the Dying Emperor* (Pantheon Books, New York, 1991)

Gill, Tom, *Men of Uncertainty: The Social Organization of Day Laborers in Contemporary Japan* (State University of New York Press, New York, 2001)

Haley, John O., 'The Myth of the Reluctant Litigant', *Journal of Japanese Studies*, 4, 2 (1978), pp. 359–90

—— 'Unsheathing the Sword: Law without Sanctions', *Journal of Japanese Studies*, 8, 2 (1982), pp. 265–81

Henderson, Dan Fenno, *Conciliation and Japanese Law* (2 vols., University of Washington Press, Seattle, 1965)

Herbert, Wolfgang, 'The *Yakuza* and the Law', in J.S. Eades, Tom Gill and Harumi Befu, *Globalization and Social Change in Contemporary Japan* (Trans-Pacific Press, Melbourne, 2000), pp. 143–58

Isazawa, Yuji, *International Law, Human Rights and Japanese Law: The Impact of International Law on Japanese Law* (Clarendon Press, Oxford, 1998)

Ishida, Takeshi, 'Conflict and its Accommodation: *omote-ura* and *uchi–soto* Relations', in E.S. Krauss, T.P. Rohlen and P.G. Steinhoff, *Conflict in Japan* (University of Hawaii Press, Honolulu, 1984), pp. 16–38

Itō, Kimio, 'The Invention of *Wa* and the Transformation of the Image of Prince Shōtoku in Modern Japan', in Stephen Vlastos, *Mirror of Modernity: Invented Traditions of Modern Japan* (University of California Press, Berkeley, Los Angeles and London, 1998)

Johnson, Elmer H. with Carol H. Johnson, *Linking Community and Corrections in Japan* (Southern Illinois University Press, Carbondale and Edwardsville, 2000)

Kawashima, Takeyoshi, 'Dispute Resolution in Contemporary Japan', in A. von Mehren (ed.), *Law in Japan* (Harvard University Press, Cambridge, MA, 1963), pp. 41–72

—— 'The Status of the Individual in the Notion of Law, Right, and Social Order in Japan', in Charles A. Moore (ed.), *The Japanese Mind* (University of Hawaii Press, Honolulu, 1967)

Koschmann, J. Victor, 'The Idioms of Contemporary Japan VIII: *Tatemae to Honne*', The Japan Interpreter, 9 (1974), pp. 98–104

Krauss, Ellis S., T.P. Rohlen and P.G. Steinhoff, *Conflict in Japan* (University of Hawaii Press, Honolulu, 1984)

Miyazawa, Setsuo, trans. Frank G. Bennett, Jr with John O. Haley, *Policing in Japan: A Study on Making Crime* (State University of New York Press, New York, 1992)

Moeran, Brian, *A Far Valley* (Kodansha International, Tokyo, New York and London, 1998)

Neary, Ian, *Human Rights in Japan, South Korea and Taiwan* (Routledge, London, 2002b)

Noda, Yosiyuki, *Introduction to Japanese Law* (trans. and ed. Anthony H. Angelo, University of Tokyo Press, Tokyo, 1976)

Oda, Hiroshi, *Japanese Law* (Butterworth, London, 1992)

Parker, L. Craig, *The Japanese Police System Today: An American Perspective* (Kodansha International, Tokyo, 1984)

Pharr, Susan, *Losing Face: Status Politics in Japan* (University of California Press, Berkeley, 1990)

Raz, Jacob, *Aspects of Otherness in Japanese Culture* (Institute for the Study of Languages and Cultures of Asia and Africa, Tokyo, 1992a)

—— 'Self-presentation and Performance in the *Yakuza* Way of Life', in Roger Goodman and Kirsten Refsing (eds), *Ideology and Practice in Modern Japan* (Routledge, London, 1992b)

Roberts, Simon, *Order and Dispute* (Penguin, Harmondsworth, 1979)

Shinomiya, Satoru, 'Adversarial Procedure without a Jury: Is Japan's System Adversarial, Inquisitorial or Something Else?', in Malcolm M. Feeley and Setsuo Miyazawa, *The Japanese Adversary System in Context: Controversies and Comparisons* (Palgrave Macmillan, Basingstoke and New York, 2002), pp. 114–27

Smith, Robert J., *Japanese Society: Tradition, Self and the Social Order* (Cambridge University Press, Cambridge, 1984)

Upham, Frank, *Law and Social Change in Postwar Japan* (Harvard University Press, Cambridge, MA, 1987)

Von Mehren, A. (ed.), *Law in Japan: The Legal Order in a Changing Society* (Harvard University Press, Cambridge, MA, 1963)

LIGHTER READING

Crichton, M., *Rising Sun* (Century Arrow, London, 1992)

Saga Junichi, *The Gambler's Tale* (Kodansha International, Tokyo, 1989)

FILMS

'*Hana-bi*' (1997 'Beat' Takeshi)

Twelve Sweet Japanese (*12 nin no yasashii nihonjin*) (1991 Shun Nakahara)

Conclusion

At the beginning of this book the conclusion was anticipated as the place where some common features of different areas of Japanese society would be brought together. So far we have skimmed across an enormous range of topics pertaining to a very complex and complicated society. We have ranged from the microscopic to the macroscopic, and back again. We have grown up with a Japanese child, we have gone out to work, to play, to pray and to vote, and we have learned how to deal with disputes. The question now remains: have we succeeded in gaining some kind of understanding? In these final pages, the aim will be to summarise a few important classificatory principles which have emerged again and again in the course of this book. It is my contention that an understanding of these principles will go a long way towards aiding an understanding of Japanese behaviour at any level.

First of all, it is important to reiterate the point made in the previous chapter that much social interaction takes place at a face-to-face level. Within the largest corporations, universities, political parties, gangs, even the self-defence forces, two related principles operate to ensure that most important transactions may be made between people who know and understand each other, who can rely on each other and predict each other's behaviour. The first principle is the hierarchical one – which we have been referring to as Nakane's inverted V principle, although it has been described by plenty of other people – namely that recruits to any large organisation, as well as many smaller ones, establish long-term links with a particular superior; in turn, these inferiors will become linked to newer recruits as their superiors, and the whole enterprise can be pictured as a series of personal, individual links.

The second principle is even more widespread. It is the principle of establishing and belonging to *uchi* groups. These may be represented for any individual as a series of concentric circles, with the smallest, most intimate group in the middle, and the largest probably being the *uchi* group of all

Japanese people. The primary school curriculum reflects this model as children are taught in social studies about the family in the first year, the neighbourhood in the second, the wider city, town or village in the third, the prefecture in the fourth, Japan in the fifth and only in the sixth year do they begin to learn about the rest of the world. As the attachments get larger, there is less likelihood of seeing an entire group together at any one time, but there are various symbolic ways in which they may be represented, and in which their members may make known their common allegiance. Flags, badges and company songs are but a few examples. In fact, an individual probably spends most of his or her life with members of the closer groups, but in appropriate circumstances, principles of behaviour can be applied to more distant acquaintances on the basis of common membership in an *uchi* group at any level.

The consequences of this emphasis on face-to-face interaction are various and far-reaching. They are also particularly amenable to social anthropological analysis because much of the training of social anthropologists involves the study of small-scale, face-to-face groups of the kind that the Japanese have managed to maintain. I have made this point rather forcibly in the introduction to *Interpreting Japanese Society* (Hendry 1998), a collection of papers written by anthropologists about Japan, and referred to several times in this book. In particular, much of the effectiveness of mechanisms of social control relies, in the Japanese case, on principles that are more commonly found in small communities of Polynesia and South-east Asia than in the industrial societies with which Japan is usually compared.

These are diffuse sanctions like gossip, ridicule and ostracism as negative reactions to unacceptable behaviour, and prestige and status as positive benefits that accrue to those who live according to the shared value system. These sanctions lose their power if people are easily able to move out of a community or other *uchi* group, but as was pointed out in Chapter 12, Japanese society makes it very difficult to do this. Of course, in urban areas, the pressures are much less great within a residential area, and some occupations are more constraining than others in this respect, but for many, the opinion of neighbours, friends and workmates counts for a great deal. This is true of many peoples throughout the world, within their own face-to-face circles, but it is emphasised here because the importance of long-term relations is so pervasive in the case of Japan.

Operating to maintain these face-to-face relations, then, are further principles that we have already discussed at intervals throughout the book. One is reciprocity. Again, this is a universal characteristic of social interaction, particularly important in long-term relations. Appropriate exchanges are usually very clearly decided in any particular dyad, and an imbalance in material goods usually implies that there is something intangible like help or loyalty moving in the other direction in its place, although prestige and status are often demonstrated materially by the receipt of an excess of goods. It is not unusual for people in Japan to keep a record of the value of goods that have been received, so that an appropriate amount may be spent when the time comes to make a return. There are certain fixed occasions when gifts will be made, and regular exchanges serve to reconfirm the relationships.

At a non-material level, there are other clear expectations of reciprocity in pairs of relationships, the most striking being the exchange of loyalty for benevolence between an inferior and superior in many different circumstances. This type of exchange may not be manifest in packets and parcels, but it is none the less binding. These rules may be discussed in terms of 'debts' (*giri* and *on*) but some relationships might even be regarded as too close for the application of such cold-sounding concepts. As was pointed out in Chapter 12, the *ninjō* of human feelings must not be forgotten. This might seem like a let-out clause allowing for the neglect of reciprocity, but it is precisely in relations close enough for human feelings to be taken into consideration that the force of obligation actually seems to be strongest.

Another important principle in the maintenance of long-term relations is, of course, the hierarchical one itself. Along with the exchanges involved, there are also fixed rules about who defers to whom, how much and when such deference may be relaxed. The contextual nature of hierarchy is interesting in the Japanese case, as is the virtual guarantee that one is almost always in a position to be superior to someone as well as inferior to someone else. Possibly before they are even aware of such differences, almost any member of Japanese society automatically receives a certain amount of deference merely on the strength of his or her age, whether it be 2 years or 82 years, and as long as one remains within the value system, one usually accumulates further status by living through the normal experiences of life. This is particularly the case in long-term relations, which provides an incentive for maintaining them smoothly.

Much of the expression of deference may be rather elaborate role-play, but this is an essential part of the maintenance of harmony in social relations, another principle that is, of course, highly prized. This role-play is part of the exercise of *tatemae* in human relations, the presentation of an appropriate face for any particular situation, and this aspect of Japanese interaction again runs through most arenas. It helps to make possible the phenomenon described as consensus decision-making, the appearance of an amazing degree of social order, even among society's misfits and cast-offs, and it also helps to make possible the communication of less pleasant things, which would be quite unspeakable in ordinary language, simply by adjustment in the use of the various levels of politeness available.

Equality must not be forgotten, of course, and this is another principle that is important in certain circumstances, as was illustrated particularly in Chapter 5 on education. The assumption that is made about the ability of any child to keep up with the class, given the right approach and a measure of persistence and perseverance, is fundamentally much more egalitarian than the emphasis on innate intelligence which is found in many other countries, although it is not to be denied that Japanese teachers are aware of such differences. The same principle is found in the arts, when the study of any skill is expected to involve long and arduous training rather than being a 'talent' which one is encouraged to feel one either has or doesn't have. The 'automatic' aspects of hierarchy, like those based on age and experience, also temper the differences with an egalitarian quality. We have also seen the symbolic expression of equality in the kindergarten and in the neighbourhood.

The principle of cooperation is also given a high rating in a Japanese list of value priorities, and this emphasis on putting the needs of a group of some sort before one's own personal desires tends to sound unattractive to people brought up in a society that emphasises individualism. The security gained through membership in such *uchi* groups necessarily involves a certain loss of individual freedom, but socialisation is such that the needs of the wider group are presented as one's own needs, and a certain sense of satisfaction seems to be associated with the contribution an individual can make to the workings of a larger endeavour. In fact, if the system works properly, there should be no need for the self-assertive aspect of individualism, since close relations and associates, in whatever arenas they operate, should be taking care to consider each other's interests.

With regard to the development of an individual 'self', this is not denied, indeed it is encouraged from an early age, and there are plenty of Japanese 'individuals' to disprove any theory that would attempt to suggest it could. To take but one example, the almost universal pursuit of arts and hobbies, from youth through to long past retirement from economically productive activities, provides members of Japanese society with an abundance of possibilities to pursue individual interests and select companions outside those with whom one must necessarily pass a good deal of time. The close bonds that are formed within a face-to-face society also make possible a degree of deep understanding that may never be achieved in a more anonymous world. Indeed, the pervasive use of *tatemae* behaviour, and its apparently clear separation from *honne*, even offers the possibility of an ultimate individual freedom that may perhaps be denied to people who fail to recognise such a distinction.

In the end, we have distilled out a small number of principles that help us to understand social interaction in Japan, though they are certainly not uniquely Japanese. The creation of us/them dichotomies – as we could term the *uchi/soto* distinction – is a feature of human society found all over the world. The separation of real feelings from one's 'face to the world' – as the *tatemae/honne* distinction does – is also a recognisable human practice, though the degree of social support it receives is a variable feature. Even the development of *seishin*, an inner spiritual strength, is a concept by no means alien to other cultural systems. What is unique – although only as unique as any other specific form of life – is the way particular combinations of these elements may be found in particular parts of Japanese society, and recognised as Japanese. Like any other member of the global village, Japan has its own history and its own internal diversity, and it forms part of the human world we all share. Members of Japanese society draw on all these resources to shape their own system of values, responding to outside change and moulding internal change. In this way, they continue to contribute to the rich diversity of the world at large.

Index

Page references for figures are in *italics*

256 *Index*